American Power and the Prospects for International Order

AMERICAN POWER AND THE PROSPECTS FOR INTERNATIONAL ORDER

SIMON BROMLEY

polity

Copyright © Simon Bromley 2008

The right of Simon Bromley to be identified as Author of this Work has been asserted in accordance with the UK Copyright, Designs and Patents Act 1988.

First published in 2008 by Polity Press

Polity Press
65 Bridge Street
Cambridge CB2 1UR, UK.

Polity Press
350 Main Street
Malden, MA 02148, USA

ISBN-13: 978-0-7456-4238-3
ISBN-13: 978-0-7456-4239-0 (pb)

A catalogue record for this book is available from the British Library.

Typeset in 10.5 on 12 pt Times NR
by SNP Best-set Typesetter Ltd., Hong Kong
Printed and bound in Great Britain by MPG Books Ltd, Bodmin
Cornwall

The publisher has used its best endeavours to ensure that the URLs for external websites referred to in this book are correct and active at the time of going to press. However, the publisher has no responsibility for the websites and can make no guarantee that a site will remain live or that the content is or will remain appropriate.

Every effort has been made to trace all copyright holders, but if any have been inadvertently overlooked the publishers will be pleased to include any necessary credits in any subsequent reprint or edition.

For further information on Polity, visit our website: www.polity.co.uk

CONTENTS

TABLES AND FIGURES

TABLES

FIGURES

PREFACE

The nature of American power and its place in shaping the international order is a large and and complex question and I did not exactly set out to write a study of it. This book is, rather, the product of a series of smaller projects that worried away at bits of the puzzle for long enough for me to realize that if I put some of the pieces together a picture might emerge that helps us to see American power and its role in the world in new ways. In retrospect the basic claims of the book seem obvious enough to me, but since they took a while to uncover and because they are sufficiently different from those found in most other studies of the subject, I hope that their publication contributes to the debates on these questions. For I firmly believe that the future relationship of the United States to the rest of the world is one of the key questions facing the lives of many people, and that public debate about that role – in the United States and elsewhere – needs not only to be better informed but also to be guided by a genuine understanding of what American power might and might not be capable of achieving. If the present study prompts readers to question some of the assumptions about American power that I explore and to see the pertinence of some of the different questions I ask, it will have served its purpose.

Writing a book like this is not easy in the present research-assessment-driven climate – very little of what follows draws on work published in scholarly journals – and it is a tribute to the collegial, relaxed and genuinely open academic culture of the Open University and especially its Faculty of Social Sciences that I have had the space to complete the project. I cannot imagine how I would have written this anywhere else.

I also know that it would never have been finished without the love and support of my family, Vanessa and our two boys, Thomas and Robert. Vanessa has been wonderful throughout as ever and the boys have been a constant, delightful distraction – though they did choose the cover – and I'm very lucky to have them all.

Simon Bromley
Sheffield, February 2008

INTRODUCTION

The American Project for a Liberal International Order

At the outset of the Cold War and during the early years of post-war reconstruction, President Truman stated that the only way to 'save the world from totalitarianism' was for 'the whole world [to] adopt the American system', for 'the American system' could survive only by becoming 'a world system'.[1] And describing what he called 'isolationism inside out' in 1950, James Warburg wrote that Americans 'are willing to become citizens of the world, but only if the world becomes an extension of the United States'.[2] Shortly thereafter the magnitude of these challenges was made apparent when Chester Bowles presciently noted that 'the two-thirds of the world who live in the undeveloped continents . . . will ultimately constitute the world balance of power'.[3] Finally, speaking just nine days after the attacks of 11 September 2001, President George W. Bush said that:

> After all that has just passed – all the lives taken, and all the possibilities of hope that died with them – it is natural to wonder if America's future is one of fear. Some speak of an age of terror. I know there are struggles ahead, and dangers to face. But this country will define our times, not be defined by them. As long as the United States of America is determined and strong, this will not be an age of terror; this will be an age of liberty, here and across the world.

These remarks point to a set of concerns that have marked a fundamental constant of American geopolitics since the outbreak of the Second World War. This fixed point has taken the form of a vision of a desirable international order – and of the place of the United States within that order – and a project for accomplishing that vision. It has also sometimes seemed like a nightmare for American strategists, since, notwithstanding strenuous efforts to sustain military pre-eminence, a steady diffusion of economic power has been a guiding ambition of US foreign policy. That is to say, the United States has consistently sought to promote economic development, including inevitably catch-up development, in key parts of the rest of the capitalist world. Accordingly, it has always been recognized that the United States would be unable to contain or limit the wider diffusion of political power that would inevitably accompany these economic shifts, especially given that not all development would imitate the US model. Indeed, as Emmanuel Todd rightly says, underlying all serious American geopolitical analysis since the end of the Second World War has been a haunting vision 'of an America that, far from being invincible, must cope with *the inexorable reduction of its power within a world of rising populations and economic development*'.[4]

Put another way, it was always envisaged that the long-run decline of US economic preponderance was both cause and consequence of its attempt to transform the international order. It was precisely because *relative* economic decline was seen as inevitable that the imperative to transform the rest of the world in America's image was so strong. Moreover, the imperative to transform the rest of the world in an American direction was all the more urgent, yet difficult, as it soon became evident that liberalism was by no means the only, or even the best, vehicle for the diffusion and replication of economic development. This predicament established an enduring tension between unilateral impulses to remake the world in the US image, if necessary alone and by force (American nationalism as liberal imperialism), in an attempt to fashion cooperative international management among (an ever-growing number of) liberal capitalist powers, and worries that overseas entanglements would threaten the domestic order. As Barry Buzan rightly notes, 'like all revolutionary states, the US has been torn between proselytizing to remake international society in its own image and preserving its own purity against foreign corruption'.[5]

As long as the Cold War persisted, however, there was no real tension between unilateralism and collective management as far as the developed capitalist world was concerned. The leading capitalist allies were willing to accept US leadership over matters that were essentially *internal* to the international capitalist economy not only because such leadership served genuinely collective interests, but also because the allies needed US forward engagement in (and protection from) a wider *external* and systemic struggle against state socialism and the power of the Soviet Union. Indeed, the bi-polar and ideological divisions of the Cold War – the United States versus the Soviet Union, liberal-democratic capitalism versus authoritarian state socialism – obscured the other project of a US-led reconstruction of the unity of the international capitalist economy in a post-colonial world of many states marked by the definitive end of formal empire. The result was that 'the Cold War system [was] subject to a dynamic – the growth of the world capitalist system – which was tangential to the Cold War itself'.[6]

With the dissolution of the Cold War, the project of extending the international capitalist order of many states under US leadership appeared to stand as the most visible vector of international politics. As a result, the tension between the unilateral impulse and the need for collective management is there for all to see. In what sense, and to what extent, then, is the American system (Truman) becoming a world system, that is, a self-sustaining international system? Where does the world balance of power (Bowles) sit in relation to the United States and the world order it seeks to fashion? These questions go to the heart of the very idea of, and the project for, a *liberal* international order. Is the latter simply the geopolitical moment of American power, an 'extension of the United States' (Warburg) – the legitimating rhetoric of US great power dominance and imperialism – or does it represent something that, while deeply bound up with American power, resonates more widely in the contemporary international system? And if liberal forms of international order do resonate widely in the world beyond America, then how and why? These are the basic questions that this study seeks to address.

Before I outline the studies to come, I want to make a couple of very brief remarks about the understanding of *international order* that is implicit in what follows. The primary goals of social life include guarantees of security, agreements and property, and the patterns of relations and interactions that achieve these goals comprise the bases of social order. At an international level, order may be maintained by a balance of power, but it may also be maintained, as the adherents of the English school of International Relations theory rightly insist, 'by a sense of common interests in those elementary or primary goals; by rules which prescribe the pattern of behaviour that sustains them; and by institutions which make these rules effective'.[7] So, we can think of international order as the result of the balance of power in an anarchical states-system, in which the (potentially) coercive power of one or more states is ranged against that of others; this kind of order arises from power checking power or from the strong dominating the weak. But we can also conceive of international order as a result of common interests arising from various forms of positive-sum interdependence; in this latter case, order is a collective property of states that are able to coordinate some of their interactions to mutual advantage. How far the resulting norms and institutions serve to shape the social purposes of states and the dominant social groups within them is, of course, a central question in constructivist and institutionalist debates.[8]

I am mainly concerned with power and interdependence as routes to international order, and I see rules and institutions as some of the forms in which powers and interdependencies are variously configured. This does not mean that rules and institutions are unimportant – on the contrary – but it is to claim that they are manifestations of patterns of social power and interdependence, not something separate from and additional to these. Put differently, to study power and interdependence is, in part, to study how they are rule-governed and how they are institutionalized. My particular focus is how political and economic power are configured, rule-governed and institutionalized in broadly liberal capitalist forms in an international economy of many *de jure* sovereign states.

The chapters that follow explore a range of different aspects of the American project for a liberal international order. Chapter 1 – 'The American Ideology: Modernization Theory and the Neo-Conservatives' – argues that the orienting framework of US foreign policy after the Second World War was not just realism but also modernization theory. That is to say, calculations of interests and the balance of power were situated in a wider vision of, and project for, the transformation of international order. This was an attempt not so much to transcend the anarchic competition of power politics, but rather to temper this by means of creating forms of coordinated economic interdependence, based in part on the replication of aspects of the American model of capitalism in the rest of the capitalist world, from which many states could derive positive benefit. One key implication of this kind of thinking was that policy had to be directed not only towards the essentially military balance of power but also towards the internal, social constitution of states as well as the forms of their engagement with the international economy. In its most optimistic moments, this view held that such a project might effectively displace struggles over relative power by a collective endeavour geared towards absolute forms of empowerment. Chapter 1 ends with a discussion of the neo-conservatives and some of the debates around the policies of the Bush administration in order to show both the continuities between the neo-conservative vision and a (pessimistic) reading of modernization theory as well as the ways in which the Bush doctrine dramatically departed from some of that theory's core insights.

Chapter 2 – 'America's Transatlantic Empire: Where in the World Is America?' – takes a critical look at the American ideology and the extension of what Gramsci called 'Americanism' to the rest of the world. After taking issue with the analytical basis of radical and realist claims that notions of a liberal international order are, in effect, little more than increasingly transparent and ineffective legitimations of American coercive power, I consider, first, a question about the nature of the US constitutional project and how this has been internationalized in certain key respects, and, secondly, a question about where Americanism may be found in the rest of the world, and what effects it exerts. I seek to develop an historical understanding of the sources of US power in the contemporary international economy – at least insofar as this relates to the developed capitalist parts of the world, principally the transatlantic arena (but also including Japan). I then look in some detail at the nature of transatlantic integration, from the perspective of the development and international orientation of the European Union, and show that American power involves the resources or assets of the territorial United States, the ways in which US capitalism and society have continued to function as sources of potentially generic practices and institutions that have been and continue to be replicated in the rest of the capitalist world, and the positive-sum coordination of these two 'Americas'. While the historical core of this world has been the transatlantic region, it has steadily expanded despite the relative decline of the weight of the US economy in the world economy and even after the end of the Cold War.

Radical and realist arguments about the importance of the competitive struggle for control and the continuing importance of great power or inter-imperial rivalries often consider the United States' attempts to control world oil as a key issue. In Chapter 3 – 'American Oil, World Oil: Resources, Conflicts, Control and Scarcity' – I examine these and other arguments in some detail. Was the need to control Iraq's oil an important consideration in the invasion of 2003? How do America's attempts to control world oil relate to the 'long war' being waged across much of North Africa, the Middle East, Central Asia and beyond? What is the form of 'control' that the United States is seeking to establish, and to what purpose? Was future scarcity of oil, in conjunction with projected increases in demand from China, India and others, a motivating factor in the unilateral and belligerent turn of George W. Bush's first term in office? Through an analysis of the changing geopolitical and economics of international oil, and of the place of US policy in relation to this, I address these questions and argue that the kind of control that the United States is attempting to establish is generally benign for the other major powers and that scarcity is not a real or serious concern for the foreseeable future. Reading overall US strategy through the lens of the war in Iraq, and seeing that war as a premonition of inter-imperialist or great power rivalry, are likely to prove poor guides to future alignments.

Next, in Chapter 4 – 'American Power, the Future of the Dollar and the Challenge of China' – I consider two potential challenges to the future of US power. It is often argued that the international role of the dollar is a key source of US power and that the European Union and its currency, the euro, might challenge that role, to the detriment of the United States. I develop an analysis of the dollar's role and evaluate the balance sheet of costs and benefits that the United States derives from this. I show that while the use of the dollar by other countries provides clear net benefits to the United States, it also provides many benefits to others. And I argue that the ability of the American authorities to control the future role of the dollar on a unilateral basis is now considerably diminished as compared to the era of Bretton Woods. The emergence of the euro, and the continuing monetary and financial integration in the eurozone, as well as the surpluses of emerging Asia (and, more recently, the major oil exporters), constrain the US ability to exploit what President de Gaulle famously called the 'exorbitant privilege' of the dollar. To sustain the dollar's international role, the United States will have to cooperate with others.

The issue of emerging Asia, especially China's rapid industrial development, has raised the prospect of great power or inter-imperial rivalries dominating the international scene once again. Prominent US realist analysts have called for the United States to abandon its economic engagement with China and seek what in effect amounts to a new policy of containment directed at the rise of Chinese power. (Many radical analyses see China as the real target of the war in Iraq and the drive to control world oil.) I situate this question in the context of both the emergence of industrial capitalism in Asia and the wider theatre of Asian geopolitics, arguing that it makes no sense to seek a 'containment' of China or to pursue zero-sum – let alone negative-sum – inter-imperial rivalry against it. On the one hand, it is far from clear that the United States could find a consistent and stable set of allies in such endeavours. And on the other hand, the implicit parallel with the containment of Soviet power ignores the categorical distinction between the social purposes of Soviet and Chinese power: the Soviet Union withdrew from and sought to overthrow an integrated international capitalist economic order; China is seeking to join it. Accommodating the rise of China's economic power will doubtless bring many changes and potential challenges, but confrontation with China, or retreat from the Asian theatre, can only damage US interests. That said, there is no reason to suppose that the United States will retreat from its pursuit of a military capability 'beyond challenge'.

In a brief conclusion – 'The Prospects for a Liberal International Order' – I argue that in the coming decades the key to international politics will be how the United States seeks to manage the tensions between economic multi-polarity and military uni-polarity, and that, in turn, the answer to this will be as much determined by domestic American politics as by the actions of powerful geopolitical actors in the rest of the world. Notwithstanding the unilateralism and militarism of the Bush administration, I argue that constructive engagement by the United States will be essential to managing a series of very real challenges to international order. The powerful tendencies towards cooperation in a coordinated international capitalist order have outgrown the reach of American coercive power, but the United States still has much to gain from an extension of that order. Whether the United States will remain actively engaged with the project for a liberal international order or succumb to the politics of fear remains an open question.

1 THE AMERICAN IDEOLOGY

Modernization Theory and the Neo-Conservatives

Introduction

Social and political theory, said Marx, is but the attempt at 'the self-clarification of the struggles and wishes of the age'.[1] As such, modern social theory in the 'West' has been strongly tied to a notion of progress. Whether or not future historians will endorse modern conceptions of the uniqueness of European modernity – there are already many questioning that thesis in interesting ways – a belief in that uniqueness and its intimate connections to a notion of progress was certainly a *social* fact during the nineteenth and twentieth centuries. At the same time, the scars of colonial violence and racism, the carnage of the First World War, the full enormity of European fascism and the inter-imperialist rivalries of the Second World War, the ever-present threat of nuclear annihilation during the Cold War, and the massive inequalities and poverty of the contemporary international economy bring us face to face with the darkness and irrationality of that modernity. 'A taut dialogue between pessimism and optimism, reason and unreason, defines social theory in the twentieth century,' says Jeffrey Alexander: 'Suspended between perfection and apocalypse, what marks off the greatest of [the twentieth] century's theorists is their attempt to mediate these dichotomies.'[2]

Against this background, Alexander continues, 'it is American thought . . . that has been exceptional, precisely because it has been so untutored and perfectionist, so confident in the unobstructed access to rationality in modern life'.[3] Interestingly, Alexander cites Talcott Parsons and John Rawls as exemplars of this rationalist optimism: the one, the ur-figure of modernization theory; the other, the leading exponent of post-war Anglo-American constitutional political liberalism. This is far from coincidental, so I will argue, because it was modernization theory (not realism) which provided the intellectual matrix for the conduct of American geopolitics after Pearl Harbor and which continues to guide the most seductive of roadmaps for the future of American power. (And Rawls' liberalism was indeed the most distinguished political codification of the constitutional elements of the American ideology.)

The encounter of modernization theory with non-liberal societies and polities, both in theory and in practice, also contained an in-built tendency towards imperialism, as had the earlier tradition of European liberalism from which American modernization theory itself descended. The dominant motif of 'development' in modernization theory turned on seeing the 'South' as different in the sense of historically anterior, situated at an earlier stage of development than that which the 'West' had already left behind, and as requiring instruction – even tutelage – on how to emulate the achievements of the latter. Thus, while modernization theory, and the practice it guided, recognized the *de jure* sovereignty of developing states, its practitioners were never overly bothered by the *de facto* requirements of gaining consent for their projects of change. More or less wherever the balance of coercive power was sufficiently disposed to make liberal imperialism possible, and whenever the need for it was sufficiently pressing, it was actual.[4] Setting this fact to one side for now, I want to explore some of the fortunes of this way of thinking about geopolitics in the one state that claims to have made it fully its own – namely, the United States.

In what follows, I begin by outlining the main contours of modernization theory considered as a general social theory. Then I argue that the conception of 'development' to be found in modernization theory played an important – indeed central – role in the strategy of containment, especially as geopolitical competition moved beyond the stabilization of post-war Europe towards the South. I also argue that 'modernization as development' was not only a project of domestic transformation for Southern states, but also a strategy of geopolitical management as well as a vision of transformation for international order. In order to illustrate this argument, I look in detail at the work of Walt Rostow and investigate the contours of this vision. On the basis of that investigation, I then show that modernization theory – more precisely, that part of the theory that dealt with questions of world order – anticipated both the 'end of history' discourses of the post-Cold War epoch and the raft of theses associated with contemporary liberal ideas about a transformed 'international order. I conclude this chapter by noting the clear echoes of modernization theory in the agenda of today's neo-conservatives as well as the ways in which the Bush doctrine has failed to register some of its key insights.

What was Modernization Theory?

Theoretically speaking, modernization theory derived from a reworking of classical European social theory by a generation of intellectuals formed in Europe's inter-war crisis, subsequently exiled to Britain and the United States. It also had a fairly direct set of social and political correlates, both nationally and internationally, in the immediate post-war conjuncture. By the close of the 1950s, the process of modernization was taken to be all but completed within North America and Western Europe: market economies, liberal-democratic political systems and rational-secular cultures had all sunk deep roots. (The participative and redistributive pressures of European social democracy certainly provided a contrast with the more liberal and elitist political order in the United States, but these could readily be seen as variations on a theme, rather than as constituting alternative kinds of society.) In the East a different set of social arrangements certainly prevailed, even if its culture was if anything more militantly rational and secular, but this could be understood as a form of reactive (and therefore more directly state-controlled) modernization, which with time and good fortune might still converge with that of the West. It was only in the South that the future seemed unsure, where the process of modernization had not yet taken root, and where there would likely be competition and conflict over the direction that future development would take. Indeed, it was above all challenges to (Western) modernization in the South that provided both the impetus to reformulate classical formulations of the theory and the context for the emergence of its eventual rivals and temporary successors – dependency and world systems theories.

Later variants of the theory, therefore, introduced many refinements, characterized by a growing mood of uncertainty: the category of 'traditional' societies was opened up and the diversity of pre-modern societies and cultures explored; the idea of the 'modern' was also expressed in less ethnocentric terms and the range of institutional and cultural variation within modern societies recognized; the transition from the traditional to the modern was investigated and found to be more complex – less endogenous and less uni-linear – than originally supposed, such that it was no longer even clear that all societies could modernize; and, finally, the coherence and stability of the end-point – modernity itself – was called into question, as ideas of modernity gave way to proclamations of post-modernity. Under the weight of this immense internal modification, modernization theory seemed to collapse, even to evaporate, to be revealed as little more than a rationalization of Western domination in the period of US ascendancy after the Second World War. Modernization theory, Alexander says, 'died sometime in the mid-1960s' – only to be reborn in the 1980s.[5] How did all this come to pass? Let us begin by taking a closer look at the theoretical coordinates of the theory itself.

Modernization theory came in many shapes and sizes, but it is possible to discern a core set of theses shared by most of its variants.[6] To begin with the obvious, the approach was founded on a binary classification of societies into the 'traditional' and the 'modern'. Although this simple taxonomy of societies was central to the narrative coherence of modernization theory, serving both to define the present in relation to the past and to legitimate the *project* of modernization as policy, many theorists clearly recognized the degree of simplification involved in such a schema. It was apparent, for example, that there was a considerable degree of social variation within each of these categories. Equally, some theorists preferred to see the 'modern' and the 'traditional' as two poles of a continuum rather than as mutually exclusive alternatives. Nevertheless, the theory argued that at an appropriate level of generality the differences between the two were both singular and decisive for social development.

Underpinning this partitioning of the multitude of historically existing social arrangements was a quite specific conception of *societies* 'as coherently organized systems whose subsystems were closely interdependent'.[7] The original general theoretical framework organizing this conceptualization was, of course, Parsonian structural functionalism, but this was not an essential feature of the enterprise and it was resisted by many of its adherents. What was more important than an attachment to any specific general theory was an understanding of societies as bounded entities in geographical space and historical time; an insistence that the various components of a given society were not only related to one another in systematic ways but also shared a common set of attributes, qualities which defined the nature of the society in question; and a tendency to characterize those defining features in singular terms – modern versus traditional.

These unified and integrated societies were conceived substantively in terms of the theory of industrial society. Institutionally, the character of the modern was defined in terms of a number of central themes, such as: the decline of traditional 'community' and the rise of urbanism as a way of life; the consequences for work and family life of the demographic transition; the extension and deepening of the division of labour based upon industrialization; the concentration of political authority in the state and the associated rise of notions of popular participation and political equality; and the secularization of culture.[8] In sum, the modern comprised an industrial division of labour coordinated by market exchange, bureaucratic and rational-legal forms of political organization, and a secular culture founded on the triumph of modern science – in short, a generic, universalistic, means–ends-oriented rationality of social and individual action.

Whether attention was focused on the realm of culture and norms, on the one hand, or on institutions and structures, on the other, modern societies were said to be 'rational' in the sense employed by Max Weber. For Weber, rational conduct is based on the knowledge provided by systematic, empirical science; a rational social order is one characterized by the objectification and depersonalization of power; and rational control is that which is achieved through the application of rules in fixed procedures.[9] Science, law and bureaucracy were the defining features of the modern. For the most part, the 'traditional' was designated by means of a negative and residual contrast to these aspects of modernity.

Modernization

The *process* of social change from the traditional to the modern, modernization as such, was understood in a broadly evolutionary fashion, with societies as the units of selection, adaptation as functional specialization, and an ever more complex division of labour as the means. Specifically, the process of modernization tended to be viewed in terms of a highly stylized, and hence selective, account of (north-west) European development since the late eighteenth century. In this story, modernization was divided into a sequence in which each stage of adaptation formed a prerequisite for higher levels of development, where the change from one stage to another was generally irreversible, and through which all societies potentially might pass. The detailed specification of the stages and the precise mechanism(s) of adaptation varied from one theorist to another, but an evolutionary, linear and, in some senses, endogenous account of social development undoubtedly characterized the theory as a whole. This implied not only a certain similarity of development in different places at different times, but also the idea that the process of modernization itself could in principle be generalized to *all* societies.

Located at the end-point of this evolutionary process, the modern societies of the West, the theory contended, represented a culmination of social development. While social change and conflict were certain to continue with the further dynamic rationalization of modernity (by the late 1950s theorists were already outlining the contours of the new, *post*-industrial society), the social order of modernity was said to be fundamentally bereft of the kind of contradiction or dysfunction which promoted *qualitative* transformation. Modernization theory, even in its structural-functionalist form, was not inherently conservative; and its Parsonian formulation was soon complemented by an emphasis on material determinations (as well as cultural norms) and on conflict (as well as consensus). Robert Merton in particular cautioned against theoretically assuming, rather than empirically demonstrating, too high a degree of functional rationality in social arrangements. The central interpretative claim, however, was an argument to the effect that the tensions and conflicts associated with structural differentiation, functional specialization and the growth of social complexity were secondary to the new forms of collective empowerment and individual autonomy which were thereby and simultaneously promoted.

There was a pronounced tendency to identify the modern, geographically and historically speaking, with the 'West', though the precise sense in which modernization theory was Eurocentric requires clarification. Shmuel Eisenstadt has argued that originally modernization was perceived 'as the final stage in the fulfilment of the evolutionary potential common to *all* societies – of which the European experience was the most important and succinct manifestation and paradigm'.[10] But in the intellectual and political climate of the time it was only a small step from this vision to another, in which

> modernization (or modernity) should be viewed as one specific civilization or phenomenon. Originating in Europe, it has spread in its economic, political and ideological aspects all over the world. . . . The crystallization of this new type of civilization was not unlike the spread of the great religions, or the great imperial expansions, but because modernization almost always combined economic, political, and ideological aspects and forces, its impact was by far the greatest.[11]

Modernization theory in fact contained both positions or, more accurately, never clearly formulated the distinction Eisenstadt is attending
to, and certainly never pondered its implications.

In any case, the geographical, temporal and social designation of
the West was somewhat opaque: it might be the Judaeo-Greek inheritance from Antiquity or it might be the industrial revolution of the
late eighteenth century, or indeed several other points in between –
the Renaissance, the Voyages of Discovery, the Reformation, the rise
of modern science in the seventeenth century, and the secular process
of enlightenment in the eighteenth – or some combination of all of
these. Not only was the designation of the West and its rise to modernity problematic – as Aijaz Ahmad has put it: '*When* did this First
World become First: in the pre-Christian centuries, or after World
War II?'[12] – but also the status of several other major regions (Japan
and Turkey, for example) remained unclear.

Notwithstanding these ambiguities, in practice the modern was
identified with the West. A simple syllogism followed inevitably.
Within the binary framework of the theory, the equation of the
modern and the Western obviously meant that the non-Western was
'traditional'. Given that modern societies were uniquely dynamic,
generating distinctive levels of social power, modernization was destined to spread from one society to another, placing pressure on traditional societies to modernize. Therefore, as the traditional became
the modern, so the non-Western would become Western.[13] Was convergence upon Western norms and institutions, then, the comforting
end-point of a world-wide process of modernization? In order to see
how the theory answered this question, we must look at the understanding of development that was embedded in the geopolitical doctrine of containment.

Containment and 'Development'

The doctrine of 'containment' is rightly seen as lying at the centre of
US policy making after the Second World War, but its connections
with the origins of 'development' have been less often remarked upon.
Much of the debate about the character of containment has shifted
between a realist focus on questions of military security, centred on
the containment of Soviet military power and the stabilization of the
balance of power through the division of Europe (and Germany) and
the formation of more or less global alliance frameworks, on the one
side, and a series of revisionist counter-arguments that economic and

political considerations, related to reconstructing export markets for US business and marginalizing the Left in Western Europe, dominated US concerns, on the other.

Both of these perspectives are based on an unrealistic separation of the 'geopolitical' from the 'economic' and focus too exclusively on Europe. In practical terms, such a separation and narrow focus could not be sustained, for two main reasons. In the first place, US policy makers were agreed that the military security of the United States depended on the denial of control of the Eurasian region to any single power, and that this required a strategy of 'defence in depth', an ability to deploy and project power on a global basis. Secondly, and more importantly, the main threat to such a strategy was not seen solely in terms of a Soviet military challenge in Eurasia, but also in the inability of the capitalist world to reproduce itself economically, socially and politically.[14] The threat of communism was as much *social* as it was military; it came from the *failures* of capitalist development in the South, not just from the strength of the Soviet armed forces in the East. Notwithstanding its subsequent militarization, the doctrine of containment never lost these underlying concerns with the problems of social development and capitalist stabilization. And while stability was fairly soon established in Europe, in the South things were to take rather longer.

At the root of the US conception of the post-war order was what Robert Pollard has called the 'quest for "economic security"'.[15] This was an attempt to use US economic power, together with its asymmetric position in international markets, to reconstruct the international economy based on essentially liberal polities. If the 'strategic' lesson of the two world wars was that the United States could not allow a single power to dominate the Eurasian region, the 'economic' origin of these conflicts was traced to the politicization of the economic, or market-based, mechanisms of capitalist reproduction. Excessive state intervention in, and regulation of, markets resulted in widespread social conflict over the conduct of economic policy within the leading capitalist powers, as well as the interlinking of economic and territorial competition and rivalry between them. What the post-war order needed, therefore, was a set of domestic and international arrangements which would allow investment, production and – above all – trade to operate relatively unhindered by direct state-political control. In turn, this would necessitate the reconstruction of national economies and their integration into international markets in those regions where capitalist development was already established, and the 'development' of capitalist forms where they were absent.

Of course, such arrangements were expected to bolster the position of the United States and of US businesses, but their deepest rationale was that they would provide security, understood as the stable reproduction of an increasingly open and liberal world economy and states-system. In turn, the world-wide spread of such arrangements, which entailed the spread of capitalist relations of production and their institutionalization in the more or less liberal form of the 'market' and the 'sovereign' state, was to be the central element in the containment of Soviet power. Military power was deployed primarily in the service of these aims.

As far as what was to become the 'Third World' was concerned, the central issue for the United States was how to manage the processes of decolonization and of economic orientation to the world market in the context of widespread social mobilization within the periphery, declining European power in the colonial world and an increasingly global Cold War rivalry. It was in this context that the post-war question of 'development' was formulated. Considered politically, the United States had long supported the *de jure*, or formal, sovereign independence of national states, subject to the governments of those countries observing capitalist property rights and a certain degree of openness to international markets in general and to the economic rights of US nationals in particular. Where property rights were not or could not be upheld, policies of pre-emptive imperialism, or support for the imperialism of others ('jackal' imperialism), had been followed.[16] Economically, the newly independent world was expected to maintain its position in the international division of labour, albeit with a reorientation towards the US economy, providing a market for European and US exports, earning dollars through raw material exports to the United States and acting as a site for US overseas investment.[17] By these means, international markets could be reconstructed, as Europe and the Third World earned enough dollars to allow a significant opening of their economies; and the growth of this liberal world would simultaneously combat the social and political challenge posed by communism.

In the early post-war decades, the United States gave little attention to the role that the key multilateral institutions (the World Bank, the International Monetary Fund and the General Agreement on Tariffs and Trade) might play in relation to Third World development, preferring to concentrate on bilateral ties to selected states and on bilateral aid dispensed for military and economic objectives. (This stance ran in parallel to the position in Western Europe, where the multilateral institutions only played a significant role *after* post-war reconstruction was substantially accomplished.) Development strategy centred on two key concerns: first, securing adequate political power and authority to contain the social pressures that accompanied the early phases of capitalist development; and, second, gaining access to sufficient foreign exchange to pay for imports necessary to modernize the economy and arm the security forces.

This composite agenda intersected in complex ways with that of the newly independent states in the Third World. Lacking substantial political independence at the time of their integration into international markets, in many instances Southern states failed to develop and integrate coherent *national* markets before the Second World War. This resulted in the consolidation of social forces (both foreign and domestic) whose mode of accumulation and reproduction was not geared to encompassing projects of national development. Thus once political independence was attained, and often before, projects to dispossess or bypass such groups became the centre-piece of state-led nationalist models of development. Moreover, since the social forces which linked the developing world to the dominant metropolitan centres were also those that controlled access to political power, *nationalist development was also and necessarily a process of state formation and nation building.* It was this coincidence of the need to form new states and consolidate state power through opposition to local and international powers, to establish the authority and legitimacy of new regimes by the construction of new bases of support and to inaugurate industrial development from a subordinate position in the international division of labour which placed the state at the core of nearly all Third World development projects.

Just as the linked drive for state formation and industrial development constituted the domestic agenda for Third World politics in the post-war era, so there were equally clear parallels in the international system: namely, the pursuit of a degree of independence vis-à-vis the superpowers and the exigencies of the Cold War, on the one side, and the attempt to lift some of the burdens imposed by survival in the world market, on the other. One of the main constraints limiting the room for manoeuvre in both of these domains was the difficulty of securing access to foreign exchange. This difficulty could be eased by access to bilateral aid (either economic or military), multilateral lending, foreign direct investment and (later) borrowing from international banks. Whatever combination was pursued, the shortage of foreign exchange often resulted in a central role for the state in rationing it to local producers, and hence also a significant degree of control over the mobilization of complementary domestic savings for investment.

Another powerful constraint on the actions of newly established states was the overall security (political and military) of the regime. The threat to the newly established post-colonial regimes was as often domestic as inter-state. Nevertheless, the new recognition of sovereignty by the major powers, together with the pressures to assist economic development and military security driven by the bipolar competition of the Cold War rivalry, solidified the tenure of extant states. This reinforcement of Third World sovereignty by the new disposition of the international system meant that polities which in many other respects often lacked the practical capacity for statehood nevertheless survived.[18] But once again, these arrangements meant that the resources and levels of organization of the state apparatus were augmented in relation to the social organization of other forces within Third World economies and societies and that the position of the military within the state was similarly strengthened.[19]

Managing Development

These considerations serve to explain what became a clear tension – even a paradox – for US strategy towards developing countries. On the one hand, development carried through under popular nationalist auspices tended to favour state-led, indeed in some cases state-capitalist, models of growth. Anti-imperialist, but not anti-capitalist, these none the less often involved significant degrees of state ownership and control of assets, high levels of protection against international markets and the exclusion of foreign ownership from large sectors of the economy. The social and political requirements of successful state formation and tolerable rates of socio-economic development seemed to be more or less inconsistent with high levels of participation in the *liberal* forms of the economic order that lay at the centre of US designs for the post-war world. Precisely the kind of nationally protected, state-led capitalism that post-war reconstruction in Western Europe was designed to avoid (and to a considerable extent did avoid) appeared to be the dominant model in the South. On the other hand, where this model of development worked, at least it was capitalist. In the context of the Cold War, and in an era of pronounced social and national mobilization in the developing world, there was often little alternative but to accommodate to these basic trends, while seeking to influence policy in more liberal directions at the margins. In fact, in many cases, even liberal reforms were opposed for fear that they might empower radical and potentially anti-capitalist forces. In this way, the logic of containment served further to support the active, generally authoritarian, role of the state in Third World development.

Many of these broad determinants of post-war development were reflected in the specific policies and institutions that governed Western aid relations with the emerging Third World. Two aspects are particularly noteworthy: first, the overall US dominance of the Western aid regime; and, secondly, the focus on strengthening the role of the state in securing the conditions for socio-economic transformation. Early US aid policy grew out of the post-war, bilateral reconstruction initiatives that were organized by the Mutual Security Agency, which only changed its name to the US Agency for International Development (USAID) in the early 1960s. USAID provided bilateral development assistance to low-income countries and the Treasury Department took responsibility for policy towards the multilateral organizations. (The vast majority of US aid has always been in the form of bilateral aid and much of this has been 'tied'.) In the 1950s and 1960s US aid policy effectively dominated the West's agenda. According to Anne Krueger: 'In 1960 the United States provided 85 per cent of all bilateral aid, or 55 per cent of total development assistance. . . . As late as 1965 U.S. foreign aid accounted for 51 per cent of all long-term capital flows to developing countries.'[20]

During this period, US aid disbursements were dominated by Cold War considerations and were oriented towards the immediate consolidation of state power and the pursuit of growth that could deliver both socio-economic benefits to the population and finance to the state. Given these priorities, it was more or less inevitable that most aid would be for the provision of public infrastructure, for basic industrial investment initiatives and for balance of payments support, on the one hand, and for bolstering the military and the police, on the other. Economic aid therefore focused to a large extent on project-based lending to finance individual development projects, often located in the public sector. Through to the end of the 1970s, most multilateral lending was also project-based. Thus the dominance of the United States in the Western aid regime and its Cold War orientation also served to buttress the position of the state in the development process – in line with the deeper pressures stemming from the requirements of state formation, regime consolidation and industrial development on the domestic front, and the new sovereignty regime and superpower Cold War rivalry in the international arena.

The key geopolitical question posed by this complex entanglement of containment and development was whether the *international* order of modernity would be as bereft of contradictions and tensions as the theory of modernization stated was the case for the domestic order. It is to this question, the world-wide aspects of the theory of modernization, that I now want to turn. Critical discussions of modernization theory have generally concentrated on the adequacy of its account of the modern in terms of the theory of industrial society (often in a debate with Marxist accounts of *capitalist* society) as well as its theses on the endogenous and evolutionary transition out of 'traditional' society (in large measure a debate with dependency theory). What is often overlooked in these frankly sterile encounters is the fact that modernization theory not only provided an account of modern, Western societies and of how 'traditional', non-Western countries might emulate their patterns of development, but also formulated an explanation of the character of international order that would be produced by the world-wide diffusion of modernity. This neglect is not justified.

Modernization Theory and World Order

Consider, for example, Walt Rostow's famous work *The Stages of Economic Growth* (1960), perhaps the defining text of modernization theory as applied to the problem of world order. After the war, Rostow served briefly in the State Department (1945–6) and at the United Nations Economic Commission for Europe in Geneva (1947–9), before returning to academic life. However, it was in his capacity as a policy adviser to the Kennedy administration that came into office in 1961, in his role as Chairman of the Policy Planning Council at the Department of State (a position that the architect of the doctrine of containment, George Kennan, had also held), and as President Johnson's National Security Adviser in 1966, that Rostow was to exercise his most significant influence. By the time his 'non-Communist Manifesto' appeared in 1960 he had already published important and influential analyses of Soviet communism, *The Dynamics of Soviet Society* (1952/4); China, *The Prospects for Communist China* (1954); and the international role of the United States, *The United States in the World Arena* (1960). Shortly after leaving office and returning to his academic career, as an economic historian, Rostow published a study of the political and geopolitical aspects of modernization, *Politics and the Stages of Growth* (1971). Taken as a whole, Rostow's work not only provided specific

analyses for the guidance of US foreign policy, up-dating and modify-
ing the doctrine of containment to cope with the geopolitical emergence of the 'South', but it also established an overall account of the
character and evolution of the post-war, international order.

This is of some importance, since John Lewis Gaddis points out
that Rostow's 'draft statement of "Basic National Security Policy"'
may be seen 'as the most comprehensive guide to what the administration [and that of Kennedy's successor, Johnson] thought it was trying
to do in world affairs'.[21] The importance of Rostow (and many other
academics involved in post-war US foreign policy) has been challenged by Bruce Kuklick in his very valuable study of intellectuals
and war from Kennan to Kissinger.[22] Kuklick maintains, not implau-
sibly, that none of the decisions about the Vietnam war was directly
affected by the input of academic analysis from figures like Rostow.
That may well be the case, though other historians have concluded
otherwise, but it is scarcely the point. Rostow is an important figure,
not because his specific ideas made a *difference* to policy making
about war (and it is important to note that Kuklick's focus is exclusively war and Cold War, not the wider engagement of the United
States with the post-war international capitalist order), but because
he articulated a vision of America's role in the world which, in less
articulate forms, was widely shared by the US foreign policy elite.
This is why I will now examine this vision in some detail.

Formulated shortly after the end of the Second World War,
Kennan's doctrine of containment had argued that since four out
of the five major centres of industrial and military power in the
world – the United States, Great Britain, Germany and Japan – lay
outside the Soviet bloc, the key objective of Western (and, specifically,
United States) geopolitical management was to ensure that none of
these fell under Soviet control, using essentially economic means to
isolate the USSR. With these aims accomplished, it would then be only
a matter of waiting for economic failure and national antagonisms to
undermine both the unity of the international communist world in
general and the stability of the Soviet state in particular. Kennan's
notion of containment was, therefore, asymmetric: he did not believe
that the United States needed to contest Soviet and communist power
equally across all dimensions – ideological, military and economic – in
all areas of the world. Specifically, Kennan recommended that the
United States should operate most assertively in those domains where
it had a comparative advantage vis-à-vis the Soviet Union, essentially
in the economic sphere, and he concentrated on securing the centres
of industrial power for the West, paying little attention to the internal

character of social development in the less powerful – though more populous – regions of the world. The doctrine of containment that was actually implemented differed somewhat from Kennan's original ideas, since in practice it soon took on a strong military dimension, as the United States engaged in an arms-race and searched for military allies around the perimeter of the Soviet sphere of influence.

More importantly, however, by the time the Kennedy administration came to power, and certainly after the Berlin (1961) and Cuban (1962) crises, policy makers increasingly came to the view that:

> The struggle [against Soviet communism] had been switched from Europe to Asia, Africa, and Latin America, from nuclear and conventional weaponry to irregular warfare, insurrection, and subversion, but it was not less real for that. . . . Rostow had become convinced that the future struggle between communism and capitalism would take the form of contests to demonstrate the relevance of each ideology to the development process in the Third World. . . . Rostow liked to describe communists unflatteringly as 'scavengers of the modernization process'; the unavoidable traumas of that process made developing countries susceptible to this 'disease of the transition to modernization'.[23]

It was in this context that Rostow developed his theory of modernization and applied it, first, to the problems of 'development', and, secondly, to the overarching character of world order.

Rostow's Non-Communist Manifesto

Rostow began by arguing that economic growth was 'one manifestation of a much wider process of modernization', in which the emergence of new forms of property and markets, together with the 'building of an effective centralized national state', were of central importance.[24] Underpinning Rostow's particular view of the stages of modernization – from the cultural and technological restrictions of traditional society to the 'search for quality' in the age of high mass consumption, passing through the preconditions for take-off, the take-off itself and the drive to maturity along the way – was a twofold definition of the process of modernization. In the first place, development was seen as a cultural or, more accurately, a cognitive change, involving an acceptance of the view that the physical world was both knowable and subject to human manipulation. It was above all this 'Newtonian' cognitive shift 'which distinguishes the modern world from all previous history'.[25] This was so because, secondly, modernization was also defined in terms of the industrial revolution, since: 'What distinguishes the world since the industrial revolution from the world before is the systematic, regular, and progressive application of science and technology to the production of goods and services.'[26] The ability to exploit the resulting flow of innovation effectively added an additional factor to production, an 'indefinitely expansible' technological resource which lifted both the 'Ricardian diminishing returns to land and the Malthusian spectre'.[27] In the pre-Newtonian world, by contrast, the technological ceiling meant that 'constraints operated: on the level of agricultural production; the level of output and employment in urban industry; the level of population that could be sustained; the level of taxable income; and the consequent capacity of governments to carry forward their security, welfare, and constitutional objectives'.[28]

Rostow argued that many of the economic, political and even cultural preconditions for take-off were observed in a range of traditional empires, but they could never escape these technological restraints. Thus: 'The British take-off – and its diffusion – broke, at last, the cyclical pattern under which men had lived for all of previous recorded history.'[29] Modernization originated in developments in Europe (and, especially, England) during the seventeenth and eighteenth centuries. But while European in its origins, the process of modernization was of world-wide significance, since it was both an irreversible, evolutionary advance in the level of material production as well as social and cultural organization and, therefore, an immensely powerful lever of change for all the other societies which remained in the grip of tradition. Once a society had accomplished the take-off into modernity, Rostow believed that 'a definitive transition' began, as the 'deeper fundamentals required for an effective take-off appear sufficiently powerful to make growth an ongoing process', even if there was 'nothing automatic and easy about the inner mechanisms – the logistics, as it were – of sustained growth'.[30] Rostow clearly recognized that the take-off might be very difficult, that it was often limited initially to a few sectors and regions in a society, and that sustained growth required it to be repeated across society as a whole, but he argued that it was 'forced upon more backward nations by the consequences of failing to modernize in an inherently competitive and contentious arena of world power'.[31] In this respect, Rostow claimed that:

> The strongest force that has operated to induce and diffuse the impulse to growth has been the intrusion of the more advanced nations on the

less advanced. ... The profit motive played its part in the spread of modern growth; but it was Alexander Hamilton's insight that was critical in one nation after another down to the present day: 'not only the wealth but the independence and security of a country appears to be materially connected with the prosperity of manufactures'.[32]

The mechanisms of modernization were rarely, therefore, endogenous to a particular society. Although the essence of modernization was a social and cultural process, one which initiated the path through the stages of growth, the original take-off only occurred endogenously in Europe (perhaps only in Britain – and even in the British case Rostow suggested that it was in part a response to the threats emanating from the wider theatre of European power and competition). Thereafter, 'in the more general case, the take-off awaited not only the build-up of social overhead capital and a surge of technological development in industry and agriculture, but also the emergence to political power of a group prepared to regard the modernization of the economy as serious, high-order political business'.[33] That is to say, modern development in general was derived from, driven by, reactive nationalism in an inherently competitive world order, a 'ruthless arena of world power', where 'a slackening of effort, stagnation, or drawing back have brought danger from those abroad who persisted and moved relatively ahead'.[34] Modernization, in short, required a strong and determined machinery of state.[35] (Rostow noted that: 'Hamilton's Report on Manufactures of 1791 is a fundamental extension of the *Wealth of Nations* [1776] to the case of a relatively underdeveloped nation intent on catching up with an already existing industrial front-runner. ... it is the beginning of the modern literature on development'.[36])

So much critical attention has focused on whether take-offs can be identified (that is, sectorally and historically) in Rostow's relatively precise sense that his broader message has been missed. For at least as important as the economic argument about the composition and direction of investment were the political and geopolitical dimensions of the analysis. Given that the take-off was both difficult and limited to begin with, that it needed to be repeatedly generalized across ever wider areas of society, and given also the importance to modern economic growth of social overhead capital – national infrastructures of markets, basic industries and energy supplies, transport and communication networks, welfare arrangements, etc. – Rostow insisted that only a well-organized and -resourced modern state could hope to achieve a successful drive to maturity, especially in those many cases where development was essentially reactive.

Uneven Modernization, Conflict and War

Even more important was Rostow's recognition that, considered as an international process, the politics and geopolitics of modernization were unlikely to be harmonious, and this for a number of reasons. To begin with, the path through the stages of modernization was fraught with difficulties in those many instances where it was exogenously driven. Politically speaking, the consolidation of the preconditions for modernization was likely to favour the military and the bureaucrats as well as the pre-modern commercial and industrial elites and it therefore 'did not lend itself easily to stable democratic rule'.[37] Where the external pressure to modernize was not so strong as to destroy the 'conservative transitional regimes', there was often a considerable capacity for incremental modernization, scope for revolution from above; but where 'foreign intrusion, in effect, humiliates before its own people the conservative transitional regime, more violent and palpably revolutionary change occurs'.[38] Once take-off had been accomplished and a society was moving towards mature modernity, the prospects for democracy were much better, although the disruption of war and the vicissitudes of ideological and political conflict associated with the modernization process itself could still produce political revolutions and authoritarian rule. In the long run, however, Rostow argued that wherever people were allowed a genuine choice of rule, the only political arrangements consistent with the Newtonian order were liberal-democratic ones.

In addition to this often tortuous path through the successive stages of modernization, there was also the fact that different societies would be at different stages at any given time, implying that their geopolitical interaction would be characterized by significant imbalances of power and wealth. Since the resources made available to states by the drive to maturity after take-off could be used for warfare, conquest and external expansion as well as for improving public welfare and personal consumption at home, this unevenly paced development, when compounded into an international process of modernization, suggested considerable scope for inter-state conflict.

Putting these political and geopolitical considerations together, Rostow identified (in broad outlines) several distinct phases in the evolution of the modern international order based on the changing nature of the interaction between the uneven movement of states through the stages of growth, on the one side, and the competitive struggle for power, on the other. In the first, colonial phase, competition between the European powers in conjunction with the weakness of the colonized societies resulted in direct or indirect European control of most non-European peoples. However, the very act of colonial rule prepared some of the preconditions for take-off in non-European societies. Overlapping this first phase, yet also marking a significant shift in the nature of world order, was the era of wars of regional aggression associated with the late preconditions and early take-off periods, in which societies were tempted to channel their new-found wealth and power towards external expansion, as in the case of America in the 1840s (and briefly in the 1890s), Germany in the 1860s, Japan and Russia in the period 1890–1905 and various 'other ambitious regional expansionists in the 1950s and 1960s' in the new states of the Third World.[39] Finally, there were what Rostow characterized as the wars for control of the Eurasian landmass, as powers driving towards maturity encountered weaker societies on their borders and sought to control them, resulting in the two world wars and the Cold War.

These dynamics helped to shape the character of world order in the twentieth century. As Rostow explained:

> America's role on the world scene in the twentieth century did not stem . . . from the brief phase of old-fashioned imperialism that welled up in the 1890s . . . [but] from the march of the stages of growth, yielding particular situations which were to enforce on Americans a sense of vulnerability and danger. . . . In the three decades after the Civil War, four great areas – Germany, Japan, Russia and the United States – moved rapidly forward in industrialization: Germany and the United States to industrial maturity, Japan and Russia into take-off. The interplay among them was to determine the world's balance of power in the first half of the twentieth century. . . . In the end, it was the relative weakness of Eastern Europe and China, when flanked by industrially mature societies . . . which provided the occasion for the great armed struggles of the first half of the twentieth century.[40]

The post-war epoch, according to Rostow, represented a fundamental departure from this association between uneven development and warfare. Wars remained an ever-present reality; but system-wide conflict was increasingly unlikely. Most obviously, the self-deterring character of nuclear weapons strengthened the position of the weaker powers in the system, despite superpower dominance and rivalry. But much more importantly, Rostow averred, 'the central fact about the future of world power is the acceleration of the preconditions or the beginnings of take-off in the southern half of the world', such that the world was fast approaching a situation of 'diffused power, in which the image of Eurasian hegemony . . . will lose its reality'.[41] Decolonization put an end to wars of conquest; wars of regional aggression remained possible but their benefits were reduced and their costs raised by the steady march through the stages of growth in one society after another; and attempts to seize the balance of power in Europe or Asia were no longer credible. As the United States gradually relinquished its hegemony over the West and constructed a wider multilateral order, the era of hegemonic powers would at some point pass.

Modernizing Containment

In these circumstances, the Cold War was increasingly tangential to the direction of world development: it only persisted because the Soviet system was built around internal repression, the mobilization against an external threat and the diversion of resources to heavy industry and military purposes. Hence any redirection of resources towards welfare and private consumption would compromise the political monopoly and control of the communist party. But the Cold War could not last, Rostow believed, since the Soviet economy significantly lagged behind that of the United States and its growth rate was running down. Communist forms of organization were powerful means of generalizing the take-off and driving the economy towards basic industrial maturity because they served to consolidate and heighten the control of the state over society. Rostow noted that the rise of Soviet power came after the Russian take-off of the late nineteenth and early twentieth centuries, and that Mao's China had been subjected to an 'abortive' take-off (a remarkable counter-point to developments in Taiwan), suggesting that the socialist collectivization of agriculture constituted an obstacle to effective modernization. If there was to be a convergence of industrial societies in the later stages of growth, Rostow was clear that it would be on largely capitalist terms.

In fact, even before the death of Stalin (1953), the judgement of US specialists studying the Soviet economy was that his revolution from above was inherently limited as a growth strategy. Rostow summarized the consensus when he argued that, by means of 'a system of political and social control capable of mobilizing a high proportion of national income for capital investment, by depressing the level of consumption', the Stalinist model was able to call upon a backlog of investment and technological opportunities, a temporarily favourable population-to-food-supply balance, and extensive, unexploited resources of labour, land and raw materials.[42] Aside from the coercive apparatus of social and political control, 'all of these advantages are transient', destined to succumb to extensive limits and declining marginal returns. In addition, the priority accorded to heavy industry and armaments at the expense of agriculture and consumer goods industries, as well as the repression of incentives implicit in the administrative system, limited the scope for intensive growth. Rostow interpreted Khrushchev's report to the Central Committee (September 1953) as clear evidence that these problems were well understood by the post-Stalin leadership, and he concluded: 'the day is almost past when the crude extensive methods applied by Stalin can sustain the Soviet rate of growth. . . . The stability of Soviet policy since the mid-1930s is artificial.'[43]

Until the Cold War was won, however, containment would have to become more symmetric, oriented towards managing the development process in the South, altering internal social arrangements – if necessary by direct intervention, military or otherwise – in order to enable them to withstand the pressures of change without falling under communist control. Politics in the developing world would for some time be conducted under the shadow of Cold War, in circumstances where societies had rapidly to absorb a huge backlog of technology (sometimes assisted by foreign aid), as well as meet pressing demands for economic growth, social improvement and political participation, and cope with large state sectors and unstable political systems. As Rostow wrote on the eve of the Kennedy administration:

> It is in such a setting of political and social confusion, before the take-off is achieved and consolidated politically and socially as well as economically, that the seizure of power by Communist conspiracy is easiest; and it is in such a setting that a centralized dictatorship may supply an essential technical precondition for take-off and a sustained drive to maturity: an effective modern state organization. . . . the fate of those of us who now live in the stage of high mass consumption [North America, Western Europe and Japan] is going to be substantially determined by the nature of the preconditions process and the take-off in distant nations, processes which our societies experienced well over a century ago, in less searching and difficult forms.[44]

In this, as in so many respects, Rostow was ahead of the game. While Samuel Huntington's famous *Foreign Affairs* article on 'The Bases of

Accommodation' (1968, originally a memo to the State Department in December 1967), advocating a policy of 'forced draft urbanization', is well known and has been much criticized in the academic community, it was Rostow who promulgated similar positions from the outset and from within government; playing a significant role in both the Kennedy and Johnson administrations; consistently arguing for an escalation of the US military commitment to and involvement in Vietnam, right through to the end of Johnson's term; and hawkishly encouraging the President's 'devotion to bombing' – not for nothing did a colleague describe Rostow as 'Chester Bowles with machine guns'.[45]

However, if the process were successfully managed, if the West could demonstrate that capitalist modernization in the South was indeed feasible, then the long-run prospects were encouraging. In a world where power was more evenly balanced, where the high mass-consumption societies were increasingly disinclined to pursue aggressive external ventures, and where modernization brought the mass of the population into the political realm even in relatively poor countries, a qualitatively different kind of international order might yet emerge.

At this point, it is instructive to note both the fundamental continuity in the assessment of the geopolitical significance of the Soviet experience in the minds of Kennan and Rostow as well as the difference occasioned by the increased geopolitical salience of the South in the mind of the latter. In his now famous (and originally anonymous) article of 1947 in *Foreign Affairs* ('The Sources of Soviet Conduct'), Kennan wrote that:

> the maintenance of this pattern of Soviet power, namely, the pursuit of unlimited authority domestically, accompanied by the cultivation of the semi-myth of implacable foreign hostility, has gone far to shape the actual machinery of Soviet power as we know it today. . . . [The antagonistic] characteristics of Soviet policy, like the postulate from which they flow, are basic to the internal nature of Soviet power, and will be with us, whether in the foreground or the background, until the internal nature of Soviet power is changed.[46]

As we have seen, this is a judgement that Rostow fully shared. Kennan, however, tended to see the revolutionary ideology of the Soviet state in terms of the political debates and conflicts of the European socialist and communist movements. Without discounting the importance of this component, the clear implication of Rostow's assessment was that the international significance of 1917 had to be read in a somewhat wider perspective of attempts by the non-European world to catch up with the modernity of the West. As Theodore von Laue put it in explaining *Why Lenin? Why Stalin?* in 1964:

> Mass politics, an ever-faster tempo of technological change, and the intensive interaction between Europeans and non-Europeans, 'civilized' and 'underdeveloped,' combined to produce a more explosive instability than had ever arisen in all the past millennia of human existence. The story of the Bolshevik Revolution is the core of the terrifying transition begun in those years. . . . Underneath the travail of revolution and counterrevolution that broke over a bewildered and driven people, of terror and counter-terror, the deeper necessity took its course. [That 'deeper necessity' was twofold:] the need for identification between rulers and ruled and the need for industrialization. . . . [Russia] could meet the common challenge of the global power competition only by a special effort of imitation. Under the face-saving guise of a superior norm it had to copy the ability of [earlier] models to mobilize the energies of their citizens to the full.[47]

Von Laue also shared Rostow's confidence that the challenge, while real, was spent, for, given the circumstances, 'the culmination of western achievement, the secure combination of spontaneity for the individual with global power for the state, of civic freedom with the ability of society to set a universal norm, tends forever to elude the Soviet regime'.[48]

If the ideological conflicts of the Cold War could be dissolved, or rather resolved by a convergence on Western terms, then two key issues would remain as serious 'unfinished business', forming potential impediments to the world-wide triumph of modernity. In the first place, only about one-fifth of the world's population lived in areas where the take-off had been successfully accomplished, and the task of ensuring that the preconditions for take-off and the take-off itself were secured for the remaining four-fifths would not be easy. However, there was nothing in the experience of those societies which had made the transition to suggest that others could not follow in their path. Secondly, within the societies characterized by high mass consumption, important shifts in social structure and values were underway. On the one hand, to the extent that modernization ended fears of absolute material insecurity, the marginal benefit of economic goods declined and a post-material, service-oriented 'search for quality' was coming to dominate the political scene. And on the other, important social groups – in the United States Rostow singled out Blacks and the increasingly highly educated young – were still marginal to the socio-economic processes of modernization. In circumstances of democratic politics, the rise of new issues and the demands of new social groupings would likely exist in some tension with an older (industrial and class-based) set of political forces and institutions.

That is to say, the principal question for the world-wide consolidation of modernity would become not whether it would overcome traditional resistance from without, nor even whether the rival communist model of modernity would succeed against it, but whether modernity could become genuinely universal from *within* and include all and not just some in its orbit, both internationally and domestically. Nevertheless, scarcely a decade after voicing his concerns about 'the fate of those of us who now live in the stage of high mass consumption', Rostow felt able to deliver a more optimistic assessment of where the overall process of modernization was headed, suggesting that there was at least the potential for a new kind of international order to emerge. In this connection, Rostow pointed to 'the diffusion of responsibility for certain critical security and welfare functions from national capitals to alliances . . . and to . . . international bodies'; to the fact that 'in the sweep of history the nation state, as we know it, came late' and, therefore, that loyalties might again come to be focused not only towards it, but also distributed both above and below it; to the ways in which 'modern science and technology have rendered all men brothers whether they like it or not; by creating a network of intimate interaction which links the domestic life of nations to their external dispositions as never before'; and hence to the wisdom of 'the theological and humane counsel in our [i.e., humanity's] cultures that human brotherhood is, in fact, the ultimate reality'.[49] The world-wide spread of modernity, in short, held out at least the possibility that social arrangements might evolve beyond circumstances in which ideological struggles between different ways of living issue in violent conflicts within and across societies, where the strong forcibly subdue the weak in the competitive world between states.

Modernity Is *Not* the 'End of History'

The judgements of Kennan and Rostow that a combination of long-run relative economic failure, nationalist rivalry and a basic lack of political legitimacy would both fragment the communist world and undermine the Soviet state proved remarkably prescient. Looking back after the end of the Cold War, Rostow argued that the collapse of communism confirmed his long-held scepticism about the ability of the Soviet system to sustain a transition to high mass consumption, as well as demonstrating the inability of highly administered economies productively to assimilate the advanced technologies of a knowledge-based economy. The course of China's four modernizations confirmed his thesis about the inability of communism to generalize the take-off and its agricultural inefficiency. (Rostow later noted that when he gave the lectures that formed the basis of *The Stages of Economic Growth* in 1958, 'those concerned with international affairs were much affected by the image projected by the Soviet launching a year earlier of the first Sputnik, which suffused the Communist world with an optimistic sense of rising relative power. That mood was heightened by the display of apparently greater momentum in Mao's China, then in the grip of the Great Leap Forward, than in Nehru's democratic India.'[50])

The coming to maturity of a 'fourth graduating take-off class' of states in the capitalist world – Argentina, Turkey, Brazil, Mexico, Iran, India, China, Taiwan, Thailand and South Korea – would continue to diffuse power across the world, definitively ending the prospects for hegemony, but possibly with destabilizing consequences on a regional basis. At the same time, a serious challenge remained insofar as many societies in the South (in the 1990s accounting for perhaps one-fifth of the world's population) had still not emerged from the preconditions for take-off into the decisive take-off stage, rendering the problem of 'development' as urgent as ever. Rostow also suggested that the 'indefinitely expansible' growth made possible by the industrial revolution might be called into question by the existence of resource and environmental constraints. Would the lifting of the Ricardian and Malthusian constraints by industrialization prove to be a temporary interlude in the ecological-cum-demographic structuring of human history? And finally, 'the credibility of the national state [was] being attenuated from above and below' because of increasing global connections between societies and the uneven progress of modernization within them.[51] According to Rostow, it was these issues of regional stability in the wake of the end of the Cold War and the eventual erosion of US hegemony, the continuing problems of 'development', environmental limits and the challenges of global connections and national fragmentation that defined a new global agenda.

Whether the existing high mass-consumption societies would be able to manage the difficulties thrown up by these issues remained to be seen, but Rostow remained cautiously optimistic: 'the end of this millennium is not the end of history but rather a time to resume a quest we cannot abandon'.[52] The basis for this consistently optimistic assessment of the post-war order was a constant of Rostow's vision: namely, the end-state implicit in the theory itself. As we have seen, for Rostow, modernization inaugurated a competitive, world-wide transformation of societies and cultures, driven forward by the impetus of reactive nationalism and mercantilist policies in the backward regions of the world. Beneath all the 'bruising' and 'convulsive' events of this 'extraordinary two centuries' flowed the principal currents of an internationally compounded process, the progressive expansion of the number of mature, or maturing, modern societies, with each one following more or less the same path of development, or at least confronting the same set of choices. (The advent of modernization 'did not decree a single pattern of evolution to which each society has conformed; but it did, at each stage, pose a similar set of choices for each society'.[53])

Most importantly, as a result of the expansion and induced replication of the process of modernization, the overall direction of development was towards an increasingly homogeneous set of national societies linked together through economic independence and an historically unprecedented degree of political cooperation. Measured against the noble ambitions of the United Nations Charter, the achievements of the post-war order might seem limited, but:

> the world community, viewed as a political system, has succeeded in surviving for a quarter-century without major war. . . . This negative achievement is not trivial. The environment . . . has been the most dangerous man has ever known: a convergent struggle for power and ideology; the nuclear sword of Damocles; the bringing into the world political system of all the continents largely neutralized or out of play between 1815 and 1914 – continents which had all the explosive potential of the Balkans before the First World War.[54]

It should be clear from the discussion so far that the common assertion to the effect that modernization theory relies on an endogenous and evolutionary notion of societal change scarcely does justice to the complexity of its account. To be sure, we have seen that the process of modernization was conceived of in essentially intra-societal terms, with social, cultural and cognitive change pushing societies through a fixed sequence, and that the end-point of the evolution of different societies is basically similar. (Rostow did not believe that modernization erased cultural differences as such, but he did assert that it was only finally consistent with a common secular, rational and liberal-democratic culture.)

But we have also noted that most (perhaps all) modernization is in part exogenously derived, driven by inter-societal and inter-state competition, and that in practice significantly differing patterns of development have characterized the West, the communist world and the South. What this shows, I think, is the sharp distinction the theory drew between the uneven and varied processes of modernization, on the one hand, and the single end-point of modernity, on the other. That is to say, modernization theory conformed to the methodological tenets of evolutionary theories in general, separating its account of the particular variations found in the historical record from its explanation of why – in the long run – social change approximates a given sequence with a determinate end-point. The central claim was (and is) really one about the survival value or resilience of modernity in competition with other social orders.

The theory said that the long-run dynamic of modernity terminates in an homogeneous end-state, with an absence of contradictions, if not conflict, both within and between societies. And the theory had a story to tell about how this came about. The process of modernization began at a societal level, perhaps already influenced by comparatively weak inter-societal pressures. At this point, inter-societal influences were weak because traditional societies could not generate sufficient resources for major projects of external transformation. Traditional empires certainly expanded over considerable distances, and persisted for significant spans of historical time, but their fundamental logic was adaptive and, eventually, cyclical. (The more diffuse expansion of the great religions did have a notable transformative impact, but this was confined to the realm of belief.)

However, as the process of modernization gathered pace, so the capacity of the new societies to challenge the military, economic and cultural integrity of the old expanded accordingly. Notwithstanding the strong inter-societal, or systemic, thrust thereby imparted to the now international and indeed world-wide process of modernization, it remained also a societal phenomenon because it operated – if it occurred at all – on the territory of a particular political authority, at the behest of, and on the terrain defined by, a modern *state*. At the end of the ensuing series of modernizations, the world would be populated by modern states, an international order in which the advent of mature modernity makes societies inherently peaceful from within, and where the diffusion of industrial (and hence military) power among states renders imperial ambitions increasingly anachronistic from without.

More specifically, modern industrial growth presupposes a basically 'Newtonian' cognitive disposition, at least insofar as culture is allowed to bear on economic questions. The most efficient deployment of this Newtonian attitude occurs when economic institutions are organized in a de-centralized and competitive way, with the market-driven allocation of (private) property rights as the best means of guaranteeing this on an ongoing basis. However, this scientific and market-based order requires a durable and general form of public power both to underwrite the 'private' freedoms whose 'unsocial sociability' (Kant) it seeks to exploit and to perform certain inherently social and collective functions which purely private interests cannot secure. The necessary means for these tasks are found in the modern nation-state, preferably in its constitutional, liberal-democratic form. This economic and political order of capitalist industrialism generates qualitatively distinct levels of social power, both for its 'private' and 'public' spheres within and for its engagements with non-capitalist and pre-industrial societies without, such that it confers an evolutionary advantage in the struggle for power over all rival modes of social organization.

The Modernization of the International

Once initiated, therefore, these 'Newtonian' and 'industrial' revolutions inaugurate a new and irreversible phase in human history, marked by five new features of inter-societal interaction:

1. The power that societies can mobilize in their engagements with one another is increasingly generated by their level and rate of technological development, and, deriving from this, by those specific cultural forms and institutional arrangements which most conduce to technological progress.
2. Relations between societies become more extensive, more intensive and operate more rapidly and powerfully – in short, what it is now *de rigueur* to call 'globalization' begins.
3. Technological progress, and the institutional means of exploiting and enhancing it, together narrowly limit the feasible range of social arrangements, such that the inter-societal system will be characterized by strong tendencies towards homogeneity *within* and *among* societies – thus ensuring a degree of cultural and political convergence.

4. Since the basis of technology is essentially knowledge, and since a high degree of openness is required to produce and use knowledge effectively, there will also be a strong tendency towards the diffusion of technology and hence power *between* societies – thereby bringing about (relative) convergence economically and (eventually) militarily.
5. The combination of the technological and institutional basis of power, on the one side, and the composite convergence derived from it, on the other, will produce an inter-societal order characterized by increasing acceptance of universal principles and hence wider and deeper forms of cooperation.

That is to say, what have subsequently become somewhat separate discussions, located in different intellectual fields, of various features of the world order – (1) the changing nature of international power; (2) the globalization of the international system; (3) the long-run convergence between the rival systems in the Cold War (on Western terms); (4) the pattern and determinants of economic (and military) development within the world system; and (5) the prospects for multilateral forms of liberal governance – were originally several aspects of an encompassing theory of the direction of development within, and the ultimate character of, the post-war order.[55] Modernization theory embedded its account of each of these distinct features or aspects of world order within its more general theory of modernity and its particular claims about the survival value of modern institutions and practices.

The stable end-state of the process of modernization – a more or less pacified liberal international order – is thus attributed to this dual internal and external, domestic and inter-state, transformation of traditional social orders. In this respect, modernization theory restates limited aspects of the classical liberal argument adumbrated in the political writings of Kant and Bentham, as well as in the more sociological works of Saint-Simon and Spencer and the economic manifestos typified by Cobden and Bright. It should be obvious that a bastard version of this line of thought leads fairly directly to the theses of the 'end of history' associated with Francis Fukuyama.[56] Indeed, Fukuyama's elaborate *divertissement* on the desire for recognition and the demands of science and technology bears an uncanny resemblance to von Laue's altogether more prosaic identification of the twofold 'deeper necessity' underlying the process of modernization: namely, 'the need for identification between rulers and ruled' and 'the need for industrialization'.

But for all that, Rostow's comment that the end of the second millennium was 'not the end of history but rather a time to resume a quest we cannot abandon' should remind us of the other side of that vision. For while modernization theory predicted a peaceful international order as the *telos* of modern development, the path taken to that end was inevitably 'uneven and combined' – in Trotsky's pregnant phrase: uneven because the onset of modernization and all that entailed is an historically staggered series of events; and combined because the doings and means of the more powerful inevitably intrude on and thereby alter those of the less powerful. The course of world development, therefore, could *not* be read by analogy to that of domestic transformations. The moment of geopolitics, what Justin Rosenberg has identified as the 'problematic of the international',[57] was an ever-present feature of the modernization theory I have been discussing, even if this recognition did not intrude on the basic conception of social development. Taking stock of the development of the modern international system, Rostow concluded:

> This had been an extraordinary two centuries in human experience. Doctrines of nationalism and human liberty, of revolutionary egalitarianism and manifest destiny have combined with the diffusion of modern science and technology to transform the world, for the first time in history, into a single, sensitively interacting community. This transformation was not mainly the result of an antiseptic diffusion of knowledge or search for profit. It occurred through an interacting series of intrusions from abroad and convulsive transformations of societies at home, in reaction to those intrusions. The working ideologies of men . . . are the product of that cumulative, bruising reactive experience. The question is this: As memories of past humiliations fade, as efforts to achieve domination over others lead to frustration, as old ideologies prove themselves irrelevant, is it possible that more human perspectives will develop among men across international boundaries?[58]

Modernization Theory, the Neo-Conservatives and the Bush Doctrine

It is so much an article of faith in International Relations that realism has served as the guiding theory of US foreign policy – its operative ideology if you prefer – that post-war (and thus also Cold War) realism has even been illuminatingly characterized as an 'American' social science.[59] Nevertheless, it remains the case that all the major figures directly associated with the intellectual articulation of US foreign policy – Kennan, Dulles, Rostow, Kissinger and Brzezinski, for example – as well as all of its key strategic planning frameworks, have also been guided by a dynamic and broadly liberal vision of the fundamental *transformation* of international order set in train by the advent of modernity, understood more or less in the terms set by modernization theory. For American modernization theory – and this is the key point – the process of modernization brought about by policies of development, imperialist or otherwise, was viewed not just in terms of its impact on particular societies, but also in terms of its consequences for the international system as a whole, that is, the world order comprised of the interactions and mutual relations of modernized and modernizing states and societies. The realist discourse and calculations of power and balancing have always existed alongside – perhaps, more accurately, inside – an encompassing liberal vision of the modernization, development and transformation of world order.

These observations are especially pertinent given the rise of the neo-conservative moment in recent American foreign policy. The neo-conservative moment in US foreign policy, which was to some extent embodied in the emergence of the 'Bush doctrine', certainly marked a departure from the interregnum presided over by presidents George H. Bush and Bill Clinton. The interregnum was marked by an apparent (neo-)liberal triumphalism, on the one hand, and an inchoate succession of geo-strategic roadmaps, on the other. If Fukuyama was the most visible exponent of the former,[60] the latter ranged from realist premonitions of imperial overstretch and decline,[61] the renewal of multi-polar rivalry and the age of the United States as the sole regional power with global power ambitions,[62] through chauvinist accounts of the coming clash of civilizations,[63] to sundry accounts of globalization,[64] on the one side, and escalating chaos,[65] on the other. None of these roadmaps, however, played a significant role in the formulation of US foreign policy during the interregnum.

Moreover, with the signal exception of the realists, all of these contributions essayed distinctly *anti*-geopolitical readings of the post-Cold War conjuncture in international politics. The temper of the times, perhaps also reflecting some real features of the international system, was marked not only by an aversion to geopolitical thinking, but also by a questioning of the very idea of seeking to analyse a single international system. Even Henry Kissinger argued that there were four international systems: relations between the great powers, principally in the Asian theatre; a pacified zone among the capitalist democracies of the Western Hemisphere; ethnic and religious strife in the Middle East; and 'the continent for which there is no precedent in European history . . . Africa'.[66] Similarly, Barry Buzan argued that no 'single model of social structure can capture the contemporary international system'.[67]

Modernization Theory Redux

Set against this pluralism, by virtue of its focus on an alleged US primacy, neo-conservatism reasserted the idea of a unitary and unifying characterization of the source of order in the international system – the combination of universal values and unrivalled military power embodied in the United States. Christian Reus-Smit says that the neo-conservatives believe that 'America's material preponderance and universal values give Washington the means and the right to reshape world order'.[68] This is true but, as we have seen, this belief is shared much more widely in US political culture. Indeed, it has some claim to be a defining element of the American ideology. As such, neo-conservatism offered, self-consciously, a diagnosis of the threats, forces and opportunities at work in contemporary geopolitics as well as a forceful reassertion of the importance of America's role in making international order.

Notwithstanding its apparent novelty, the neo-conservative moment in US foreign policy was, in fact, a return to normalcy. Despite its untutored brashness and sometimes strident expression, it was a vision that was in large measure fully in tune with the dominant post-war paradigms of American geopolitical thinking. Where it differed from the optimistic reading of earlier modernization theory was in its assessment of how far the transformative impulses of liberal modernity had worked their effects across the skein of international politics; in its evaluation of the current recalcitrance of the non-liberal world in the face of the all too evident inducements and attractions of the same; and, most especially, in its estimation of the role of military power in fostering yet more liberal transformation, especially in the one region that was both strategically critical to but poorly integrated with the liberal core – the Middle East.

Seen from this perspective, it is clear that the strategic vision of the neo-conservatives was 'one of fear':[69] it was based in the view that, notwithstanding the capitalist and US victory in the Cold War, liberal values and institutions were not widely shared outside the United States and they would have to be (if necessary forcibly) imposed if

America was to have a benign, long-term geo-strategic environment. This was, I believe, a 'fear' grounded in a realistic premonition of potential future geopolitical misfortune. It was a result of what I take to have been an accurate recognition of the fact that the dissolution of the Cold War on US terms was not at all the same thing as the rest of the world adopting the 'American system', let alone becoming an 'extension of the United States'. Neo-conservatism, in short, was haunted by the worry that the project of US-led modernization was far from complete, that it may be forever incomplete, and that American geopolitics must be guided accordingly.

The fact that for some of its advocates (and for rather too many of its critics) the neo-conservative vision was also bound up with a specifically Straussian pessimism about the fate of liberalism – bizarrely seen by some as the phantasmagorical mirror image of Sayyid Qutb's Islamic authoritarianism – is neither here nor there. If there were common intellectual ancestors to the neo-conservatives, they were a Hegelian or Marxist confidence in the ability to read the course of world-historical development, on the one hand, and Albert Wohlstetter, on the other – the latter the game-theoretic geo-strategic thinker who was the architect of 1950s paranoia about US vulnerability to a Soviet first-strike and the 'missile gap'. As Bruno Tertrais says, Wohlstetter focused on 'the pursuit of invulnerability in the face of risks of surprise attacks' and a 'search for means of making the military tool, even at the nuclear level, usable by military leaders'.[70] With Fred Ikle, Wohlstetter was also the co-rapporteur of *Discriminate Deterrence* (1988) – itself the forerunner of the now notorious 1992 *Defense Planning Guidance*.[71] This worldview is pretty close to the 'RAND Zeitgeist', memorably described by John Nash's biographer, Sylvia Nasar, in terms of 'its worship of the rational life and quantification, its geopolitical obsessions, and its weirdly compelling mix of Olympian detachment, paranoia, and megalomania'.[72]

In fact, whatever unity exists among the neo-conservatives is better understood in political and geopolitical terms, rather than in terms of any particular intellectual antecedents. The domestic support for George W. Bush's international posture was a mixture of the neo-conservatives, the Christian right and the nationalist right. Domestically, the Christian right had forged an alliance with the big business elements of the Republican Party. Meantime, the opportunity afforded by the events of 11 September 2001 (9/11) and unfinished business vis-à-vis Iraq made an alliance of convenience between the neo-conservatives and the nationalist right. The Christian right had also given unqualified support to Israel's policies in the Middle East.

Together, these elements consolidated the domestic basis for a form of populist foreign policy, that is, a policy that reflected popular concerns rather than those of the elites of the North East, that was hostile to any external constraint or oversight on the US constitution, and that valued the military as the most legitimate institution of the state. Its social base lay in the South and the Mountain West – Bush's core electoral constituency – and it fed on anxieties about the loss of control over society by the WASP population. It also had the support of much of the capitalist class for its *domestic* agenda. Big business, however, was less than enthusiastic in its support for the Iraq adventure (notwithstanding the cheer-leading of the *Wall Street Journal*) but went along with Bush as the price to be paid for domestic pay-offs.[73] Indeed, significant elements of the capitalist class became seriously worried that, as Anatol Lieven puts it more generally, 'American nationalism [was] beginning to conflict very seriously with any enlightened, viable or even rational version of American imperialism'.[74]

Whatever the details of their cultural and political attachments, the specific geo-strategic challenges identified by the neo-conservatives were the emergence of China as a potentially hostile power; the troubled identity and future orientation of Russia; the continuing regional threats posed by Iraq, Iran, Serbia and North Korea; and the relative 'neglect' of US military supremacy after 1991. But behind this particular list there was a deeper reading of the emerging geo-strategic predicament that animated both the neo-conservatives and, at least after the events of 9/11, nearly all conservative American nationalists. The overarching framework of this reading remained that of (liberal) modernization theory, but a series of pessimistic concerns that were always present, if never foregrounded, in the original formulation moved to centre-stage.

A first set of concerns related to the ability of the most powerful states in the system to maintain more or less exclusive control over the means of mass destruction. On the one hand, proliferation threatened to undermine the nuclear oligopoly, thereby creating a more competitive environment in which less stable and potentially revisionist powers gained access to nuclear (and other) weapons and ballistic missile systems. On the other hand, a rising level of general technological competence and capacity meant that technologies of mass destruction were becoming more widely accessible, including to non-state actors. This latter concern was not merely an artefact of 9/11, still less an opportunist manipulation of the same.[75] These worries were the origins of the notion of preventative action, since both kinds of proliferation were seen as a threat not just to the United States, 'but to the whole system of interstate relations'. And, as the unabashed liberal imperialist, Robert Cooper, explained: 'A system in which preventative action is required will be stable only under the condition that it is dominated by a single power or a concert of powers. The doctrine of prevention therefore needs to be complemented by a doctrine of enduring strategic superiority.'[76] The aim of maintaining strategic superiority in perpetuity has, of course, been a constant of all post-war US administrations. And what kind of state, inheriting the military balance that the end of the Cold War delivered to the United States, would do anything other than seek to maintain and even extend this position, wherever this could be done at acceptable economic cost?

The second concern was that the rise of new regional powers under the impetus of 'reactive modernization' was likely to be a source of instability and potential conflict in the international system. While the neo-conservatives were somewhat confident of the ability of the United States to maintain its role as the sole global military power, the fall of Russia and the rise of China (and, to a lesser extent, India) were seen as profoundly unsettling for the Eurasian theatre. In this context, while Fukuyama might in principle trump Huntington in the longer term, nationalism was the wild card in the game of democratic (or capitalist) peace. The future alignments of such powers as Turkey, Ukraine, Iran, and the like, were also of concern, states that were themselves not of the first rank but whose strategic choices and alignments were crucial for the system as a whole. The fear was that there were 'many countries that could become too powerful or too aggressive for regional balance'.[77]

The third worry was that the unitary leadership of the United States that was forged during the Cold War, bringing together the balance of power (or terror) between East and West and an empire by invitation within the West, was unravelling. The most specific worry was that Europe – that is, the European Union – was set on a perilous course of internal indulgence and external neglect.[78] NATO had always had an important element of internal intra-Western confidence building about it, but it was also, during the Cold War, a functioning strategic and military alliance. But Kosovo convinced *all* US geo-strategic opinion – and, perhaps more importantly, the Pentagon – that NATO was now only a means of extending the zone of peace in Europe, a loose form of collective security; even Brzezinski saw, and Kissinger lamented, that it was no longer a functioning military alliance. More reassuringly, there was considerable confidence that, for the foreseeable future, Japan would stick to its alliance with the United States, given its potentially threatening competition with China.

In addition to the likely problems of managing regional theatres and adjusting alliances to a post-Cold War world, there was the altogether wider question of the general diffusion of economic power away from the United States and the yawning gap between military and economic considerations. This was the true Achilles' heel of American power. Thus, there was a clear-sighted recognition that talk of uni-polarity was only a partial description of the configurations of international politics. Clearly, the United States would not face a *global* competitor any time soon – loose talk about multi-polarity from China, Russia and even France and Germany was at best a wish that the United States would exercise its prerogatives in accordance with the *status quo* pieties of the UN Security Council. Yet, the position of the United States itself – in the Asia-Pacific, North Atlantic and Western Hemisphere – depended on the legitimacy created by institutionalizing *shared* interests such that none of these regions sought to act independently, let alone counter to American priorities. (In this respect, the Middle East was the outlier: a region where the United States was unavoidably and deeply entangled because of oil and Israel, but where it had no institutionalized presence and precious few common interests.)

This need to take account of the interests of those one sought to lead, even while deterring the emergence of a peer competitor, was explicitly recognized by the Defense Planning Guidance of 1992. Thus, while the neo-conservatives placed a significant emphasis on the autonomy and efficacy of US military power, and while the main thrust of the 1992 *Defense Planning Guidance* was to prevent the emergence of any hostile power dominating a region whose resources could generate global power and to use force to 'preclude threats', including the spread of nuclear weapons, that same document also noted that:

There are three additional aspects to this objective. First, the US must *show the leadership necessary to establish and protect a new order that holds the promise of convincing potential competitors that they need not aspire to a greater role or pursue a more aggressive posture to protect their legitimate interests.* Second, in the non-defense areas, we must *account sufficiently for the interests of the advanced industrial nations to discourage them from challenging our leadership or seeking to overturn the established political and economic order.* Finally, we must maintain the mechanisms for deterring competitors from even aspiring to a larger regional or global role.[79]

That is to say, it was explicitly recognized that strategic restraint and an inclusive and long-term definition of US interests, making space for the interests of others, were important if military primacy was not to promote potentially adverse competition and perhaps direct challenges in the future to the further institutionalization of US leadership.

Entirely consistent with the main thrust of modernization theory, the neo-conservatives discounted the idea that these challenges could be met merely by a (realist) geopolitics of power balancing and a reaffirmation of state sovereignty. It was not just that the scale of military uni-polarity removed some of the potential for balancing – as realists like William Wohlforth rightly noted[80] – but also that taming the threats of proliferation from 'rogues' and 'evil-doers', bending rising regional powers towards the *status quo* and forging a new basis for US international leadership all required addressing the internal or domestic constitution of states and societies as well as the obvious brigading of the foreign policies of friends and enemies alike. Indeed, one powerful line of continuity between the neo-conservative vision and that of earlier modernizers was the argument that targeting the domestic social order of states as a means of rendering the international environment benign according to American lights should become first-order geopolitical business.[81]

Gaddis has suggested that the national security doctrine of President George W. Bush, as developed after 9/11, could be 'the most important reformulation of US grand strategy in over half a century'.[82] This may yet be so, but it is important to recognize the degree to which the new doctrine represented, in part, a return to unfinished business, the resuming of a quest that the United States could not easily afford to abandon – to paraphrase Walt Rostow. Even the doctrine of military – and perhaps even nuclear – supremacy can be seen, to some extent, as a resumption of postures from the late 1940s and 1950s, that is, postures in place before the Soviet Union attained a degree of strategic parity (a secure second-strike capability) in the early 1960s. Still, it is also important to note that the circumstances in which that quest has been resumed, and the strategic environments in which older strategic postures have been revived, are radically different from either that of the immediate post-war moment or that which animated Rostow and others in the 1960s.

If the emphasis on the autonomy of military power and, hence, the need to extend US supremacy was a neo-conservative innovation, the growing unilateralism of foreign policy was not. From the beginning of the Clinton administration, Congress – operating in response to the lobbying of domestic interest groups, both economic and ethnic – was instrumental in setting the terms of US unilateralism on a bipartisan basis.[83] But even given the renewed emphasis on military power, what was also distinctive (at least in the first term of George W. Bush and especially in relation to Iraq) was the belief that the costs of cooperation with others were greater than the benefits, as well as the notion that where the US led then others would follow. If there was a Bush doctrine, beyond asserting the legitimacy of unilateral preventative war and a determination to maintain military strength 'beyond challenge', then, it was broadly speaking as follows: that a unilateral and coercive exercise of US power, especially military power, could reshape the world to America's advantage such that others would be compelled to follow continued US leadership. The underlying premise was that the uni-polar moment, which was essentially a military phenomenon, could be transformed – in part by dint of the events of 9/11 – into an unchallenged and unchallengeable *geopolitical* leadership.

So, while the neo-conservative vision was shaped, in substantial part, by some pessimistic reflections on the fortunes of modernization and by a determination to resume the transformative impulse which that vision expressed and gave voice to, the emphasis on the unilateral exercise of coercive power that stood centre-stage in the Bush doctrine was at odds with the wider realities of international development that modernization theory sought to analyse. Commenting on the original vision, Francis Fukuyama says that during the 'heyday of classical modernization theory, development . . . was seen as a means of inoculating populations from the appeal of communism, a way to stabilize allies and anchor American influence around the world'.[84] As Fukuyama also notes, this strand of US foreign policy has not carried over into the neo-conservative agenda or the policies of the Bush administration.

To be sure, the Bush doctrine itself would not have got very far without two things: first, 9/11 and the probably temporary mobilization of US public opinion behind an aggressive and assertive foreign policy that this made possible; and, second, the alliance with the nationalist right.[85] Whereas the neo-conservatives were liberal imperialists, the nationalist right had a more limited agenda – the visceral antipathy to international entanglements was, in fact, the distinctive contribution of the nationalist right to the Bush doctrine – but the two could coalesce partly because of specific shared concerns about Iraq.[86] They were also united in that nearly all strands of American nationalism share the view that the United States is a unique power whose national interest is more or less synonymous with the global interest.[87]

The rationale for the Bush doctrine was, of course, eminently contestable and vigorously contested by many in the US geo-strategic establishment. Joseph Nye, among others, was a powerful critic of the view that the costs of cooperation were always greater than the gains, especially in relation to matters economic and issues that constituted international collective action problems such as terrorism. Nye also noted that the unilateral exercise of coercive military power could undermine US 'soft' power, that is, the ways in which broader elements of US society and culture act as a target of imitation and pole of attraction for other forces and states in the international system. Many realists, as well as the likes of Kissinger and Brzezinski, pointed out that even in the military sphere, in conditions of strategic interdependence, the United States might gain more in the longer term by exercising strategic restraint, thereby forestalling the tendency of other power centres to balance against it.

Others questioned the *political* efficacy of military power. There are inherent limitations to the fungibility of military power in a postcolonial world in which economic power is dispersed – and fast dispersing – as never before. Michael Mann wrote of an 'incoherent empire' that was incapable of producing durable political rule or even widespread economic order. Military supremacy, said Mann, is 'not nuclear weapons or weight of numbers but global deployment and fire power', but this cannot guarantee desired political outcomes, only a 'massive intimidatory presence . . . vis-à-vis any which dares to stand up to it'.[88] But if this is so, 'What kind of Empire is this?' It is, surely, a form of military supremacy that does not deliver autonomy of initiative, let alone outcome, either in relation to economic questions or in respect of genuinely collective problems, including transnational terrorism. Similarly, Todd charted the sharp economic and demographic constraints on US global power, speaking of a 'theatrical micromilitarism' that was becoming less and less convincing.[89]

Moreover, while the 'return to force' was 'accompanied by a reaffirmation of the *arma cedant togae* principle'[90] – that is, enhanced presidential initiative and autonomy in the use of force – the continuing price to be paid for the Vietnam war and a vibrant and pluralist civil society was that this also entailed, operationally speaking, the subordination of political ends to military means and tactics. In turn, this implied the eclipse of State Department planning by Pentagon concerns with force protection and the maintenance of an unbridled hierarchy of military command in 'combat' situations – in effect, anywhere where there are American bodies in uniform. Not surprisingly, therefore, critics also questioned whether the relations between means and ends were sustainable given domestic opposition to unilateral militarism and the role of special interests as well as the nature of American domestic politics in the making (and frustrating) of US foreign policy.

Questioning Neo-Conservatism

In fine, the limits of the Bush doctrine were those of liberal imperialism as pursued by a single, liberal capitalist power in the contemporary international system, in which military uni-polarity coexists with economic multi-polarity and in which the age of empire is definitively over. In the first place, the Bush doctrine had nothing to say about the management and ordering of an increasingly multi-polar international economy in which military supremacy cannot, for the most part, be parlayed into political leadership in dealings with established partners in Europe and Japan and emerging powers in China and India. In such a world, leadership has to be hegemonic. This truth was well understood by modernization theory, and its recognition was – paradoxically – what originally animated the fear of the neo-conservatives.

So it is perhaps not surprising that the point was soon acknowledged by Bush's second term as well as by almost all serious commentators on US power. Noting that a general trend towards 'a diminishing appetite for international engagement [among US elites and publics] is being accompanied by a second potent trend – increased unilateralism', Charles Kupchan argued that 'Washington cannot have it both ways. It must either engage widely and run the show. . . . Or it must step back and shed some of its international burdens . . . and accept the resulting loss of influence.'[91] Similarly, G. John Ikenberry pointed out that: 'The Bush administration wants both to serve as the global provider of security and simultaneously to pursue a traditional conservative foreign policy based on narrowly defined self-interest. . . . It cannot do both – it must choose.'[92] Noting that the functional imperatives of managing interdependence as well as the gains to the United States from strategic restraint, which serve to shape the interests and reactions of weaker states, Ikenberry argued that uni-polarity would more likely lead to a redefinition of multi-lateralism, not to a general retreat to unilateralism.[93] And Buzan concluded that: 'If the US seriously weakens or destroys the social structures that it inherited from the Cold War, it risks undermining one of the key foundations of its own status – its ability to embed itself in the regional structures of Europe and East Asia, and thereby to play the swing-power role that gives it a unique position of influence in world politics.'[94]

A second shortcoming of the Bush doctrine was, as Washington discovered, that 'regime change and nation building [were] not after all distinct activities'; that 'while the United States might be capable of unilateral (or at least UN-less) regime change, it was not capable of nation building on its own'.[95] By the same token, as Mann noted, vis-à-vis Iraq: 'Most of the world felt it did not *need* the American Empire. . . . Correspondingly, against such a small adversary, the US did not need Europe or anyone else.' In fact, nation building and state formation were policies without any discernible agency to direct them at all: while the aftermath to the Iraq war made it clear even to the Bush administration that a UN mandate significantly contributes to 'unconditional permission to use foreign bases, allied troops, the cash to fund the venture and, above all, legitimacy', it would be hard to argue that the institutions of the United Nations – that is, in effect, the machinery for the collective management of decolonization – have any real experience or competence in these respects.[96]

For all this, if the invasions of Afghanistan and Iraq were to amount to 'nation building' – even nation-building 'lite' in Michael Ignatieff's apt phrase[97] – if they were to be anything more than punitive expeditions,[98] then internationally responsive political rule had to be established in their territories in the aftermath. The point is that flows of money and knowledge leave US interests open to attack from any territory where the government cannot (or will not) be held internationally accountable for the actions of those within its borders. As the *New York Times* columnist Thomas Friedman never tired of saying, if you don't visit bad neighbourhoods, they will visit you.[99] But domestic constraints and local conditions imply that direct imperial rule is extremely difficult, so local actors know that the US forces cannot stay long on the ground (save confined to heavily fortified bases cut off from the surrounding society); and, therefore, the United States cannot find reliable local collaborators capable of establishing domestic legitimacy.

Military power, then, does not, for the most part, translate at all directly into durable political influence. Coercion doesn't work. Bases, 'proconsuls', and the like, do not rule the local society. They don't even protect local rulers (they may even render them less legitimate in the eyes of locals), so the United States cannot coerce those rulers by threatening to withdraw its support. Contrary to the suggestions of Andrew Bacevich,[100] the world-wide network of US bases, as well as the regional commands they are linked to, do not function as 'garrisons' in the Roman sense of that term. As General Wesley Clark pointed out in response to this kind of argument:

> the worldwide dispersion of U.S. troops in small training and assistance packets . . . [and] elite teams of special forces personnel . . . [are] far more effective at maintaining Pentagon 'access' than promoting a broader, values-based agenda. . . . we are heading towards a less powerful and relevant America, regardless of the number of stealth bombers we deployed or countries we 'accessed'.[101]

It follows, then, that even a temporary, indirect form of empire is difficult to establish: for even if indirect rule doesn't presuppose the possibility of full-blown empire, it does at least require a process of *political construction* in the aftermath of *military destruction*. As Niall Ferguson lamented:

> there are three fundamental deficits that together explain why the United States has been a less effective empire than its British predecessor. They are its economic deficit [its inability to extract unrequited tribute, cf. the British and India], its manpower deficit [the Pentagon doesn't do 'nation-building'] and – the most serious of the three – its attention deficit [what kind of imperial power, for example, supports the routing of the Soviets in Afghanistan and then allows Pakistan's Inter-Services Intelligence to install the Taliban?].

The United States, he continued, 'is not only an empire without settlers, but also an empire without administrators. . . . you simply cannot have an empire without imperialists – out there, on the spot – to run it'.[102] (The plaintive tone – 'you simply cannot have an empire without imperialists' – is most revealing and overlooks the fact that nowadays far too many 'men on the spot' would be needed for this to be anything other than an anachronistic fantasy, though Paul Bremer was indeed a pale imitation of Lord Curzon – a fully fledged man on the spot's 'man on the spot'.) In short, while US military power after the Cold War is, indeed, historically unique as compared to other states, as compared to European imperialism taken as a whole, its ability to reorder politics on the ground is feeble. The contemporary international order is a fully post-colonial order – *politically* speaking. Empire, in the sense of the extension of durable rule from one territory and people to another, is no longer a viable option in a world in which the means of capitalist development and state building are widely diffused and in which masses of the population in all states have been drawn into the (proto-)national public realm. The imperialism of the age of empire has gone for good and we live in an age of nation-states and nationalism that is overwhelmingly hostile to any attempted efforts in the direction of colonial rule. In that sense, as Mann rightly said, 'The Age of Empire has gone.'[103] Imperialism without empire – that is, liberal *militarism* – is now the American way.[104]

Conclusions

Thus, insofar as it amounted to a coherent grand strategy – and that is something that is all too easily overestimated; Fred Halliday, for one, has referred to 'grand strategy' as a 'pompous term much used in Washington to describe and give bogus coherence to random bits of aggressive and bellicose fantasy'[105] – the Bush doctrine had little to contribute to these two fundamental constraints on unilateral liberal imperialism. Todd may go too far in the opposite direction but there is considerable truth when he writes:

> If we want to understand what is happening, we must absolutely lay aside the idea of an America acting on the basis of a global plan that has been rationally thought through and methodically applied. American foreign policy has a direction, but it is about as directed as the current of a river. . . . Things are no doubt moving but without the least bit of thinking or mastery. This is now the American way – the way of a superpower, there is no question, but one powerless to maintain control over a world that is too big and whose diversity is too strong for it.[106]

In fact, rather than seeing the Bush doctrine as a *general roadmap* for US grand strategy, it is probably better seen as an opportunistic response to the events of 9/11 and a reckless attempt to deal with some very specific, but real and long-standing, problems of US strategy in the Middle East. If the Bush doctrine had ever been implemented consistently across the field of global geopolitics, it would have been bound to fail. Reading US strategy *in toto* through the optic of military uni-polarity – in particular through the 'war on terror' and specifically the invasions of Afghanistan and Iraq – is to get things the wrong way around.

That most perceptive of American commentators and social critics, Richard Hofstadter, once said that: 'The most prominent and pervasive failing [of American political culture] is a certain proneness to fits of moral crusading that would be fatal if they were not sooner or later tempered with a measure of apathy and common sense.'[107] Perhaps fortunately, domestic opposition (as well as apathy) and geo-strategic commonsense soon tempered the application of the Bush doctrine, though the consequences of and for Iraq will be long-standing. The basic reason for this is that, leaving to one side the very real question, raised by Todd and others, of whether the United States is now capable of sustaining a coherent grand strategy, the fact of economic multi-polarity in an international capitalist order of many states is as much the key to the future of world politics as is military uni-polarity. I will argue that US *military* pre-eminence can only be effectively parlayed into a stable and durable *political* leadership when it advances the coordinated interests of an expanding, yet still imperial, liberal capitalist economic order. Of course, US military power can be exercised unilaterally in certain circumstances, but it will only contribute to US hegemonic leadership when it addresses the common interests of the dominant centres of capital accumulation and their international economic relationships.

2 AMERICA'S TRANSATLANTIC EMPIRE

Where in the World Is America?

Introduction

'Modernization' is once again alive and well, and Jeffrey Alexander has provided an insightful genealogy of this remarkable recovery in the domain of general social theory.[1] Be that as it may, my concern has been with the role played by modernization theory in formulating accounts of the *international* order. As we have seen, many of the themes at play in the current raft of liberal theses concerning the transformation of the international order were foreshadowed by this way of thinking. Most importantly, for present purposes, the strategic vision of the neo-conservatives can be seen to have drawn upon a pessimistic reading of that worldview. This is no doubt due, in part, to the fact that the theory represented a very considerable intellectual achievement, an enduring formulation of great perspicacity. But it also comprised a means of interpreting the world, a narrative structure that informed and guided the conduct of public policy both nationally and internationally. Its critics were not wrong when they identified the (scarcely concealed) legitimating role of classical modernization theory and, in particular, its imbrications with the geopolitics of the United States. Nowadays, as Alexander notes, it is no longer 'modernization' that is invoked and promoted but rather the conjunction of 'markets', 'human rights' and 'democracy'. And this rhetoric of 'neo-'modernization theory no longer speaks in the name of US foreign policy alone but as the voice of the 'international community' *tout court*.

So, as social theory and as an international political project, where does modernization theory stand today? Is its current revival merely the ideological complement of an untrammelled and unrivalled US hegemony, as many radical critics suggest, or does its use to frame a course for a world beyond American supremacy indicate that something more is at stake? According to its critics, material inequalities, exploitative interdependence and cultural and political particularisms show that the universal pretensions of liberal modernity are particular instantiations of power – of the North over the South and of privileged groups in the North. Liberalism, on this reading, amounts to little more than what Immanuel Wallerstein called the 'legitimating geoculture' of historical capitalism. Ever ready to appropriate the conceptual weapons of his political adversaries, Samuel Huntington echoed the point: 'Universalism is the ideology of the West for confrontations with non-Western cultures. . . . The non-West sees as Western what the West sees as universal.'[2]

To this extent, then, (neo-)modernization theory and contemporary radical analyses of American geopolitics represent mirror images of one another, the one affirming what the other denies. At one level this simply registers a difference of political evaluation and endorsement. But beneath that difference there are two differences of substance that properly distinguish these views. The first is that there is a genuine disagreement about the purchase of the American ideology. There is no dispute, I hope, about the fact that the American national ideology – that is, the symbolic representation of the *national* interest of a particular nation-state – presents itself in very peculiar terms. Perry Anderson comments as follows:

> Internationalism, in conventional parlance, traditionally had as its opposite some version . . . of nationalism. In the US, however, . . . the term internationalism acquired a pregnantly different antonym: here its opposite was isolationism. The antithesis of the two terms – internationalism/isolationism – makes clear their common presupposition: at stake was never the primacy of national interest, which formed the common ground of both, but simply the best way of realizing it. The historical origin of the couplet lies in the peculiar combination created by the American ideology of a republic simultaneously exceptional and universal: unique in the good fortune of its institutions and endowments, and exemplary in the power of its radiation and attraction.[3]

Or, as Richard Hofstader once noted: 'It has been our fate as a nation not to have ideologies, but to be one.'[4] Clyde Prestowitz adds that 'America is the only country with an "ism" attached to its name'.[5] The disagreement, I think, turns on the extent to which Americanism is genuinely 'exemplary in the power of its radiation and attraction'. After all, not all great powers have functioned in this manner. Secondly, there is a basic disagreement about the place and role of military power in the contemporary international system. Where, in what ways, and to what extent, does military coercion work?

In what follows, I first seek to analyse the character of the American empire by looking at what Gramsci and other Europeans called Americanism (something rooted in but much more than Taylorism plus Fordism), the nature of the US constitutional project, and the ways in which both played out in the rest of the capitalist world. Secondly, I consider the question of imperialism in order to focus on the role played by coercive military power in the American-led international order. Having looked at these debates about the nature of US power, thirdly, I turn to a more formal analysis of anarchy, rivalry and interdependence in the capitalist world before, fourthly, exploring how these issues look in the transatlantic order.

The American Empire

Perhaps the most breathless estimation of the transformative power and radiance of the American ideology is represented by Michael Hardt and Antonio Negri's *Empire*. The key theses of that work are simply stated: first, the global order of capital is regulated by a new logic and structure of rule, a new form of 'sovereignty'; and, secondly, this logic and structure of rule is glued together by the society of the spectacle, in which power resides ultimately in the multitude. 'Empire establishes no territorial centre of power and does not rely on fixed boundaries or barriers.'[6] And while US 'hegemony over the global use of force' stands at the top of the pyramid of the 'global constitution' that governs this order, 'the glue that holds together the diverse functions and bodies of the hybrid constitution is what Guy Debord called the spectacle, an integrated and diffuse apparatus of images and ideas that produces and regulates public discourse and opinion'.[7] 'Empire', then, involves a hierarchy of power within the capitalist world, but this is anchored in a 'global constitution', rather than in imperial control of some political-territorial units over others. Whereas imperialism was associated with an extension of political control from one territory to another – 'imperialism was really an extension of the sovereignty of the European nation-states beyond their own boundaries'[8] – empire is an essentially deterritorialized field of economic and cultural relationships.

This is 'empire' as seen in the mirror of Rome, and as found in both the pre-Roman culture of ancient Greece and the post-Roman culture of Christian Europe, as a hierarchy of polities that guarantees a universal order based on shared identities, values and interests, in which one power, the hegemonic power, is raised above others, not so much by force as by force of example, or as exemplar. It is the notion of empire as, in Dominic Lieven's terms, 'first and foremost, a very great power that has left its mark on the international relations of its era'.[9] It is empire as a form of rule over many territories and peoples that works by incorporation, associated with an economic and cultural order that proclaims itself the basis of a universal civilization.

The novelty of Hardt and Negri's characterization is the insistence that this empire is now universal and that its power is no longer anchored in a fixed, territorial centre, since power – the glue of the 'global constitution' – is primarily cultural and economic, not political. This is a form of 'sovereignty' (if indeed that is the correct term for what is being identified), in which power is configured in fluid and transnational networks of cultural and economic relations rather than in the legitimate authorities of the political and territorial order. There is, then, already a tension in this account, never properly explored let alone resolved, between the recognition that the United States exercises 'hegemony over the global use of force' and the wider idea of a universal empire. It is almost as if – in accordance with the central conceit of globalization theory – the mobile character of economic and cultural transactions has somehow cancelled the anchorage of politics in control over peoples and territories, thereby simultaneously effacing the moment of geopolitics that derives from the coexistence and interaction of multiple polities.

Still, there is no doubt that this image captures important aspects of contemporary American power. As Joseph Joffe has argued, American culture 'radiates outward' as its 'market . . . draws inward', with two very important implications. In the first place, insofar as American power resides in economic and cultural networks operating within and beyond the territory of the United States, and to the extent that the political form of the US state conforms to liberal constitutional norms, these are kinds of power that 'cannot be aggregated'. Secondly, insofar as these forms of power work in large part by their powers of attraction – what Joffe calls 'pull, not push' – they 'cannot be balanced', save by withdrawal from key elements of the international system and, most especially, the international economy.[10] G. John Ikenberry makes the related point that the US political system has traditionally been open to the concerns of its allies in

various ways, and that this helped to cement a liberal form of hegemony. (Ikenberry also notes the other side of US post-war influence
among its capitalist allies: namely, the reduction of (West) Germany
and Japan to semi-sovereign status by virtue of the post-war, Cold
War constitutional settlements imposed on the defeated Axis powers.[11])
Let us now examine the attractive nature of US power in a little more
detail.

Americanism

The United States certainly claims an exceptional role in world affairs,
uniquely defining its national interest as more or less synonymous
with that of the international community *tout ensemble*. Its liberal
advocates concur: 'America's national interest . . . offers the closest
match there is to a world interest.'[12] This image draws upon a particular reading of American history that emphasizes the formation of the
United States as a result of the networks of trade, people, conquest,
settlement and ideas that circulated in the Atlantic economy, linking
north-west Europe, the Americas and Africa, during the seventeenth
and eighteenth centuries. After the independence of thirteen colonies
from Britain in the American Revolution of 1776, the subsequent
development of the United States was, in part, an indirect continuation of that process – both globalizing and imperial – of European
expansion into the non-European world.

At the same time, however, this expansion was also defined as anti-
colonial and republican and, as such, its self-identify was that of the
New World rather than the old European order. Unlike the major
European states, the United States became a major power without a
formal overseas empire. Rather, independence cleared the way for
westward expansion and settlement such that 'the whole *internal*
history of United States imperialism was one vast process of territorial seizure and occupation'.[13] As John Adams, the second President
of the new Republic (1797–1801), had expressed it in 1774, the purpose
of American independence was to pursue the formation of an
'independent American empire'. 'After all', says Bernard Lewis, 'the
American Revolution . . . was not a victory against colonialism, but
the ultimate triumph of colonialism.'[14]

It is only by presenting this 'internal colonialism' as an expansion
into uninhabited or freely alienated lands that the American ideology
of 'exceptionalism' could take root. But among the overwhelmingly
European majority of the population, such an idea did strike a deep
chord. This ideology of exceptionalism encompassed two sets of

ideas: first, that the United States was uniquely fortunate in having escaped the patterns of historical development characteristic of the old order in Europe and in being able to create anew a society based on security, liberty and justice; and, secondly, that it was an exemplary power, representing a model that was universally applicable to the rest of mankind. In this way, the United States has been able to present its national interest as simultaneously unique and universal, as entirely consistent with a form of cosmopolitan internationalism.

The consolidation of the sovereignty of the Union after the Civil War and the development of the national market, based on federal transfers of land to private ownership, laid the basis for the later development of a mass society: the US pioneered the culture of mass consumption as well as the consumption of mass culture, both of which were based in mass production, or what foreigners simply called 'Americanism'. The age of mass destruction followed shortly after, as the United States pioneered the combination of the mass production of high-explosive weapons and massive increases in the mobility of means of their delivery. This is what a 'superpower' originally meant, defined by William Fox as 'great power plus great mobility of power'.[15]

Subsequently, substantial elements of this model proved to be transferable to other capitalist countries. This meant that the leading economy in the world became a pole of attraction for others, as Perry Anderson, following Antonio Gramsci, has rightly emphasized.[16] It was this generalization of the US model, its partial replication outside the territory of the United States, which gave its unique ideology of exceptionalism – the only national interest that presents itself as a universal, cosmopolitan interest – such a powerful grip.

In a highly prescient analysis of 'Americanism and Fordism' in his *Prison Notebooks*, Gramsci asked 'whether America, through the implacable weight of its economic production (and therefore indirectly), will compel or is already compelling Europe to overturn its excessively antiquated economic and social basis'.[17] Gramsci's conclusion was that this was indeed the case, but that it represented 'an organic extension and an intensification of European civilization, which has simply acquired a new coating in the American climate'.[18] That is to say, just as the creation of the United States itself was, in part, a product of European capitalist imperialism, of colonial settlement in the Americas, so European capitalism was now being reshaped by the more advanced economic order in America.

Gramsci also saw clearly that Americanism was not simply a new mode of mass production and mass consumption, but also a new form of social structure and state:

> Americanism requires a particular environment, a particular social structure (or at least a determined intention to create it) and a certain type of State. The State is the liberal State, not in the sense of free-trade liberalism or of effective political liberty, but in the more fundamental sense of free initiative and of economic individualism which, with its own means, on the level of 'civil society', through historical development, itself arrives at a regime of industrial concentration and monopoly.[19]

At the time he was writing, Gramsci observed the beginnings of Americanism in Europe – in Berlin and Milan, less so in Paris, he thought – but this was to become a much more important development after the Second World War. With the unprecedented political and geopolitical unity imposed within the developed capitalist world by the communist challenge from without, Americanism was reproduced externally on the back of the defeat of rival imperialisms in the Second World War and the hegemonic role of the United States in post-war reconstruction.

In an essay seeking to place American history in a wider world context, Charles Bright and Michael Meyer describe the consequences after 1945 as follows:

> The postwar American sovereign, built on territories of production, had created vectors along which elements of the U.S. state and American civil society could move off into the world and benefit from the permanent projections of American power overseas. . . . The tools of control – military (the alliance systems and violence), economic (dollar aid and investments), political (the leverage and sanctions of a superpower), and ideological (the image of the United States as leader of the free world) – were tremendously powerful, and the ideological imaginary of the territories of production, with its emphasis on material progress and democracy, proved extraordinarily attractive.[20]

Hence, Bright and Meyer's question, 'Where in the World is America?', has two parts: what is the position of the (territorial) United States in the international system; and where – and with what effect – is Americanism in the rest of the world? American power in the round, I will argue, is based on both these Americas; or, rather, the key to

US power is the *relation* between these two senses of American power.

The American Constitutional Project

Hardt and Negri generally present the historical development of the United States as one in which 'a new principle of sovereignty is affirmed, different from the European one: liberty is made sovereign and sovereignty is defined as radically democratic within an open and continuous process of expansion'.[21] In relation to this project, Native and African Americans represent externally and internally subordinated peoples. Recognition of this prompts a further thought. 'Perhaps what we have presented as *exceptions* to the development of imperial sovereignty', they write, 'should instead be linked together as a real tendency, an alternative within the history of the U.S. Constitution. In other words, perhaps the root of these imperialist practices should be traced back to the very origins of the country, to black slavery and the genocidal wars against the Native Americans.'[22] This seems to me in some ways correct. From the time of the proto-liberal thought of Thomas Hobbes, through to the more expansive notions of rights and self-government in John Locke, to the comments of John Stuart Mill on the rights of intervention of 'civilized' peoples against 'barbarians', liberalism has been entirely consistent as a theory of liberty *and* empire.[23]

Natural law, in the hands of such early enlightenment thinkers as Hobbes, was transformed from a divinely ordained external standard into the idea of subjective natural rights, universal rights that are duplicated in every individual and which no one can rationally deny to another. The natural law was thus understood as the basis of a universal moral theory. These individual rights – broadly to seek peace and uphold agreements – can be alienated to a collective body, thereby effecting a transition from the universal order of morality among rights-bearing individuals to the inevitably particular and legal order of a given state. (Hobbes remains the commanding theorist of this idiom.) The basis of political authority is thereby conceptualized in effectively secular terms, in terms of autonomous individuals, rights-bearing agents, who transfer some of their rights to the state, in order that the latter may realize and protect their freedoms. For liberalism, then, the legitimacy of the state is thereby rendered contingent on the provision of security and on law conforming to the private interests and welfare of rights-bearing, property-owning individuals. Liberalism asserts the rights of individuals against the state, and private property is central to these rights as it diffuses power.

Within Europe, these ideas constituted a powerful attack on the arbitrary power of rulers whose claim to legitimacy was either religious or absolutist. However, societies that did not uphold these rights in this way were, according to these theorists, in a sense pre-political. Considered as individuals, their people were entitled to the same (universal) moral considerations as was everyone else, but they had no legal-political status as *peoples* or nations. Even John Stuart Mill wrote, in his essay 'A Few Words on Non-Intervention' (1859), that 'barbarians have no rights as a *nation*, except a right to such treatment as may, at the earliest possible period, fit them for becoming one. The only moral laws for the relation between a civilised and a barbarous government, are the universal rules of morality between man and man.'[24]

By these means, liberal thinkers sought to reconcile notions of individual rights, private property, limited (and representative) government and the rule of law with capitalist colonial expansion and settlement in foreign lands. These ideas represented an important shift in the ruling mores and discourses of empire. In contrast to conquest empires of feudal aristocracies based on force and religious conversion, trading empires would be based on wealth and common interests – what the English in the eighteenth century liked to call 'empires of liberty'. This shift was accompanied by the enlightenment's 'powerful celebration of the civilising and humanising power of commerce'.[25] 'Civilization', rather than evangelization, thus became the official discourse of the European empires. And to be civil was to be someone who knew correctly how to interpret the natural law – nowadays extended to include the full panoply of free markets, liberal democracy and human rights. Empire, in turn, could increasingly be represented as a commonwealth of 'free' peoples enjoying individual liberties under the rule of law.

Set against this background, when Hardt and Negri say that 'the contemporary idea of Empire is born through the global expansion of the internal U.S. constitutional project',[26] there is a large element of truth in this, even if that project had its origins in the prior expansion of seventeenth- and eighteenth-century European, and especially English, society. But this does not mean that the process has no centre. Nor does it imply the effacement of the conjunctural development of geopolitics by the global flows of networked societies. In fact, it has a hierarchy of centres located in an increasingly coordinated set of territorial states, that is, compulsory apparatuses of political power, in which the power of the United States plays a complex and ambiguous role, sometimes directing collective forms of empowerment to mutual advantage, sometimes using its coercive power to deter and compel adversaries, and sometimes using both to engineer an imperialist creation of new forms of capitalism.

This is, I will argue, a form of liberal imperialism with deep roots, and a more or less continuous presence, in the history of capitalist development since the late seventeenth century; it is motored by the economic dynamics of the restless expansion of capitalism, and by the competitive (yet partly coordinated) states-system, which provides its political armature. What glues this system together is less Guy Debord's spectacle than the common verities of material interests; the coordinated power of a liberal international capitalist order; and, acting on behalf of this, in the last instance (and sometimes it now seems in the first instance), the coercively deployed military power of the United States.

Imperialism

Empire, according to Hardt and Negri, is to be contrasted with imperialism, the latter being defined in terms of the 'extension of the sovereignty of the European nation-states beyond their own boundaries', that is, in terms of its political form, rather than in terms of its economic mechanisms. However, by defining imperialism in political-territorial terms, Hardt and Negri, in effect, concede much of the liberal self-understanding of a world of independent states: empire represents a global expansion of the US constitutional project and US – now globalized – forms of economy and culture, but America is not imperialist. Of course, capitalist imperialism (often) involved 'an extension of the sovereignty of the European nation-states beyond their own boundaries'; but, even where it did so, it was also an *economic* (and cultural) process, which established relations of economic domination – 'specifically, the formal or informal control over local economic resources in a manner advantageous to the metropolitan power, and at the expense of the local economy'.[27] Indeed, as Ellen Meiksins Wood has pointed out, 'capitalist imperialism eventually became almost entirely a matter of economic domination, in which market imperatives, manipulated by the dominant capitalist powers, were made to do the work no longer done by imperial states or colonial settlers'.[28]

Capitalist imperialism, on this understanding, is a set of coercive power relations established between different parts of the world economy, such that one region benefits at the expense of another. Its central mechanisms are economic and involve the ability of one region to manipulate market imperatives to its advantage. These economic mechanisms – operating by means of control over trade, investment or labour migration – may or may not involve the extension of political-military control by one polity over another. In any case, colonial rule is only one form of empire, for, as Charles Maier, rightly says: 'Empire is a form of political organization in which the social elements that rule in the dominant state . . . create a network of allied elites in regions abroad who accept subordination in international affairs in return for the security of their position in their own administrative unit.'[29]

Now, it is a commonplace that the United States currently exercises something close to a global monopoly over the international use of force and, moreover, that this state of affairs is likely to persist for some considerable time. At least as far as military power is concerned, William Odom and Robert Dujarric are surely correct to say that the 'quantity and dimensions of U.S. power are so overwhelming that no other state or potential coalition of states can reasonably hope to counter-balance it'.[30] It is much less clear, however, just what this fact signifies for the conduct of contemporary international politics and even for the future of US grand strategy towards the international capitalist order. For many the Bush administration's 'war on terror' was a composite, even if contradictory, attempt to assert permanent US dominance over other states and the system of states as a means of expanding, and policing, a liberal imperialist international capitalist order. 'The primary principle of [US] foreign policy, rooted in Wilsonian idealism and carried over from Clinton to Bush II', says Noam Chomsky, 'is *the imperative of America's mission as the vanguard of history, transforming the global order and, in doing so, perpetuating its own dominance*" guided by "*the imperative of military supremacy, maintained in perpetuity and projected globally*".[31]

Chomsky identifies one powerful reason for maintaining and asserting such primacy in the need to defend a position of domination in a context of widening global inequalities. Chomsky quotes the US National Intelligence Council to the effect that as neo-liberal globalization continues, so 'deepening economic stagnation, political instability, and cultural alienation [will] foster ethnic, ideological and religious extremism, along with the violence that often accompanies it'.[32] 'The most fundamental and antagonistic contradiction of all those that US supremacy entails', says Stephen Gill, is 'the fact that for a growing proportion of the world's population the deepening power of capital expropriates and undermines the basic means of livelihood.'[33] 'What has long been understood [by US planners]', says Chomsky, is that 'the rich and powerful are no longer assured of the near monopoly of violence that has largely prevailed throughout history.'[34] Similarly, Paul Rogers interprets the post-Cold War strategy of the United States as a response to the conjunction of global inequalities and an erosion of the West's monopoly of the means of violence.[35] With the passing of the Cold War, which in any case many identify in largely inter-imperial or North–South terms, the imperatives for the United States to dominate the South and to discipline competitors and allies in the North have not changed.[36] Indeed, as global inequalities deepen and as a tri-polar *economic* order has become 'more firm' (Chomsky), those imperatives may be even more pressing.

In a similar manner, Emmanuel Todd has argued that with the end of the Cold War the United States has retreated from whatever universalism it once promoted, both domestically and internationally. Describing this retreat as the 'central ideological tendency of America today', Todd says that:

> the pressure of the rival empire [viz. the Soviet Union] had pushed the United States beyond what it was really capable of achieving in the area of universalism [both domestically and internationally]. The disappearance of this pressure is . . . reducing the circumference of the mental circle that will unite those still to be included within the American 'universal'.[37]

Taken together, the potential instabilities generated by global inequalities and an incipient erosion of the monopoly over the use of violence, the rise of other centres of economic power, and the retreat from universalism imply that 'what America proposes now is not the protection of a [world of] liberal democracy, but instead more money and power for those who are already the wealthiest and the most powerful'.[38] The 'principal beneficiaries' of the coercive US drive to subordinate all states to the private forces of civil society, avers Gill, are 'the global plutocracy of the mega-rich'.[39] The end result is a drive for permanent, global military supremacy and the institutionalization of 'a permanent state of war across the globe' under the pretext of the 'war on terror'.[40]

Some argue that through the ideologies of 'human rights' and the 'international community', the United States has had some considerable success in usurping the right to violate the sovereignty of others, while jealously protecting its own sovereignty from any external scrutiny or challenge. Thus, Perry Anderson has suggested that 'in the absence of any alternative or countervailing power, American hegemony has for the first time been able to impose its self-description as a global norm. . . . its synonym is simply – nothing less than – the "international community" itself'.[41] Others argue that the United States is increasingly unable to legitimate its international role. In the absence of such legitimacy, the patently coercive face of military power assumes a greater salience. It is 'not clear', says David Harvey, 'that the US will follow the rules' of the open, liberal post-war order: America has 'given up on hegemony through consent and resorts more and more to domination through coercion', in large part precisely because the 'capitalist logic . . . points to the draining away of economic power from the United States'.[42]

Notwithstanding these differences of interpretation of the balance of force and consent, there is widespread agreement that: first, the neo-liberal globalization pursued by the United States serves to widen international inequalities and deepen global conflicts; secondly, with the passing of the Cold War, America's motives in subordinating the South and disciplining allies and potential rivals are becoming increasingly clear; thirdly, relations of coercive power, and especially those of military force, are supplanting forms of cooperation and collective empowerment in the shaping of international order; and hence, fourthly, America's protestations of Wilsonian idealism (the liberal-democratic imperialism of the neo-conservatives) are little more than increasingly threadbare attempts to legitimate US global power.

So there is, as ever, a neat inversion of the conceits of liberal modernization theory in all of this. America's mission, says Andrew Bacevich, is one of 'transforming the global order and, in doing so, perpetuating its own dominance'.[43] But this is precisely what modernization theory regarded as a contradiction in terms. It was just because the United States could *not* expect permanent dominance that the imperative to transform the rest of the world was so strong. The purpose of transformation was to make the world safe for an America whose power was sure to diminish. This is the ever-present paranoia in American politics that continues to haunt the neo-conservative imagination. But on the radical reading, while this may be true in respect of *economic* matters, it is not the whole story, since transformation and *military* supremacy are perfectly consistent with one another. Indeed, for radical analyses, it is because transformation has been associated with a relative decline of American economic power that the assertion of a coercive military superiority has become all the more important.

Finally, this is so because, as Chomsky puts it, 'violence is a powerful instrument of control' and 'coercion works'.[44] On this count, the 'war on terror' (now the 'long war') is but the latest in a series of umbrellas under which a project of perpetual dominance has been pursued since the end of the Cold War. Variously named – 'a perpetual war for perpetual peace' (Gore Vidal following Charles Beard), 'a permanent state of war across the globe' (Todd), an 'infinite war' that is 'without end' (Ellen Meiksins Wood after Thomas Hobbes) – it dramatically signifies the unashamed claim to global leadership and exclusive status that has long been at the core of American self- and national-identity and foreign policy.

The motivations behind this project have been construed in a variety of ways: to sustain the military-industrial complex within the United States; to bolster a wider domestic, right-wing and nationalist, agenda; to visit exemplary terror in punitive expeditions; to establish an international norm of preventative war, exercised exclusively and unilaterally; to effect regime change in 'rogue' states; to discipline allies and (potential) regional competitors – in each case, however, 'the overriding objective is to demonstrate and consolidate US domination over the system of multiple states'.[45] And while some have contended that the empire over which this power seeks to hold sway is a deterritorialized, globalized field of *economic* and *cultural* power (Hardt and Negri), most sober observers insist that it is nevertheless an 'empire that must be administered by institutions and powers which do indeed have territorial boundaries', that is, an order of *politically independent nation-states*.[46] Indeed, it is also something of a commonplace that the *differentia specifica* of US capitalist imperialism is that it is exercised indirectly through, between and among states that maintain their *de jure* sovereignty, rather than through direct – that is, colonial – imposition. It is, in short, an empire fully attuned to a post-colonial world.

These elements of common understanding conceal a range of important differences of interpretation and some unresolved questions. Is US grand strategy aimed at a classically offensive realist posture, designed to increase its essentially military and coercive power within the system of states, as a means of perpetuating its role as the sole regional power with global ambitions and forestalling the emergence of any regional powers that can challenge that pre-eminence?[47] Or is it, rather, that it is 'this endless *possibility* of war that imperial capital [that is, capital that operates within and between the developed capitalist states and which dominates peripheral capital] needs to sustain its hegemony over the global system of multiple states'?[48] And if it is the latter, how does 'imperial capital' relate to US capital – where, if anywhere, are the inter-imperial rivalries now? – and how do both relate to the geopolitics of the United States? Is the military pre-eminence of the United States a precondition for the hegemony of imperial capital over the post-colonial states-system?

Behind these questions lurk others: what are the sources of US power, and how do they operate in an international capitalist economy and system of nation-states? Both realists and many radical critics, including Marxists, are prone to take military uni-polarity as an all-encompassing fact about world politics. 'It is often misleading to focus on one region of the world,' says Chomsky, 'forgetting that global planning is in Washington.'[49] For realists this is to be expected since realism contends that the overriding goal of great powers is to maximize their share of world power and the ultimate currency of power among states is relative military capability.

For radical and Marxist analysts the argument takes a different form: either a claim that uni-polarity in effect produces a form of US super-imperialism as a means of disciplining potential inter-imperialist economic rivalries, as military power compensates for economic weakness; or an argument about the function of exemplary violence in disciplining recalcitrant states, as the US military can go anywhere at any time and visit destruction, even if it cannot establish stable political rule in the aftermath; or the claim that military competition is the one domain where the US lead is unassailable: since America's existing military advantages are certain to produce attempts to gain a deterrent by its geopolitical adversaries, the US is reaching for global power by eroding the firewall between nuclear and conventional weapons and attempting to monopolize the military use of space for offensive purposes.[50] In each case, however, it is assumed that military power is the harbinger of political power.

Anarchy, Rivalry and Interdependence

Alongside the ideological competition between the capitalist and communist worlds and the military rivalry between the superpowers, post-war American power involved three different kinds of relationship with the rest of the capitalist world:

1. *a marked asymmetry of coercive power resources*: in both the military and the economic spheres the United States was uniquely and asymmetrically able to impose costs on others;
2. *a pole of attraction*: US society – its economy, culture and even aspects of its politics – served as a model that radiated outwards and attracted inwards, providing a 'target of imitation' that others sought to replicate or emulate; and
3. *hegemonic leadership*: US political and ideological leadership offered positive-sum solutions to many of the collective action problems for the leading capitalist states through a coordinated, if not consensual, hegemonically ordered international division of political labour.

Now that the Cold War is over, many have argued – if somewhat formulaically – as follows: the success of the United States as a pole of attraction has undermined the uniqueness and asymmetry of its coercive economic power, thereby eroding the conditions for US hegemony. Specifically, it has been argued that:

1. the United States did indeed function as a pole of attraction, but the replication or emulation of elements of the American model outside the territory of the United States has resulted in a process of catching up and hence growing competition, thereby diminishing US coercive economic power over states that have been both economic rivals and geopolitical allies;
2. as other states or regions have caught up with the United States, so they have been tempted to assert their political and ideological independence and, with the external (i.e. Cold War) needs for unity dissolved, to refuse American direction as to their role in the international division of political labour – in short, economic rivalry tends also to geopolitical competition;
3. the result is that the United States is increasingly driven to use its remaining (essentially military) coercive power to maintain its position against potential challengers; bereft of overwhelming economic supremacy it is attempting to convert military uni-polarity into political supremacy.

There is clearly much that is right with this analysis; it is, after all, one part of the official version of US foreign policy as codified by Brzezinski and many others. But it harks back to a world – of inter-imperialist rivalries – that has gone and it is, I think, insufficiently attuned to the contemporary 'spatial fix' of capitalist development, which is that of a world of many states in which nationalism, not empire, is the dominant political and ideological force.

Consider the nature of capitalism in a world of many states. David Harvey has pointed out that historically specific, spatial agglomerations of capital necessarily give rise to uneven development and 'regionality', so that 'inter-regional competition and specialization in and among these regional economies consequently becomes a fundamental feature of how capitalism works'.[51] I don't want to quibble about the word 'fundamental', but it is surely even more important that each of these regions now subsists and depends for its reproduction on increasingly open and interdependent – though not integrated – international markets ('integrated' implies a technically efficient division of labour; 'interdepedent' carries no such burden). As Marx put it in the *Grundrisse*:

> while capital must on one side strive to tear down every spatial barrier to intercourse, i.e., to exchange, and conquer the whole earth for its market, it strives on the other side to annihilate this space with time. . . . The result is: the tendentially and potentially general development of the forces of production . . . as a basis; likewise, the universality of intercourse, hence the world market as a basis.[52]

Today, the borders of capitalist states are, at least in the more open, liberal economies, no longer 'fixed boundaries or barriers' to the flows of the circuits of capital; they are increasingly open and permeable to such flows of trade, investment and money – though not, of course, to flows of labour. But this mobility of capital across borders presupposes the definition, regulation and enforcement of rights of contract and rights to property, and much else besides, *within* and, crucially, *between* many territorially ordered centres of political power. It is the increasingly liberal codification of these rights and contracts among a growing number of capitalist states, and, perhaps even more importantly, the coordinated processes of aligning each such jurisdiction with the others, which makes possible the very mobility of capital that creates tendencies towards the 'world market as a basis'. Note, however, that the 'world market as a basis' is at most a set of tendencies of capitalist development; it has never (yet) been an accomplished fact.

So an equally fundamental fact about the international capitalist economy, in the post-colonial world of nation-states, is that capitalist development and the circuits of capital that sustain its expanded reproduction are ever more dispersed across the globe and ever more connected across multiple politically defined and administered territories, such that the logic of contemporary capital accumulation and technological innovation is less and less under American control. In the contemporary epoch this means that the logic of capitalist competition, accumulation and innovation increasingly depends on *many* states, such that each state – including increasingly even the United States – is compelled to take responsibility for managing its domestic order and external policies in ways that sustain the international conditions of capitalist development. It also implies that the regional competition that Harvey rightly highlights is primarily about the terms on which the uneven international circulation of capital is to take place. That is to say, underlying the sound and fury of the competitive game is a wider common interest in managing interdependence through an increasingly coordinated liberal capitalist international order of multiple, juridically sovereign nation-states.

The extent to which mutual interests are in fact served is, of course, an open, empirical question because the dependence of all states on internationally circulating capital is just the other side of the gains from specialization and exchange in that the concept of dependence refers to the opportunity costs of forgoing those potential gains. What Albert Hirschman said of trade applies to capitalist specialization and exchange more generally:

> The influence which country A acquires in country B by foreign trade depends in the first place upon the total gain which B derives from that trade; the total gain from trade for any country is indeed nothing but another expression for the total impoverishment which would be inflicted upon it by a stoppage of trade. In this sense the classical concept, gain from trade, and the power concept, dependence on trade, ... are seen to be merely two aspects of the same phenomenon.[53]

And given that the nexus among the competitors is highly asymmetric – after all, interdependence is just mutual dependence and mutual does not imply equal – interdependence creates the possibilities for some to control the actions of others. That is to say, the interdependence and dependence involved in the 'world market as a basis' is not simply that 'in which an effect is contingent on or conditioned by something else' (so-called 'sensitivity dependence'), but rather indicates 'a relationship of subordination in which one thing is supported by something else or must rely upon something else for fulfillment of a need' ('vulnerability dependence').[54] In this latter case – that is, in cases of vulnerability dependence – one party to interdependence may be in a position to alter the terms of its position vis-à-vis another, either unilaterally or by acting in coalition with a third party, in such a way that its benefits exceed its costs, while the target has no option but to bear its costs. In principle, then, asymmetrical interdependence may form the basis for an exercise of coercive power. Lloyd Gruber has called the power to impose costs of this kind on another 'go-it-alone' power. Once one state has exercised (or credibly threatened to exercise) go-it-alone power, thereby changing the position of another or others, the latter may 'cooperate' in a subsequent bargain. But this bargaining takes place *after* the state with go-it-alone power has acted to *worsen* the position of the target state. Thereafter, even a cooperative bargain may not be enough to get the weaker party back to the *status quo ante*.

Often, go-it-alone power is exercised in a coalition with others, and the possibility of forming such a coalition is one basis for a credible threat to exclude target states. Those threatened with exclusion would prefer that the coalition not form; but once the latter has exercised its go-it-alone power, the outsiders have little alternative but to join as inclusion represents a better outcome than exclusion, even though inclusion represents a loss over the *status quo ante*. Gruber expresses the point as follows:

> institutionalized cooperation by one group of actors (the winners) can have the effect of restricting the options available to another group (the losers), altering the rules of the game such that members of the latter group are better off playing by the new rules despite their strong preference for the original, pre-cooperation status quo.

As a result, the exercise of go-it-alone power can give rise to a 'band-wagoning' dynamic: losers join the winners because 'accession is simply the lesser of two evils'.[55] The enlargement of the coalition then changes the situation for yet more 'outsiders' who then come to experience a similar pressure to follow suit. The central point to understand here is that, unlike a cooperative bargain, which must involve positive gains for all parties, 'cooperation' that is enforced by the use (or threat) of go-it-alone power need not be positive sum; indeed, it could in principle be negative sum overall. For the targeted outsiders it is only a cooperative, positive-sum outcome with respect to the position they find themselves in *after* the exercise of coercive, go-it-alone power. When 'cooperation' is enforced in this way, the gains of the actor or actors that initiate the sequence may be more or less than the losses of the target states. Accordingly, the central analytical question at stake here is this: what is the relation between the coordinated liberal capitalist order and the collective empowerment of states and capital thereby promoted, on the one hand, and the hierarchy of domination and subordination among its expanding membership, on the other?

This question is both empirical and counter-factual: it is empirical because the costs and benefits of asymmetric interdependence are, in theory, indeterminate; it is counter-factual because costs and benefits must be reckoned relative to feasible alternatives. At this point, a formal analysis of interdependence may help to clarify the issues at stake. For once we recognize that states subsist in conditions of interdependence, just as much as those of anarchy, and that there are costs involved in exercising coercive power, some precision is called for.

Cooperative Bargains and Coercive Power

Thus far I have been concerned to insist that alongside the anarchy of inter-state competition and the rivalries that this can create, there are also relations of mutual gain and coordination established by the facts of interdependence in an international capitalist world. (Some of the analytic issues raised by this conjunction are similar to those rehearsed in the debate between realist and liberal theories of interdependence.) To see how a focus on interdependence changes our understanding of international politics, let us consider, first, a specific model of one kind of strategic interaction: we assume that there are gains to be reaped from cooperation, that there is a positive-sum game to be played. The model is one of a family of bargaining games studied in cooperative game theory: it assumes that players can bargain with each other or walk away. One useful aspect of this kind of model for International Relations theory is that it can help us to understand what countries will likely do, given their different capacities to 'go it alone'.

For example, suppose that the United States and the European Union (EU) are considering whether to negotiate on trade and investment liberalization and that the total potential gains from liberalization are $100 billion if they cooperate in reciprocal measures. On the other hand, if they liberalize unilaterally, the United States can gain $50 billion and the EU $10 billion. Figure 2.1 illustrates how the total

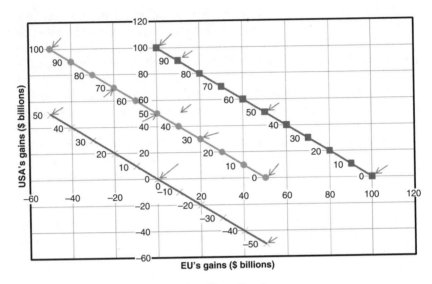

Figure 2.1. USA–European Union liberalization

gains from cooperation – that is, reciprocal liberalization – can be divided between the two parties.

Start by looking at the top right-hand quadrant of Figure 2.1. The vertical and horizontal axes measure the gains going to the United States and the EU, respectively, as a result of negotiations. At point 0,0 (the origin), the game has not started, no negotiations have taken place, so the gains are zero. Once the game starts, the United States and the EU move away from the origin, both seeking the best deal they can achieve. The points along the line 0,100–100,0 represent all the possible divisions of the total gains ($100 billion) between the United States and the EU. This can be thought of as a possibility frontier: each country seeks to achieve the best deal that it can along the frontier, by instituting reciprocal liberalization and then seeking a division of the gains that maximizes its benefits.

In order to see the range of expected outcomes, consider what might be each country's alternative to making a deal. If the EU undertakes some unilateral liberalization, its gains are $10 billion; if the United States does so, its gains are $50 billion. Then point 10,50 on Figure 2.1 represents the outcome if there is no cooperation, if the players walk away. This is sometimes called the fall-back position, or 'threat point', of the parties – what each can get in the absence of cooperation. Since the United States can get $50 billion without cooperating, it will presumably not accept a division of the joint gains that gives it less than that figure, and similarly the EU will not accept anything less than $10 billion. Neither party will accept a cooperative outcome that gives it less than its fall-back position. This implies that all points between 10,90 (where the USA gets $90 billion and the EU gets $10 billion) and 50,50 (where the USA gets $50 billion and the EU gets $50 billion) are possible outcomes. This does not tell us exactly where the division will occur, but it does illustrate the general point that we can expect the outcome of a bargaining process to be more favourable to the side with the better fall-back position, because that is what it can threaten the other side with. The party with the most to gain from cooperation is in the weaker position; *the party with the least to gain from cooperation is in the stronger bargaining position*. (Of course, such threats have to be credible.) Notice that this does *not* say that the party with the stronger bargaining position has the most to gain, relative to the *status quo*. On the contrary, it is the party with the weaker bargaining position that has the most to gain.

The bargaining game just described is a positive-sum game: there are benefits from cooperating for both parties. Clearly, not all the games relevant to international economic and political bargaining take this form. Suppose that instead the relevant available outcomes of liberalization lie along the line running from −50,50 to 50,−50. This can be thought of as a situation in which, once the barriers to trade are reduced, exports from one country drive producers in the other country out of their domestic markets, with no ensuing productive reallocation of resources. Suppose, further, that this implies that every dollar gained in the United States is a dollar lost in the EU. Then, starting from point 0,0, the countries would move out towards point −50,50 as liberalization occurred. This is a zero-sum game: no mutual benefits from cooperation are available to share. The rational response for the EU in this zero-sum game is not to liberalize, but to stick at the origin.

Now, let us return to the game represented by the frontier running from 0,100 to 100,0. Suppose that, instead of engaging in this game, the United States uses its economic weight in the world economy to change the outcomes available. It might, for example, increase its subsidies to producers before liberalization, in such a way as to impose greater costs on the EU when liberalization takes place; this, in turn, reduces the total net gains (benefits minus losses) available to the two countries from reciprocal liberalization. The line running from −50,100 to 50,0 represents the frontier of the new bargaining game.

Points along this line again represent different distributions of the gains from liberalization. It is still a positive-sum game: there are positive net gains to the parties from liberalization, relative to the starting point at the origin (0,0). To see this, start at point 0,0 and move to 0,50. Total gains are $50 billion, all going to the United States, while the EU gains or loses nothing. Then look at point –20,70, where the US gains are $70 billion and the EU's losses are $20 billion: total net gains are still $50 billion again, so the sum is positive. But the EU clearly has no incentive to cooperate in this game: it gains nothing, so it will stick to its threat point, which is point 0,0. However, the EU does have a possible bargaining tool of a different kind. By sticking to its threat point, it is depriving the United States of large gains. Conversely, if the United States can persuade the EU to liberalize reciprocally, it can afford to make a side payment and still be much better off than it was at 0,0. If the United States offers the EU $20 billion to play, the outcome would be at 20,30. The game has been effectively extended by a side payment: the parties have bargained out along the line into the top right-hand quadrant, where there are positive benefits to both countries. So in a game such as this last one, where there are positive total gains but a net loser, there is potential for a cooperative bargained outcome if the other party can find a mechanism to compensate the loser.

In the examples discussed above, neither country was able to change the threat point of the other. We established that although point –20,70 represented an outcome in a positive-sum game, the EU would not play as it could stick at 0,0 (no gains are better than losses of $20 billion). Because the EU can stick at 0,0, the United States would have to offer a side payment to move the game along the line to a point such as 20,30. However, what happens when one country, say, the United States, is in a position to change another's threat point? How might this be possible?

Let's assume that the use of force is not an option, that the system is anarchic, that is, that there is no authority shared between states and, finally, that actors know what they want and cannot be persuaded to or deceived into changing their beliefs about what is in their interests. In the absence of force, authority, persuasion and deception, the only way that one state can get another to do something that it would not otherwise have done is to change the costs and benefits associated with the range of options from which it selects. I will call the ability of one party to impose costs on another its coercive power.[56] Presumably, the United States gains from its trade with the EU and would therefore also suffer a degree of impoverishment from a stoppage. Suppose the United States was threatening protectionist measures against the EU. To assess the likely consequences of this threat, we would want to know the expected costs to *both* the United States and the EU as well as the expected US benefits of the EU changing its policies as a result of the threat (the EU's expected losses, as we shall see, do not enter the equation). The US threat makes sense only if its expected benefits exceed the costs. If benefits do exceed costs, however, the United States may impose costs on the EU by changing the terms of their interdependence in ways that the EU is unable to prevent.

We are now in a position to clarify how interdependence may operate as a source of coercive power. The United States may be in a position to alter the terms of its interdependence with the EU, either unilaterally (say, by changing its national trade policy) or by acting in coalition with a third party, in such a way that its benefits exceed its costs, while the EU has no option but to bear its costs. This is sometimes called 'asymmetrical interdependence'. In terms of Figure 2.1, suppose the United States undertakes actions that move it and the EU from the origin 0,0 to point −20,70. This is not a bargaining game; it is an exercise of coercive power. That is, US coercive power enables it to take away the EU's threat point. Once the United States has taken away its threat point, the EU now finds itself in a new situation with new options. In principle, then, asymmetrical interdependence may form the basis for an exercise of coercive power.

Bargaining now takes place *after* the state with go-it-alone power has taken a position that *worsens* the position of the weaker state. Thereafter, even cooperative bargaining may not be enough to get the weaker party back to where it was before that exercise of power. The central point to understand here, noted above, is that unlike cooperative bargaining, which must involve positive gains for all parties, 'cooperation' that is enforced by the use (or threat) of coercive power need not be positive sum; indeed, it can even be a negative-sum game overall. It is only a cooperative, positive-sum outcome with respect to the new *status quo* that arises *after* the exercise of coercive, go-it-alone power. Suppose that what the EU gains by cooperating after the United States has exercised its go-it-alone power is less than its original loss, then the EU loses overall. The US gains may be more or less than the EU's (net) losses because, as Mancur Olson explains:

The party with power gains from threatening to use or using that power if the cost of doing this is less than the value, *to that party*, of what is obtained: the losses to the victim, and even the size of the losses in relation to the gains to the party with power, do not necessarily bear on the outcome.[57]

Under what circumstances might the United States seek to impose costs on the EU rather than pursue mutually beneficial positive-sum games? There are two closely related scenarios canvassed in the realist canon. First, insofar as states are concerned with their security in what remains an essentially self-help, anarchical system, they must be concerned not just with their absolute capabilities, but also with the distribution of capabilities across the system of states. If others do relatively well, they must emulate the successful or face the possibility of threats to their survival. Kenneth Waltz calls this the 'balance-of-power theory' and says that it is the 'distinctive' theory of international politics. Similarly, the realist theorist of international cooperation, Joseph Grieco, writes that: 'Driven by an interest in survival, states are acutely sensitive to any erosion of their relative capabilities, which are the ultimate basis for their security and independence in an anarchical, self-help international context.'[58] The consequence of this, says Waltz, is that

> even the prospect of large absolute gains for both parties does not elicit their co-operation *so long as each fears how the other will use its increased capabilities.* . . . a state worries about a division of possible gains that may favour others more than itself. That is the first way in which the structure of international politics limits the cooperation of states.

Secondly, there is the idea that some forms of interdependence generate vulnerability, a form of mutual dependence that is sufficiently asymmetrical to give rise to relations of domination and subordination. This is the vulnerability dependence arising from asymmetrical interdependence that we have reviewed above. Waltz draws attention to this when he notes that 'a state . . . worries lest it become dependent on others through co-operative endeavours and exchanges of goods and services'.[59] For these reasons, realists maintain that states are concerned with their relative positions vis-à-vis one another. Waltz says, for example, that 'states spend a lot of time estimating one another's capabilities, especially their abilities to do harm'.[60] Typically, realists have military capabilities in mind. But as economic resources can be turned into military ones – ploughshares into swords, butter into guns – and as the effectiveness of military capabilities often depends on intangible features such as leadership and national will, the estimation of capabilities is not an exact science. Nevertheless, at any given time, a ranking of the major powers is usually a relatively straightforward affair.

It should be clear that the formal structure of reasoning in Leninist theories of imperialism is no different from that at work in these realist contentions. The only difference is that whereas realism traces the competition to the needs of security under conditions of inter-state anarchy, for Lenin (and Bukharin) the competition was between blocs of capital anchored to national states. But while the *dynamics* of the rivalry between states is located in the competitive struggle for markets between different nationally located capitals, the theory of imperialism (in classical Marxism) was always a theory of rival – that is, plural – national imperialism*s* and, as such, presupposed a world of *many* states. That is to say, what is an explicit premise of realist theory – namely, that many states subsist in conditions of geopolitical anarchy – is an implicit presupposition of Marxist theories of imperialism.

Now, if states evaluate their capabilities in these terms, that is, if they focus on their share of, say, the world's income (or military resources), they are locked into a zero-sum world, in which a gain for one is always a loss for another. Positive-sum interactions rapidly become constant-sum in form when evaluated in terms of relative positions.[61] The only division of the gains from cooperation that is consistent with both maintaining their relative position (measured by their *share* of world income, etc.) is one that is proportional to the original starting positions of the parties. The general point is that as soon as states start evaluating their positions relative to one another, the range of cooperative outcomes that is sustainable is dramatically limited by the fact that absolute gains tend to be converted into zero-sum conflicts – represented by the line running from −50,50 to 50,−50 in Figure 2.1. And in a zero-sum situation, there is only one point at which nobody loses (and nobody gains), that is, the point at which the relative positions are unchanged. Notice, however, that Waltz and Grieco are not arguing that states care about their relative positions directly. Rather, states care about their position in the system because of its potential impact on their welfare, security and sovereignty: they fear that a position of weakness or vulnerability may be used against them. Faced with the prospect of absolute gains from cooperation, the reason states also focus on the gains of others, writes Gruber, 'is because they fear that by falling too far behind they run the risk of incurring more than offsetting *absolute* losses at some point in the future'.[62]

In terms of the analysis developed thus far, the realist/Leninist contention is simply that states pursue absolute gains, subject to the constraint that, in an anarchic/capitalist system, a position of weakness or vulnerability may be used by another as the basis for an exercise of coercive power that imposes costs. Typically, realists have in mind the use (or threat) of force as the means of exercising coercive power. But as we have seen, asymmetrical interdependence can also provide a basis for the exercise of coercive power. And in both cases, similar considerations apply: whether force or a pattern of economic interdependence can be used depends on the threat point that a state can (credibly) establish, and that depends on the costs and benefits of using force or changing the terms of interdependence. So, it would indeed be surprising if states were concerned with only relative evaluations of capabilities. After all, relative capabilities are a means, a way of safeguarding security, not ends in themselves. In fact, realists do not maintain that states are motivated *solely* by gains in relative capabilities. Grieco, for example, argues that when considering the impact of gains from an interaction on its capabilities, a state will seek to maximize its *net* gains, which he defines as a function of its absolute gains *and* its relative gains. How states evaluate this function, that is, how they balance absolute gains and relative considerations, depends on what he calls their 'coefficient of sensitivity' to considerations of relative advantage.

In my analysis of interdependence, I assumed that states showed no consideration at all for their relative position. But consider, for example, two powerful states that start out with the same national income and identical military forces. Let us suppose that these states are also ideological and political rivals. One might expect them to be very sensitive to any division of gains from cooperation that upsets this balance, and they might also be expected to forgo potential absolute gains from cooperation if the result was that the other got a larger share and thereby improved its relative position. In this instance, the states might be concerned only with their relative positions; their coefficients of sensitivity are so large as to drive out all considerations of absolute gains. This is one highly plausible explanation for the marked lack of economic cooperation between the United States and the Soviet Union during the Cold War.

In general, however, Grieco recognizes that the coefficient of sensitivity to considerations of relative advantage will vary:

> It will be greater if a state's partner is a long-term adversary rather than a long-term ally; if the issue involves security rather than

economic well-being; if the state's relative power has been on the decline rather than on the rise; if payoffs in the particular issue area are more rather than less easily converted into capabilities within that issue area; or if these capabilities and the influence associated with them are more rather than less readily transferred to other issue areas.[63]

We can draw three general conclusions from these (admittedly rather abstract) considerations. If, first, the game is positive-sum, and if states are concerned solely with their absolute gains, there is space for cooperative bargaining to mutual advantage. In some cases, side payments may be necessary to persuade one party to play. Inter-state anarchy and capitalist competition pose no obstacles to cooperation in this world. Secondly, if states evaluate their positions purely in relation to others (measured by their share of, say, world income or the ratio of their military capabilities to those of an adversary), then all games – even positive-sum ones – are transformed into zero-sum games and there is only one mutually acceptable division of the gains: that which divides the gains in proportion to the original disparity between the parties and leaves their relative positions intact. Neither will be prepared to move away from the origin. A concern with relative position, deriving from anarchy, blocks cooperation – as in the example of the superpowers during the Cold War. And thirdly, when states care about both their absolute gains and their relative positions, the outcome is indeterminate and depends on how they weigh the one against the other. If relative considerations do not weigh too heavily in their calculations, states may still find themselves in a positive-sum game.

In other words, the concern with relative positions that is generated by anarchy is not necessarily an obstacle to cooperation when Grieco's 'coefficient of sensitivity' is sufficiently small. Even in Grieco's model, the realist claim that worries about the distribution of gains inhibits mutual cooperation emerges as but one possible outcome. It is a special case, operating where considerations of relative power dominate a concern with absolute gains. Such concerns are likely to dominate, as suggested above, when a position of relative superiority can be used to achieve greater absolute gains than those available from cooperation, or inflict greater absolute losses on another. The general point may be stated more positively. The pattern of interdependence is also part of the structure of international politics and serves to shape outcomes. Realist/Leninist considerations apply when this pattern is such that the game is zero-sum. I have argued that zero-sum games are a special case, and not the general picture. Both anarchy and interdependence matter.

As Thomas Schelling wrote in *The Strategy of Conflict*, still one of the most perceptive analyses of strategy in international politics:

> Pure conflict, in which the interests of two antagonists are completely opposed, is a special case; it would arise in war of complete extermination, otherwise not even in war. For this reason, 'winning' in a conflict does not have a strictly competitive meaning; it is not winning relative to one's adversary. It means gaining relative to one's own value system. . . . In the terminology of game theory, most interesting international conflicts are not [zero-sum] games . . . the sum of the gains of the participants is not fixed so that more for one inexorably means less for the other. There is a common interest in reaching outcomes that are mutually advantageous.[64]

In general, what explains the difficulty in achieving cooperation is not a fixed feature of anarchy – that relative evaluations (measured in ratio terms) are inherently zero-sum – but rather the likelihood that relative disparities of capability can be translated into outcomes in which one party is able to better its own position and damage the absolute capabilities of another. To reach the realist conclusions of Waltz, that international cooperation is strongly constrained by anarchy, it is necessary to assume that relative considerations weigh heavily in the calculation of states, that states fear that relative positions can be translated into absolute outcomes, specifically that one state's relative position can impose absolute losses on another while achieving gains for itself.

More generally, our analysis has the merit of making explicit what is often taken for granted in realist (and Leninist) accounts. Waltz says that the structure of the international system is defined by the distribution of capabilities between states and that structure determines outcomes in international politics. Leninist theories add that the international is also structured by economic interdependence. Yet, two international systems may have exactly the same structure (as defined by Waltz or Leninist views) and have different levels of cooperation because *their net costs of translating relative positions into absolute gains* differ from one to the other. This is another general point that is often overlooked: the exercise of power involves costs. In some circumstances, a state's share of some resource or its pattern of asymmetrical interdependence may be an accurate measure of its power, that is, its ability to impose costs on others. In terms of the analysis developed above, such a favourable position may be the basis of an ability to move the threat point of another. But this cannot be assumed, as the gains reaped from using a superior position against another may be less than the costs.

This is not, in any sense, to deny the fact that in the contemporary world the capacity for domination by means of coercion, especially by military force, is concentrated – as never before – in the hegemonic power. But it is to question whether this is either necessary or sufficient for inter-capitalist coordination among liberal capitalist states (in the sense defined by Gramsci). It is not necessary because if there is scope for coordination, that is, if there are common interests in which being coordinated is better than not being coordinated, then states can bargain to the necessary agreements: coordinated interdependence, producing positive-sum gains, is a structural feature of the capitalist world market in a post-colonial world of many states. And coercion is not sufficient because unless there is scope for coordination, in the sense just defined, then coercion does not serve the common interest. Rather, it becomes a zero- or even negative-sum game in which one state gains at the expense of another.

The Tendency to Economic Multi-Polarity

The historical core of the contemporary capitalist world – Western Europe, North America and Japan – today operates on the basis of a system of states that are partly coordinated with one another to their mutual advantage, organized in networks of international governance whose principal purpose is to enhance the openness of their territories and peoples to the competitive dynamics of capitalism. This represents a partial consolidation of a liberal capitalist order, within and among the leading capitalist states. It is, of course, a highly asymmetric order, in which there are marked disparities of coercive power, despite the more or less universal maintenance of *de jure* sovereignty. There is, in short, a hierarchy of economic and military power among the constituent states of that coordinated international order. Undoubtedly, US hegemony has played, and continues to play, a key role in bringing this order into being.

However, the very success of the United States in fashioning this order and, hence, the steady expansion of its membership is undermining the *economic* dominance of the US in the world economy. Thus, the world economy is multi-polar and will become more so in the future, even though the United States has a privileged position because of its technological lead, the scope and depth of its financial markets, the international role of its currency, and the size of its domestic market and the asymmetric integration of the latter with the world market. But the unchallenged position that the US economy enjoyed after the Second World War – technological leadership across all sectors, dominance of world output and unrivalled competitive position on the world market, the international role of the dollar as the only effective currency and the dominant place of US foreign direct investment – has changed dramatically.

The sheer size and innovative capacity of the US economy remains impressive and US economic leadership power persists, but it is a wasting asset. First, and most obviously, although the US economy is relatively insulated from events in the rest of the world market as compared with the effects of the US economy on others, this asymmetry is diminishing; secondly, the manner in which the internationalization of US capital has occurred, primarily through foreign investment rather than exports, is losing its distinctiveness as other centres of capitalist power are following suit; and, thirdly, the specific form of that internationalization, a selective and asymmetric form of liberal capitalism based on the relative separation of the economic and political moments of capitalism, also functions as part of a coordinated multi-state international order.

Moreover, it is essential to notice that the second and third of these advantages have depended on the construction and reproduction of models of capitalism more or less consistent with US priorities outside the territory of the United States. This was, in part, the legacy of the defeat of rival models of capitalist development in the Second World War, the subsequent role of the US in post-war occupation and reconstruction, and the power associated with US hegemony. But increasingly it rests on the fact that access to the world market is an essential precondition for successful accumulation and, especially, technological innovation for all capital, including US capital. In short, the governance of the world economy is something that will have to be accomplished collectively, if it is to be accomplished at all.

US Power and the Liberal Capitalist International Order

The boundaries of the liberal capitalist world are essentially political, economic and hard to define with any precision, but its historical, geographical core has been the transatlantic alliance forged after the Second World War. Among the European states of this order – that is, roughly speaking the newly expanded membership of the European Union – and those of North America, the generation of collective power plays an important role. (Japan is, of course, strongly integrated into the Atlantic order by virtue of its economic links with the West and its security arrangements with the United States. Thus, Japan is politically and economically, if not geographically, part of this order, but it also has one foot in a rather different configuration of power among the leading Asian states.) In this region, US power in the international system and that of Americanism outside the territory of the United States can be thought of in largely positive-sum terms. Most of the power generated in this arena depends upon cooperation, mutually advancing the interests of all, even if there is hard bargaining to determine the distribution of the gains. This can be seen most clearly in the case of transatlantic integration.

Transatlantic Order

The outcome of the Second World War fundamentally reshaped the balance of power in world politics. It undermined the empires of Britain, France, Belgium, Italy and the Netherlands; it (temporarily) reduced the power of the main Axis states – Germany, Italy and Japan; it massively increased the power of the main military rivals to Hitler's Germany – Stalin's Soviet Union and, above all, Roosevelt's USA; and it thereby helped to create the bi-polar international system of the post-war period. The new balance of power came to be organized around military and political competition between the two new superpowers as the Cold War competition between capitalism and communism established its sway over the field of forces in world politics. This systemic bi-polarity was reinforced by the superpowers' possession of an effective monopoly of nuclear weapons and their delivery systems. By the same token, the outcome of the Second World War also dramatically altered the nature of politics within the capitalist states of Europe. In the crisis years of the inter-war period a fear of socialism and communism persuaded many of Europe's ruling classes and elites to support authoritarian, even fascist, forms of politics, such that the liberal democracies were more or less confined to the north-western tip of the continent. However, popular mobilization and the outcome of the Second World War discredited authoritarian and fascist rule across the whole of what became Western Europe, even if democracy was not consolidated in Greece, Spain and Portugal until the 1970s and 1980s. It is no accident that the only remaining dictatorships in Western Europe – Spain and Portugal – had not been directly involved in the Second World War.

After the defeat of German (and Italian) fascism in Europe, the emplacement of Soviet power in the East and the ensuing ideological rivalry between the communist and capitalist camps changed the geopolitical and political calculations of the states of Western Europe, making the containment of Soviet and communist power the main priority. The United States was keen to encourage integration in Western Europe but wanted this integration to be 'fitted into a wider Atlantic framework'.[65] The wider Atlantic framework was defined by the United Nations (UN) and its multilateral economic organizations (that is, the General Agreement on Tariffs and Trade [GATT], the International Monetary Fund [IMF] and the World Bank); the policies of post-war economic reconstruction launched under the European Recovery Programme (the Marshall Plan) in 1948; and, most importantly, the military alliance of the North Atlantic Treaty Organization (NATO), which was established in 1949. Insofar as European integration was consistent with this wider network, US policy makers believed that it would serve a range of purposes: it would provide a means of promoting the American model of political and economic organization in the old continent; over time a stronger and more integrated Western Europe would reduce the economic and military burden on the United States of containing Soviet power; and it would limit and channel West German power – economic *and* military – in a stabilizing manner.

Although German power had been drastically reduced by defeat in the Second World War and its subsequent Cold War division into East and West, the question of how to integrate the new West Germany into the states-system of Western European and the wider Atlantic order still remained. France was particularly concerned about the future power of West Germany, and the United States was fearful that a desire for reunification might lead it to accept a neutral role, thereby effectively strengthening the Soviet position in Europe. In fact, after the outbreak of the Korean War in 1950, the United States was insistent that West Germany should be allowed to re-arm. On the economic front, it was also clear that there could be no recovery in Western Europe without the revival of the West German economy.[66] France was initially suspicious about the rebuilding of West German power and wanted to act in cooperation with Britain on defence matters to contain any future threat from Germany. For its part, Britain still had significant imperial interests and was therefore reluctant to commit military resources that could be used in other theatres solely to the defence of Western Europe. As a result, the British sought direct US involvement in rebuilding and securing Western

Europe. Finally, for the new West German state (established in 1949), security against the Soviet bloc depended on the guarantees provided by the United States within the Atlantic order. At the same time, its economic recovery and a legitimate international role required a rapprochement with France and Britain.

For all these reasons, the role of NATO was crucial. NATO was formed in 1949 as a collective military security arrangement, with an integrated military command structure in which an attack on any one member state was to be treated as an attack against all. It was organized under US political and military dominance. NATO linked states in Western Europe (Britain, France, Iceland, Norway, Denmark, Belgium, the Netherlands, Luxembourg, Portugal and Italy) to the United States and Canada. Greece and Turkey joined NATO in 1952 and Spain joined in 1982. It was an alliance directed against the Soviet Union and its European presence, a way of committing American power to Europe and a means of channelling new German power.[67] (The United States also maintained a formal military security arrangement with Japan.) Together, these states formed the core of the wider intergovernmental arrangements through which the West organized its affairs – GATT, the IMF, the World Bank and the Organization for Economic Cooperation and Development (OECD).

Because the United States guaranteed the West's security against the Soviet Union and the communist world, other Western states could concentrate their attention on essentially economic cooperation. If NATO and the wider Atlantic framework in which the West organized itself in the Cold War provided for external security, then essentially economic integration in Western Europe might help to recover the domestic authority of nation-states. The 'civilian' power of the European Union was thus created against the background of the geopolitical stabilization of Western Europe and its insertion into the US-led Atlantic order. The key question was how to organize and institutionalize (West) European cooperation. For the most part Britain and the United States assumed that Western European integration and Atlantic integration pointed in the same direction. But they differed as to the form that integration should take. The United States was keen to encourage a sharing or pooling of sovereignty by the European states in the direction of supranational, proto-federal arrangements, thereby overcoming old national differences and rivalries. Britain, by contrast, wanted cooperation to take an intergovernmental form in which nation-states retained their identities and their independent sovereign rights. In contrast to the British and US view that Atlantic and Western European integration pointed in the same direction, France believed that European and US interests might be different, and particularly resented the US military dominance of NATO and Western European security. But France shared Britain's emphasis on intergovernmental forms of cooperation that would maintain national sovereignty.

The West German position straddled both sides of the argument. On the one hand, West Germany was itself a federal state and, in any case, was not fully sovereign as a result of the political and military restraints placed upon it by the victorious Allies. West Germany thus felt less threatened by supranational arrangements than either Britain or France. It had less to lose. On the other hand, West Germany was also closely linked to the United States by virtue of their shared security concerns vis-à-vis the Soviet Union. West Germany needed European integration as a vehicle to legitimate the new state and reconstruct the economy, and the Franco-German relationship was to dominate the politics of the Union until the 1980s. France attempted to strengthen the Franco-German relationship at the expense of US influence over integration in Western Europe, especially after General de Gaulle's return to power in 1958. But when confronted with such a choice, West Germany opted for an Atlantic priority in security matters, in that it joined NATO's newly established Nuclear Planning Group in the mid-1960s, while France withdrew from the organization's integrated military command. Still, France was able to veto British membership of the European Union until the end of the 1960s, despite West German and American preferences for early British entry.

The EU and Atlantic Integration

To the extent that it governs a liberal international economic order, the EU represents a very peculiar form of political and economic organization on the international stage. So how does the EU fit into the pattern of international economic governance provided by the wider framework set by the Bretton Woods institutions? Prior to the establishment of the EEC in 1958, the member states were all individual members of the IMF and GATT. Legally and formally, this position has been maintained as the EEC has expanded and evolved into the EU and as GATT has become the WTO. The formation of the EEC coincided more or less with the final moves towards currency convertibility among the major trading economies, at a time when conditions were ripe for a significant liberalization of world trade. Post-war reconstruction was largely completed and stable, non-inflationary growth seemed to have been established. The major economies of Western Europe (and Japan) now had the capacity to earn sufficient US dollars on export markets to feel confident that currency and trade liberalization would advance their interests. The United States had encouraged European integration from the outset of post-war reconstruction, making Marshall Plan aid conditional on (West) European cooperation, and it looked favourably upon the creation of the EEC.

The Treaty of Rome (1957) aimed to create a customs union (a combination of internal free trade based on the four freedoms of goods, services, capital and people, and a common external tariff) as well as a range of common policies on agriculture, energy, transport and competition, together with limited fiscal transfers for regional development. Moreover, the Treaties of Paris and Rome set down the pattern of governance for the EU, a combination of intergovern-mental and supranational decision making under a common legal framework. With the formation of the customs union in the EEC (substantially completed by 1968), the member states no longer had national trade policies. In their place, the Community developed a Common Commercial Policy (CCP), such that the member states acted as one in concluding trade agreements with others, whether bilateral agreements with specific countries or multilateral deals under the auspices of the GATT/WTO. The CCP is part of the Com-munity pillar of the EU and, as such, responsibility for the conduct of the CCP is shared among the Commission, the Council of Minis-ters and the European Parliament.

Almost as soon as the EEC was established, there had been con-cerns that the formation of a customs union might be more trade diverting than trade creating and that the EEC might abuse its strong position in world markets to rig trade in its favour. In theory, a large trading bloc can use a tariff to limit both its imports and exports, lowering the price of the former and raising the price of the latter, thereby improving its terms of trade. If the terms of trade effect is larger than the losses that arise from the distortions to production and consumption, an 'optimal tariff' can increase overall welfare inside the bloc at the expense of outsiders. This assumes that trading partners do not retaliate with tariffs of their own. Thus an optimal tariff is a potential weapon against small trading partners but not against other large trading blocs. In any case, to forestall the latter eventuality the United States took the lead in pushing for two multi-lateral rounds of trade negotiations in GATT, the Dillon Round (1961/2) and the Kennedy Round (1964/7). Thereafter, tariffs served less and less as barriers to trade in manufactures and the focus of attention shifted to non-tariff barriers created by 'behind-the-border' measures. These were first addressed on a serious basis in the Tokyo Round of GATT (1973/9).

Although the United States was concerned about the possibilities of trade protectionism with the formation of the EEC, on balance European integration has represented a major economic opportunity for the US economy rather than a threat. We noted above that the formation of the EEC coincided with the final moves toward the convertibility of European currencies against the dollar. One important result of this was that US multinational corporations (MNCs) increased their investment in Europe. For the US economy, overseas production by MNCs became a much more important means of penetrating overseas markets than exports. By the early 1970s, when the stock of US foreign investment still accounted for just over one-half of all foreign investment, the value of production by US affiliates abroad was some four times that of US total exports. Where the US led, Western Europe and Japan followed, as real wages in these areas began to catch up with those in the USA, undermining their export competitiveness, and as European and Japanese firms achieved the necessary scale to contemplate an international presence.

That is to say, the integration of the world economy has been driven as much by foreign investment as it has by trade. Indeed, by the mid-1980s, the value produced by MNCs outside their domestic markets was greater than the value of world trade, and a significant proportion of world trade (estimates vary from around one-quarter to two-fifths) is closely linked to foreign direct investment (FDI). The growth of regional integration in the world economy, not only in the EU but also in the North American Free Trade Agreement (NAFTA) as well as various schemes for integration in the Asia-Pacific region (most notably, Asia-Pacific Economic Cooperation, APEC), is 'motivated by the desire to facilitate international investment and the operations of multinational firms as much as the desire to promote trade'.[68] Writing in the late 1990s, Gerald Meier noted that:

> The stock of US direct investment in the EU has risen much more than the value of American exports to the EU. Sales of US-owned affiliates within the EU have in recent years amounted to eight to ten times the value of exports from the USA to the EU. Moreover, a third of American exports to Europe already go to US-owned affiliates.[69]

These FDI linkages serve as a counter-balance to any tendencies towards trade rivalry between the major regions of the world economy.

For the United States, then, integration in Europe has given rise to what Gary Hufbauer called 'Opportunity Europe'.[70] Nevertheless, there are many unresolved issues in transatlantic economic integration which relate both to trade and to investment. If national and international markets function efficiently, then national treatment combined with free trade maximizes efficiency and accountability, assuming that national policies accurately reflect citizens' preferences. This combination has been called 'shallow integration' and, together with the Most Favoured Nation principle, it has been an important part of the framework of international governance developed since the end of the Second World War. (The MFN principle states that, at the border, a good or service coming from a given economic partner is treated no less favourably than the same good or service coming from any other country. Within the GATT/WTO, unconditional MFN is the norm.) In particular, it has provided the basis for much of the expansion of trade between different national economies. However, national treatment still erects barriers to international trade (and particularly investment), since it fragments the international economy into distinct national economic spaces defined by a particular framework of rules and policies. Thus even if states agree to remove all their at-the-border restrictions, to adopt completely free trade on an MFN basis, foreign firms still have to adapt to different national rules and policies behind the border in order to do business in another state.

For this reason closer market integration for the exchange of goods, and especially services, often requires something more than national treatment and open trade, and, considered in this light, the EU and its trading partners have sometimes had a different understanding of 'reciprocity' in trade negotiations. The EU interprets reciprocity to mean *national treatment* plus effective access to foreign markets. But how is 'effective access' to be defined once the principal barriers to trade and investment are no longer at-the-border tariffs but behind-the-border measures? Next, the EU and its major trading partners do not have *common standards* on issues relating to health, safety and the environment, nor do they as yet operate on the basis of *mutual recognition* of each other's standards. That is to say, policy integration between the member states of the EU has gone much further than between the EU and the United States and Japan. A related question concerns rules of origin and local content. For the purposes of the single market, the EU has defined what is to count as an EU product or service if it is produced by, say, a Japanese MNC operating in Europe. These rules can serve to restrict trade and discriminate between EU and foreign goods and services. And finally, there is considerable debate on how far public procurement, government spending on goods and services, should be opened to foreign competition, especially given that this activity often has a public service component related to issues of national culture and welfare objectives.

In the industrial sector at least, the EU has not conformed to the naïve predictions of the theory of optimal tariffs. It has certainly pursued protectionist policies in relation to specific industries (for example, cars, steel and textiles), but overall it has pursued trade liberalization for manufactured goods. Moreover, *the provision of the four freedoms in the internal market applies as much and equally to US or Japanese firms (or indeed firms from any developed market economy) as to European business.* As John Grahl says, 'in practice economic conflicts between the US and the EU have been minimal, confined to a few sectoral issues'.[71] In the case of agriculture, to be sure, it has been a different story. The Common Agricultural Policy (CAP) has, of course, been the largest single common policy of the EU, and prior to the Uruguay Round agricultural trade never came under GATT disciplines. In contrast to the EU's generally open engagement with the international trading system, Robert Lawrence says (somewhat diplomatically) that 'evidence of trade diversion is more apparent in agriculture'.[72] Indeed, conflict between the United States and the EU over bringing agricultural trade into the GATT/WTO framework nearly sank the Uruguay Round at one point in the negotiations, and the CAP is a continuing source of irritation to US trade officials and a cause of significant transatlantic trade tensions.

Catch-up – Competition But Not Rivalry

Having forged ahead of its European rivals in the first half of the twentieth century, 'American technology which was natural resource intensive, physical capital-using and scale dependent was', says Nicholas Crafts, 'frequently not the optimal choice of technique in European conditions'. It was only in the increasingly open, liberal international economy of the post-war period that '[g]reater integration of world markets, reductions in the cost advantages of domestic natural resource endowments combined with increased importance of intangible capital (R&D and education) subsequently reduced the obstacles to catch-up first within the OECD and later elsewhere in East Asia'.[73] In 1950, the United States accounted for three-fifths of the total output of the largest seven capitalist economies and 'its manufacturing industry was about twice as productive, per person employed, as that of the UK, three times as productive as German manufacturing and nine times as productive as Japanese manufacturing'.[74] Thereafter, between 1951 and 1971, US industrial production increased 122 per cent (an annual rate of 4.0 per cent) and its GDP rose 90.3 per cent (3.2 per cent per annum), whereas industrial production in Japan increased 1,092 per cent (12.4 per cent per annum) and overall GDP rose by 453 per cent (an annual rate of 8.5 per cent). The annual increase in labour productivity in manufacturing was 10.3 per cent in Japan between 1955 and 1970 and 2.3 per cent in the United States. Western Europe's convergence started from a higher base and was less dramatic but none the less substantial: for example, manufacturing labour productivity in West Germany rose 6.7 per cent per annum between 1955 and 1970.

Of course, as relative catch-up began to close the absolute gap with the United States, so further advances became more difficult. For example, 'growth in Golden Age Japan was predicated on . . . rapid mobilization of resources based on low cost rather than efficient use of capital and productivity growth concentrated on manufacturing while sheltered/non-tradable sectors of the economy sustained employment based on low productivity. By the 1990s, these features . . . [were] obstacles to further catch-up.'[75] Similarly, Glyn reports that although, by the mid-1990s, European and Japanese manufacturing productivity had reached around 80–90 per cent of US levels, thereafter it fell back to around 65–75 per cent of the US level measured per worker.[76] While the average person in the euro area was about 30 per cent poorer than in the United States in the early part of the new century, average GDP *per hour worked* was only 5 per cent lower (compared with about 30 per cent lower thirty years before); Europeans simply translated more of their increased productivity into leisure rather than income, principally by full-time workers working shorter hours.

Where the EU has attempted to compete on more or less equal terms with the United States there have been some limited but managed tensions. Consider, for example, commercial relations with the Middle East in the form of the European Union's 'Euro-Mediterranean Partnership Initiative' and Turkey's long-standing commercial agreements, including a customs union, with the EU. Turkey aims for membership of the EU and the formal position is that this remains a long-run potential, but there is considerable doubt within the Union – openly expressed in Greece, Germany, France and Italy – that it could ever qualify for accession. And even if Turkey did meet the objective criteria for membership, many still doubt that it could join, partly because its size would imply a considerable shift of power within the governance of the EU and partly on the grounds that, culturally speaking, Turkey is not a European country. The United States has consistently maintained that Turkey should become a member of the EU, in order to bind it firmly into the Western political and economic camp. Turkey's role in Central Asia after the Cold War is, as far as the United States is concerned, an important balance to Iranian and Russian influence.

At the same time, the European Union has pursued an ambitious regional cooperation agreement – centred on the creation of a free trade area between the EU and the Mediterranean countries running from Morocco to Turkey – since the EU–Med summit in Barcelona in 1995. It embraces twelve Mediterranean countries: Algeria, Cyprus, Egypt, Israel, Jordan, Lebanon, Malta, Morocco, Syria, Tunisia, Turkey and the Palestinian territories. The agenda extends beyond economic relations and includes measures to enhance regional security (especially in relation to migration) and the strengthening of cultural and educational ties. The core, however, is the drive for freer trade and investment links and this requires the EU to negotiate separate accession agreements with the twelve Mediterranean states and for the latter to negotiate similar arrangements with one another. In 2001, for example, the EU signed a 'Partnership Agreement' aimed at freeing trade (with significant exceptions in the agricultural sector) with Egypt, which in turn had concluded agreements with Lebanon, Syria, Morocco, Tunisia, Libya, Iraq and Jordan. While the original grand scheme of an EU–Mediterranean free trade area is unlikely to be realized any time soon, it has served to institutionalize a degree of cooperation on trade and aspects of development. To this end, the process also established biennial summits to monitor progress.

The United States has voiced its concerns that the EU–Mediterranean initiative should not operate at the expense of other countries, and in 1999 it formally served notice that it would not relinquish commercial opportunities to the EU or others. Given that the EU aims to make its agreements WTO-compatible, this is unlikely to involve significant conflict (except perhaps over agriculture) as both the EU and the US are pushing for freer trade and investment in the region. Indeed, immediately after the second US-led war against Iraq in 2003, President Bush announced a proposal for a free trade agreement between the Middle East and the United States and committed to assisting the states of the region to join the WTO process. To be sure, the process is immeasurably complicated by the wider Middle East 'Peace Process', in which Russia and the United Nations also have a role to play alongside the United States and the EU.

Taken as a whole, however, the larger part of the reason for the absence of major EU–US economic conflict has been the dominance of the liberal view that European competitiveness requires continental solutions: 'that market forces should operate on a continental basis, that competition policy should be tough, and mutual recognition should introduce competition between regulatory regimes'. Set against this, the more interventionist strand of thinking, which argues 'that intervention and rules should operate on a continental basis, that industrial policies should promote European competitors (rather than enforce competition), and Europe-wide regulatory, agricultural, and social policies should temper the effects of the market',[77] has been on the defensive. Thus far the former tendency has been in the ascendant: as Grahl concludes, 'European leaderships have increasingly seen Americanization as the only solution to the problems of the old continent; they have not, in recent years, envisaged divergent paths of development'.[78]

After having caught up with America economically (to a large extent), Europe might have been expected to seek political independence. 'But opposing forces pushing in the direction of a total integration within the American system also appeared in the last twenty years,' says Emmanuel Todd: 'The liberal economic revolution . . . produced at the highest European levels a new temptation.'[79] If European integration began life as a project to rescue the nation-state in the aftermath of total war, to pursue economic cooperation and to strengthen the political unity of the capitalist world in the face of the Soviet challenge, it has continued to evolve despite the dissolution of its communist adversaries. And while relations between the EU and the United States have become somewhat fractious of late – not least over the war against Iraq – there is as yet no sign that the political identity and interests of Europe are being defined outside the context of ever-increasing engagement with the world market and, *a fortiori*, increasing economic integration across the Atlantic.

Breaking with NATO?

Perhaps the central question facing US policy towards this region is how, if at all, to develop further the forms and levels of cooperation achieved thus far. At the core of this is the question of American attitudes towards the EU and NATO. Although the reproduction of Americanism in Europe provided an economic basis for transatlantic cooperation, there can be little doubt that the Cold War rivalry between the superpowers, and the competition for global influence between capitalism and communism, also served to cement political and military relations across the Atlantic. It was NATO's guarantee of the post-war division of Europe, defining the westward limit of Soviet power and settling decisively the German problem, which stabilized the states-system in Western Europe.[80] The American military presence in Western Europe, as well as the extension of the US nuclear guarantee to its NATO allies – that is, extended deterrence – may have been a form of informal empire, or hegemony, but it was also an 'empire by invitation', and it provided the framework within which the EU could develop as a 'civilian' power. European integration has, in effect, been the enemy of European military power on a wider international stage.

Under NATO's security umbrella, extensive and deep forms of economic and political cooperation prospered. Post-war recovery saw the economies of Western Europe rapidly catching up with the United States, at least until the 1970s, and the Atlantic powers appeared to consider their (collective) position vis-à-vis the Soviet Union as far more important than the relative position of each within the alliance. To be sure, at no stage was American military preponderance within NATO ever in doubt. Indeed, the continuing imbalance in military power within NATO, even as the two sides of the Atlantic became more equal economically, was and remains a major source of tension. The result has been a confused and confusing debate about 'burden sharing' that has become more serious as NATO has struggled to define a new role for itself after the Cold War.

With the end of the Cold War, the dissolution of the Soviet Union and the reunification of Germany, many concluded that NATO's original purpose had largely evaporated. NATO began a process of enlargement to include states that had formerly fallen under Soviet control in Eastern Europe, while the EU also began accession talks with many of the same countries. At the same time, the EU began to develop a Common Foreign and Security Policy (CFSP). On the European side, membership of NATO and the EU increasingly overlapped. This posed the question of the division of labour between NATO and the CFSP of the EU, in turn raising the question of the definition and purpose of NATO. NATO was established in order to commit American military power to preventing the re-emergence of a hegemonic power in Europe. It was a military alliance with a clear rationale. Enlargement has run the danger of turning it into a strategically neutral organization for collective defence, with no defined mission. Increasingly, the United States bypasses NATO for its 'out of area' operations, preferring *ad hoc* arrangements with those of its members (as well as other non-NATO states such as Australia) that join a 'coalition of the willing'. Simultaneously, some advocates of the EU's CFSP have wanted to develop procedures by which the European members of NATO might act independently of the United States. And underlying all this uncertainty has been the overwhelming military fact that the already marked imbalance between European and US military capabilities widened after the end of the Cold War. Not surprisingly, many in Washington have asked whether the United States needs NATO.

Considered in these terms, there are several possible futures. First and most likely, the CFSP will amount to little and fail to develop a serious military capability that can act independently of the United States, in which case the European members of NATO will have little option but to seek ultimate military security through the alliance. Second, the EU might become serious about military matters such that the expansions of the EU and of NATO go hand-in-hand. The obvious way of accommodating this change would be for the EU to declare an interest in safeguarding its territorial integrity and for NATO to affirm that this is one of its vital interests. NATO would then become a more equal partnership between the United States, on the one side, and the EU, on the other. While this has been the declared policy of successive US administrations, Washington's enthusiasm for this might diminish, as it became a reality. Third, the EU (or some of its members) might develop a serious military capability outside of NATO, prompting the United States to disengage militarily from Europe, in the sense of both removing the forward deployment of personnel and materiel and, by implication if not declared policy, ending the nuclear guarantee provided by extended deterrence. While the right of the Republican Party might welcome this in favour of alliances with perimeter states such as Poland and Spain as well as new links out of area such as India, it is anathema to most of the foreign policy elite in the United States, who view the transatlantic alliance as the core of American global security.

French policy has long favoured a policy pointing towards the second option noted above. The UK has always favoured the first. Prior to reunification, (West) Germany defined its foreign policy

primarily in the context of limited rearmament under NATO auspices, and secondarily, through Franco-German cooperation in the
EU. Whenever it had to choose between its NATO and EU commitments, the former came first. Now that reunification has been
achieved, whether Germany will continue to give priority to its transatlantic ties over its leadership ambitions in Europe is one of the most
important questions facing European geopolitics. (Whether Germany's decision to side with France [and Russia] over Iraq is a portent
of things to come remains to be seen.) We should note that many of
the new members of NATO and the EU, from former Eastern Europe,
regard the transatlantic commitment as especially important, as a
safeguard against potential future Russian, and even German,
domination.

A final complication is that the importance attached to global
questions of military security differs markedly on the two sides of
the Atlantic. This is, as Robert Kagan has pointed out, partly a
consequence of the massive disparity in military power. It is also
a consequence of the fact that the EU is more a regional than a
global power, whereas the converse is the case for the United States.
The EU has developed as a civilian power. Indeed, European integration has, thus far, gone hand-in-hand with a *decline* in Europe's relative military power, while that of the United States has increased.
This leaves the EU no option, for the present, but to conduct its
foreign policy through diplomacy and economic statecraft. Simply
put, it has no serious military options. Yet, it aspires to a global
role in a world that is far from dispensing with military power.
'Today's transatlantic problem', writes Kagan, 'is a [military] power
problem. America's power, and its willingness to exercise that
power – unilaterally if necessary – represents a threat to Europe's
new sense of mission. . . . American [military] power made it possible
for Europeans to believe that power was no longer important.'[81]
This is an oversimplification, since much of the transatlantic debate
– as in the dispute over how to deal with Iraq – turns on different
assessments of the long-term costs and benefits of using military
power (it also overlooks the fierce divisions *within* both Europe
and America, as evidenced by the run-up to the war in Iraq in 2003),
but it does capture an important reason why politicians across the
Atlantic often appear to talk past one another. Nevertheless, the only
power possessed by the EU is economic. The United States, by contrast, has military power as well. Consequently, the assessment of how
far to pursue some goals collectively is bound to differ from one side
of the Atlantic to the other.

Conclusions

In the Atlantic theatre, the American empire represents a novel 'regime-type: uni-polar, based on ideology rather than territorial control, voluntary in membership, and economically advantageous to all countries within it. . . . U.S. power is overwhelming, but the aggregate power of the world's liberal states is vastly greater. . . . [and] the aggregate power of the empire is greater than the sum of its parts.' The only danger to this regime in the foreseeable future lies in the policies of the one state with the power to violate its norms and rules – the United States. But while the 'United States alone has the capacity to violate the rules with impunity', it is very difficult to see how America's long-term interests can be advanced in this manner.[82] The root cause of this is not only the power resources of the territorial United States, but also its function as the pristine fount and origin of the most advanced capitalist practices and institutions that serve to spread Americanism across the system as well as the social purposes that it pursues through coordinated economic interdependence. The European allies in this regime do not react just to US power, understood in realist or Leninist terms, but also to its functionality for capitalism world-wide and the social purposes of many states that are advanced by coordinating across the Atlantic.

We can generalize this result to some extent. Faced with a high level of more or less institutionalized economic cooperation among the major capitalist powers, extending increasingly to the emerging economies in Asia and Latin America as well, many radical analyses have concluded that this reflects the impress of US imperialism in some form or other. These responses put (potential) conflict and hence considerations of coercive power at the centre of their understanding of international economic governance, seeing international economic governance as, to a large extent, a product of American power. In this, they follow a long line of realist critics of liberal theories of cooperation. The key point of that critique, as we have seen, is that states are not only, or even primarily, concerned to maximize their absolute welfare, but are also interested in their relative position vis-à-vis other states. This (realist) argument, put most carefully by Grieco, suggests that states (with a high 'coefficient of sensitivity') will only engage in mutually beneficial cooperation and coordination if, and only if, the distribution of the resulting gains does not adversely affect the relative positions of the states concerned. A subtle variant of this argument, due to Gruber, questions whether the outcomes of international cooperation really represent pareto improvements, for there is always the possibility that an 'enacting coalition', for whom cooperation produces gains, may alter the *status quo* for those *outside* the original agreement, worsening their position relative to the non-cooperative *status quo*, such that outsiders subsequently join 'voluntarily' even though they would have preferred no agreement at all. At the limit, some suggest, the enacting coalition has just one member – the United States.

Another line of argument accepts that US leadership only functions to the extent that it also serves the interests of many states in the system, but questions whose interests are being advanced. Peter Gowan, for example, says that '[i]n pursuing its world-empire project . . . the United States' business and political elites have sought to rally support as the champions not just of American business interests but of business interests and the strengthening of capitalism as a social system on a world-wide scale'. The permissive cause of this, however, is traced to the collapse of communism and hence the 'disorientation and disorganization of labour on an international scale'; it is this social retreat that has provided 'a fundamental basis for the extraordinary advance of the new Pax Americana or empire project'.[83] This is to introduce a class dimension to the determination of state interests. Whether states are pursuing absolute or relative gains, on whose behalf are they doing so? Does a state's social purpose, its welfare function, represent a reasonably just aggregation of the society it nominally represents in the international arena or is its maximand driven by the interests of a dominant group or class? Or do such interests serve as an additional constraint on what states may seek to maximize, so that they maximize national welfare conditional on the anticipated reaction of key strategic interests or groups?[84] Is it not the case that some groups benefit – internationally mobile capital (especially financial interests), skilled workers – while others lose out – relatively immobile factors of production and less skilled workers?

And finally, the central premise of the liberal story about cooperation after hegemony – namely, that the contemporary period is indeed characterized by the erosion of US hegemony – has been challenged. On this view, the erosion of US hegemony is itself a myth; or, more accurately, it only applies in a qualified way to US economic power and not at all to its military power. Therefore, there is nothing for liberal theories of post-hegemonic cooperation to explain since the United States can parlay military uni-polarity into political supremacy on key economic issues. 'Liberal' forms of international economic governance continue to survive on the basis of the continuing exercise of coercive power by the United States.

In my view, while the radical critique is often valid in specific, local instances, it is misleading as a *general* characterization of international economic governance taken in the round. Appropriately reformulated, the liberal thesis is more or less sound as long as it is understood that the central mode of ordering this realm is one of coordination, which works by producing gains over the uncoordinated *status quo*.[85] The trick is to see that we are observing the creation, *by states*, of a kind of *constitutional* order, *for states*, to govern certain limited aspects of their interaction and common interests. The question, then, becomes one of how the potential gains from cooperation and coordination are realized in an ungoverned statessystem. How is the logic of collective action overcome at the level of the inter-state system?

The answer, according to liberal theorists, is that cooperation after hegemony is possible if the international regimes and organizations, originally established under the auspices of hegemonic leadership, serve to provide a focus around which expectations can converge, an arena for information sharing and learning, a means of reducing the costs of negotiating and bargaining, and a way of making commitments credible by identifying and punishing defectors. (This is because 'tit-for-tat' is a stable, winning strategy in a repeated Prisoners' Dilemma game, provided future benefits are sufficiently valuable and the future is not discounted too heavily.[86]) The contemporary descendants of modernization theory are to be found in these discussions of (neo-)liberal interdependence and institutionalism. As originally stated, this argument left a lot to be desired. It failed to note that US hegemony was confined to the capitalist world and that the latter was ranged against, and thus unified by, an 'external' antagonist in the form of Soviet communism. And it failed to register the extent to which hegemony is as much about functioning as a pole of attraction as it is about providing leadership. But it was not wrong in identifying strong forces of cooperation in an interdependent world economy.

However, we should not think about international economic governance as a series of exchanges that can be modelled by the Prisoners' Dilemma game (as in the standard liberal accounts), or as a series of more or less constant-sum conflicts (as in the various radical contributions), but as a form of coordination on a constitutional order for international economic integration. This may seem like a nice point in game theory, but in fact it is far more important: the conditions of stability for the two types of games are radically distinct and embody two different visions of what is going on in reality. The basic point is simple but fundamental: *exchange agreements require enforcement; coordination is self-enforcing.* In circumstances of coordination, even unequal coordination, all are better off relative to the pre-coordination *status quo ante*, even if some would have preferred to have coordinated differently, and even if the gains of coordination are unequally shared. The requirements of consensus are more demanding, since consent involves a situation in which the freely chosen action of each party shares in the responsibility for the outcome.

At the international level, of course, coordination does not involve the creation of compulsory, coercive power. So, public international law, including international economic law, is limited to the regulation of those things which are genuinely common, coordinated interests of states. This order only functions to the extent that the game states are playing really is a coordination game. Coordination is not possible where there are genuine conflicts of interest, that is, where what is best for some is worst for others – in game-theoretic terms, this latter is precisely the structure of the Prisoners' Dilemma. That is why the constitutional order among states is largely limited to general, procedural rules as well as a vast array of international economic governance that has been concerned primarily with elaborating the framework for addressing matters of regulatory policy and the provision of those international public goods that do not involve significant distributive issues. But such spontaneous coordination is no less real for that.

3 AMERICAN OIL, WORLD OIL

Resources, Conflicts, Control and Scarcity

Introduction

One plausible candidate for US predatory behaviour is in respect of the world's oil and, specifically, the invasion of Iraq in 2003.* To what extent is a drive to appropriate the (rest of the) world's oil a driving force behind American foreign policy? Conversely, how might the conduct of US foreign policy shape the evolution of the international oil industry? Especially in the light of the ascendancy of a group of politicians with close links to the oil industry in Washington – most notably, President George W. Bush and Vice-President Dick Cheney – and under the shadow of the second US-led war against Iraq, many commentators argued that oil plays an important, even central, role in US foreign policy. Perhaps the most forceful exponent of this argument is Michael Klare, who has argued that

> what is undeniable . . . is that President Bush gave top priority to the enhancement of America's power projection capabilities at exactly the

---

*In most of what follows, including most of the tables and figures, I report oil statistics for and up to the year of the invasion of Iraq (2003) on the basis of the *BP Statistical Review of World Energy 2004*. Where trends have changed significantly since then, or where current data are important to the argument, I include data from the latest (autumn 2007) reports available from BP, the International Energy Agency, OPEC and other industry sources. We will see below (pp. 143–8) that the whole question of oil reserves data is subject to considerable questioning. The current version of the BP data set is available at *http://www.bp.com* and much of the IEA data – including the very useful monthly oil market report – is at *http://www.iea.org*.

same time that he endorsed an energy strategy that entails increased U.S. dependence on oil derived from areas of recurring crisis and conflict. What we have, therefore, is a two-pronged strategy that effectively governs U.S. policy toward much of the world. Although arising from different sets of concerns – one energy-driven, the other security-driven – these two strategic principles have merged into a single, integrated design for American world dominance in the 21st Century.[1]

Indeed, for Klare, ' "Blood for oil" has, in fact, become a dominant feature of the Bush Administration's military policy'.[2] 'Slowly but surely,' Klare writes in his study *Blood and Oil*, 'the U.S. military is being converted into a global oil-protection service' as 'it is getting harder to distinguish U.S. military operations designed to fight terrorism from those designed to protect energy assets . . . [the Bush administration has a] tendency to conflate the two'.[3] (Surely, the conflation, if that is what it is, also reflects the very real fact that militant groups directly target oil industry assets.) Similarly, Ian Rutledge's investigation of the consequences of America's high levels of motorized transport, *Addicted to Oil*, argues that the invasion of Iraq was first and foremost about bringing Iraq's potential reserves to international markets as a means of both augmenting world supply and undercutting American dependence on Saudi Arabia.[4] Sometimes this argument is expressed in direct, instrumentalist terms. Noting Cheney's role as CEO of Halliburton, Rutledge sees him as '[s]omeone who, given the opportunity, would not hesitate to mould U.S. foreign policy into a form conducive to the business opportunities and profit maximization so earnestly sought after by the huge energy multinationals of which his own company was a leading representative'.[5] Klare, by contrast, stresses the state interest involved and the economy-wide dependence on oil imports. Of course, the two concerns – instrumental and strategic – go together to the extent that the major US energy companies are the indispensable means by which the government achieves its energy policy ends.[6] Others argue that even if the drive for oil *per se* was not the primary reason for the war against Iraq, the United States' reassertion of its dominance over the geopolitics of the Middle East is still to be understood as part of a geopolitical manoeuvre directed against current and potential economic rivals.[7]

In what follows, I begin by separating out three different arguments about oil and the war. In order to interrogate these arguments, I next consider the place of Middle East oil in the wider picture of world supply and demand and examine the idea that 'regime change' in Baghdad might have been designed to unlock Middle Eastern supplies for the world market and the international oil companies of the main consuming nations. I then argue that the US strategy towards the Middle East and now Central Asia and beyond, while closely bound up with the politics of oil, also has other geo-strategic objectives. I argue that insofar as the intention was to unlock oil supplies, then (thus far) the strategy has failed; and that, to the extent that the strategy works, it will be of benefit to all countries that are dependent on the international oil market, not just the United States and its companies. I conclude by suggesting that struggles over access to oil are not in any case likely to be as urgent or serious as many commentators have assumed.

Reasons for War?

In the first instance, US dependence on oil imports is steadily increasing – in 1973 the United States imported about 33 per cent of its oil, today the figure is about 60 per cent, and by 2020 it may be as high as 70 per cent – and this may be seen as the 'Achilles' heel' of American power. (This is the main thrust of Klare's argument.) It is, therefore, in the interests of the United States to increase total world oil production and to encourage a diversity of sources of supply. As Rutledge rightly points out, the real issue here is dependence on *oil*, not dependence on oil *imports*, since in highly integrated international markets such as the world oil market a disruption to, or a shortage of, supply anywhere is felt everywhere through its effect on prices. We will see that the importance of oil dependence for US foreign policy depends on the projected world-wide balance of supply and demand in the world oil market, the economic and technological availability of new reserves and the alternative energy sources that might substitute for scarce oil. It is worth noting, however, that to the extent that US power, including military force, is successfully deployed to meet the ends of expanding and diversifying supplies, it serves the interests of all oil-consuming countries that are dependent on the world market.

Secondly, in pursuit of expanded and diversified sources of supply, the United States can promote the interests of its own oil companies and, more generally, the complex of interests that Rutledge calls 'oil capitalism', that is, 'companies which are not only involved in oil production but are also active in many other energy sectors'. This is a very significant sector of the economy, for, as Rutledge explains,

> only the smaller so-called 'independent' oil companies actually specialize exclusively in the upstream, oil exploration and production

business. The major oil companies are increasingly diversified energy companies with interests in natural gas production, gas pipelines and processing (natural gas liquids), gas and electricity marketing, electric power generation, solar power, etc. However since many energy products are substitutes for one another . . . over time, their prices generally tend to move in the same direction. To this extent, it is reasonable to think of oil itself – the most valuable and widely traded energy commodity – as being the ultimate energy market driver.[8]

Despite this diversification, Rutledge contends that for oil companies 'it is primarily the company's proven reserves which provide the basis for its future cash flow and profits'.[9] This, in turn, explains the relentless territorial drive to replenish and replace depleted reserves. And in a report written for the American Petroleum Institute – the industry organization of the major US oil companies – Edward Porter maintained that the greatest channel of US influence in the international oil industry 'is that of promoting free trade and investment in energy world-wide, and encouraging U.S. firms to participate in that trade and investment to the fullest extent possible'.[10] However, owing to the Organization of the Petroleum Exporting Countries (OPEC) revolution in ownership of oil reserves – far more significant than the much more visible price increases of 1973–4 and 1979 – the international oil companies of the principal consuming nations now own only a small fraction of the world's oil reserves (perhaps 7 to 8 per cent) and have production access to only about one-fifth of total proven reserves. Irrespective of the Bush–Cheney links to US oil capitalism, rolling back the OPEC revolution would indeed be a first-class objective for the US state and for the major oil companies. As above, we should note, *en passant*, that success in this endeavour would be of benefit to all the oil-consuming countries that are dependent on the world market.

Thirdly, the United States has a 'comparative advantage', relative to both its allies in Europe and Japan and its potential rivals in Russia and China, in the military and diplomatic exercise of geopolitical leverage vis-à-vis other states. Indeed, this may be as important a channel of influence in the international oil industry as that identified by Porter. The routing of pipelines, the policing of shipping lanes and the management of regional influences all depend heavily on US geopolitical and military commitments. This means, in turn, that to the extent that US companies and US geopolitics – and especially military power – remain central to ordering the world oil industry, the United States provides, in good times, a collective service to other states that enhances its overall international hegemony. In bad times, this role would provide the United States with a potential stranglehold over the economies of potential rivals. Europe and Japan have experienced this predicament since the end of the Second World War. Current US policy may ensure that China, India and others fall under the same umbrella.[11] In this respect, control of oil may be viewed as the centre of gravity of US economic hegemony, and thus the logical complement of its declared strategy of permanent, unilateral military supremacy.

According to this argument, the 'war on terror' – renamed the 'long war' in the Pentagon's 2006 *Quadrennial Defense Review* – and the wars in Afghanistan and Iraq are, in reality, part of a global strategy to reassert US dominance in the international system. Such a strategy is considered most important given the growing competition with other regions, especially the challenge posed by China and the ever-increasing importance of Middle Eastern oil. The United States is using its unquestioned military dominance to underscore its much less impressive economic position. As hegemonic leadership erodes, regional powers will seek to assert their interests and economic rivalries beckon. In this context, preventing the emergence of a 'peer competitor' – that is, China – and gaining a stranglehold over the life-blood of the world economy – Gulf oil – can be seen as core objectives for the US state. Importantly, given China's future dependence on oil imports, the latter may facilitate the former. David Harvey says that:

> Not only does [the invasion of Iraq] constitute an attempt to control the global oil spigot and hence the global economy through domination over the Middle East. It also constitutes a powerful US military bridgehead on the Eurasian land mass which, when taken together with its gathering alliances from Poland down through the Balkans, yields it a powerful geostrategic position in Eurasia with at least the potential to disrupt any consolidation of a Eurasian power.[12]

Similarly, Klare notes that China's dependence on oil flowing through waters dominated by the US Navy is a source of strategic vulnerability. This is no doubt true, but we should note that the United States *already* has the naval and air capacity to blockade China, even if no longer in its own territorial waters.

Taken together, there is, in my view, much to be said for these three approaches to understanding the invasion of Iraq and the general direction of US foreign policy since 9/11. There can be little doubt that foreign policy is, to some extent, driven by a rising concern at the state executive level about levels of oil (import) dependence and future sources of supply, by the expansionary forces of oil capitalism seeking new reserves and markets, as well as an attempt to re-establish the kind of control of the 'global oilspigot' that the United States enjoyed prior to the Iranian Revolution in 1979. But while it is true that the United States does seek to control world oil – or at least to exercise a degree of influence second to none – the *form* of that control is very ambiguous. We will see that it is, in fact, very different from the kinds of exclusive control over raw materials traditionally associated with the inter-imperial rivalries that existed in the era of European colonial empires. We will also see that gaining increased access to Middle East oil reserves may not be as essential or immediate a need for either the United States or the world economy as is often supposed.

America's Oil, World Oil

The modern oil industry first developed after the unification of the American national market that followed the consolidation of the sovereignty of the Union after the Civil War (1861–5). Alongside competitive processes of market integration, important elements of unification included federal transfers of land to private ownership, the development of railways, electrification and – between the 1890s and the First World War – the construction of a nation-wide (and originally monopolistic) oil industry. This vast and resource-rich national market could scarcely fail to forge ahead, largely unencumbered by the obstacles to capitalist development still weighing heavily on European societies, and endowed with a young, well-educated population that was able to draw upon the capital and technology of the old world. 'Shortly after the Civil War', writes Patrick O'Brien, America's 'national output exceeded those of Britain, France and Germany combined.... By the 1890s, the gap in real per capita incomes had become significant and it increased monotonically down to the middle of the twentieth century.'[13]

American capitalism not only forged ahead, but it also pioneered a new form of industrial development based on multi-divisional kinds of corporations exploiting economies of scale and scope. These corporations serviced mass markets in what within the history of industrial capitalism represent sectors of the third and fourth 'waves' of technological and organizational innovation. These waves, or phases, of development embraced the electrification of industry, transport and the domestic sphere and, later, the motorization of transport, the civilian economy and warfare. All of this laid the basis for the development of the 'mass' society and of Americanism. Alongside many other factors, an early, rapid and far-reaching shift to oil played an important role in

America's emergence as the predominant mass society of the twentieth century, since oil made possible: motive power; new kinds of industrial and agricultural possibilities based on synthetic chemicals; urbanization and, especially, suburbanization; and, perhaps most importantly, mass transportation in both the civilian and military sectors. One indicator of US precocity in these matters was that in 1929, the United States produced 85 per cent of the world's cars and 'Americans owned 78 per cent of all the autos in the world'.[14] As early as 1960, Rutledge notes, '78 per cent of American families owned at least one car and 21.5 per cent owned two or more'.[15] And where the United States led, other advanced capitalist countries soon followed. Increasingly, and especially in the United States, personal transport was dominated by the car, and cars need oil: in 2001, 69 per cent of US oil consumption was in the transport sector and 53 per cent in motor vehicles.

The rise of Standard Oil, and its divestiture after 1911, established an oligopolistic structure for the US domestic oil industry that persisted more or less untouched until the early 1970s. Internationally, the Red Line and Achnacarry Agreements of 1928,[16] in conjunction with prorationing in the US domestic market,[17] allowed the major oil companies – the four shareholders in Aramco, that is, Exxon, Mobil, Texaco and Socal (later called Chevron), plus British Petroleum, Gulf and Royal Dutch/Shell (listed in order of their entitlements to Middle East production), as well as Compagnie Française des Pétroles (CFP, later called Total)[18] – to plan investment collusively among themselves, allocating production shares to the various territories in which they had concessions in order to meet projected world-wide demand.[19] As late as 1972, these companies, five of which were American, controlled 91 per cent of Middle Eastern output and 77 per cent of the non-communist world's oil supply outside the United States. In this respect, US companies controlled the vast bulk of the supply of oil to the key allies of the United States.

Now, until the end of the Second World War, the United States was, by far, the largest oil producer in the world and self-sufficient in oil supplies. At the end of the war, the Americas – North, Central and South – accounted for just over four-fifths of world oil production. The Second World War, however, marked a turning point, for although US oil provided nearly six-sevenths of Allied oil during the war, it was clear that future supplies to Western Europe (now without access to Soviet oil) and Japan would have to come primarily from the Middle East. The changeover was dramatic: in 1947 Western Europe got 43 per cent of its oil from the Middle East, in 1948 66 per cent and by 1950 some 85 per cent, with dollar-denominated Middle East oil production expanding by 150 per cent between 1947 and 1950.[20] The overall trends in the shares of world oil production since the Second World War are shown in Figure 3.1.

Oil was increasingly to flow to Western Europe and Japan at prices below the opportunity cost of alternatives (principally coal), sourced to a large extent by US companies. It thereby played a key role in facilitating the transfer of substantial elements of the American model of mass consumption and mass production, alongside suburban living based on largely private transportation, to other capitalist countries. This meant that oil played a key role in the processes by which the most advanced economy in the world became a pole of attraction – and hence leadership – for others, as other countries sought to emulate and replicate their own national versions of mass consumption and mass production capitalism. Of course, many factors played their part in this, but oil certainly lubricated these transformations. Europe's (and Japan's) economies and societies were now being reshaped by the more advanced economic order in America, an order in which the fuel of choice for a mobile,

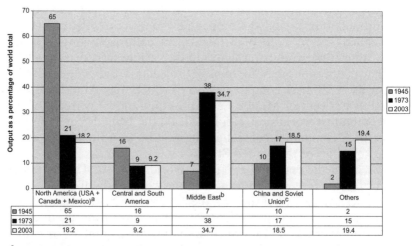

	North America (USA + Canada + Mexico)[a]	Central and South America	Middle East[b]	China and Soviet Union[c]	Others
1945	65	16	7	10	2
1973	21	9	38	17	15
2003	18.2	9.2	34.7	18.5	19.4

[a] In 2003, United States 9.2 per cent, Canada 3.8 per cent and Mexico 5.1 per cent.

[b] Figures for 2003 include Arab North Africa.

[c] In 2003, Russia 11.4 per cent, Former Soviet Union (excluding Russia) 2.5 per cent and China 4.6 per cent.

Figure 3.1. The changing balance of world oil production, 1945–2003
Source: Bromley 1991 and *BP Statistical Review of World Energy 2004*, at *http://www.bp.com.*

suburban consumer society was increasingly oil supplied from the Middle East by US firms. And the terms of trade for that oil depended on US geopolitical commitments in the Middle East.

The position of dominance in world oil production held by the United States in 1945 is now occupied by the Middle East. While it is true that the share of Middle Eastern oil in total world production was only 31 per cent in 2004 (a decline from 38 per cent in 1973 before the first major price rises), current production figures significantly underestimate the potential longer-term dominance of the region. One needs to consider that production elsewhere – that is, in the higher-cost regions outside of the Middle East – is being run down at a much faster rate, given the underlying reserve positions. Reserves to production ratios – that is, the lifetime of existing proven reserves at current rates of production – are typically an order of magnitude higher in the Middle East OPEC states than in the USA. If we look not at current production but at reserves, the longer-term decline of US oil – and thus, the eventual centrality of the Middle East – is starkly illustrated (see Figure 3.2). Clearly, OPEC producers, and,

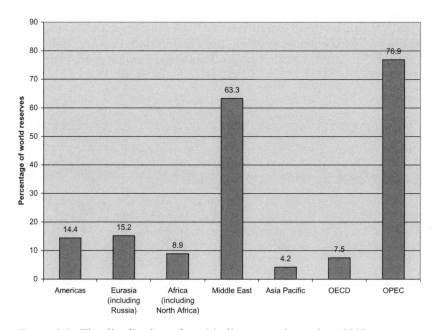

Figure 3.2. The distribution of world oil reserves by region, 2003
Source: BP Statistical Review of World Energy 2004, at *http://www.bp. com.*

within OPEC, Middle Eastern producers, control the bulk of the world's oil. That, at least, is the standard view. It is endorsed both by the organization of the main oil-consuming countries, the International Energy Agency, and by the US task force on energy conducted under the auspices of Vice-President Dick Cheney.

The International Energy Agency (IEA) and the US Department of Energy predict that the supply of OPEC oil – and,especially, Middle Eastern OPEC oil – will be critical. World oil production peaked in 1979, at approximately 65 million barrels per day (mb/d), and then declined during the 1980s. By 1993, total output had returned to 66 mb/d. Since then, output has increased steadily by an average of 1–2 mb/d each year, such that total world production was around 86 mb/d in 2007. Against this background, the US Department of Energy's *International Energy Outlook* foresees a need for an increase in world oil supply of 43 mb/d by 2020 to meet current projections of demand (see Figure 3.3).

To put that in perspective, this increase represents nearly four and a half times the current output of Saudi Arabia or five times that of Russia, and it would represent a total expansion 140 per cent faster than that achieved in the most recent period of expansion (1985–2000). It presumes an expansion of OPEC output 75 per cent faster, and non-OPEC expansion seven times faster, than that accomplished from 1985 to 2000. The IEA projections are somewhat more cautious:

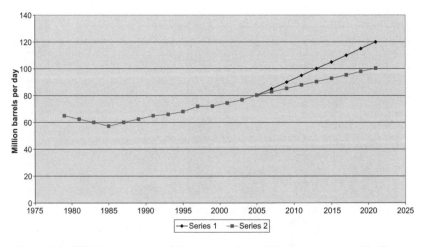

Figure 3.3. US Department of Energy projected increases in world oil production (Series 1) and world oil production at current rate of expansion (Series 2)

namely, that total world demand will reach 116 mb/d by 2030 (that is, ten years later than the US Department of Energy's estimate).[21] Most of this increase in demand – over 70 per cent according to the IEA – will come from developing countries. Recent increases in demand can be seen in Table 3.1. Assuming that the projected increases in output are achieved, the May 2001 report from the National Energy Policy Development Group in the United States, led by Vice-President Cheney, concluded that despite efforts to increase supplies from Central Asia, Africa and the Western Hemisphere, the Gulf producers still could be supplying 54–67 per cent of world exports by 2020.[22] It is predictions like these that underpin *both* the idea that rapid increases in output are needed if an ever-escalating oil price is to be avoided *and* the centrality of the Gulf to the geopolitics of oil, since Iran, Iraq, Kuwait, the United Arab Emirates and Saudi Arabia are where the bulk of the cheap, conventional oil is located.

On the demand side of the market, while the OECD bloc accounts for about 56 per cent of the total, the emerging market economies (including Russia) account for nearly 42 per cent. There are now, in fact, three roughly equally balanced regions of consumption which account for some 85 per cent of the world's total consumption: North America, Europe/Eurasia and the Asia Pacific.

Figure 3.4 shows the contemporary distribution of world oil consumption as well as refinery capacity and throughput. These 'regions' of oil consumption are also highly regionalized in their sources of supply. For example, the United States currently accounts for just over one-quarter of total consumption and a similar proportion of total world imports. To service this demand, the vast majority of oil exports from Canada, Mexico and South and Central America go to the United States; nearly half of Europe's exports cross the Atlantic (nearly three-quarters if Canada's imports are included); and nearly

Table 3.1. World oil demand changes by region, 2006–8 (thousand b/d)

	2006	2007	2008
Asia	375	641	853
North America	−232	393	347
Europe	−23	−166	275
Latin America	182	184	144
Former Soviet Union	177	−59	80
Africa	−10	130	107
World oil demand growth (mb/d)	0.76	1.42	2.10
World oil demand growth (%)	0.9	1.7	2.4

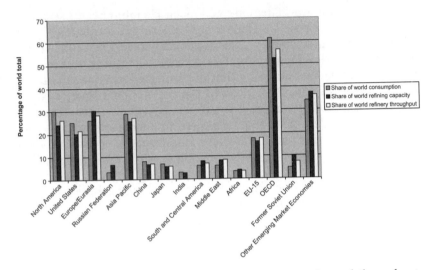

Figure 3.4. World oil consumption and refinery capacity and throughput, 2003
Source: BP Statistical Review of World Energy 2004, at *http://www.bp. com.*

two-fifths of West Africa's exports go to the United States. Europe, which also accounts for about one-quarter of total world consumption and imports, gets over four-fifths of Russian exports and over two-thirds of North African exports. Finally, nearly two-thirds of Middle East exports and roughly one-third of (the much smaller) West African exports go to the Asia Pacific region, which also accounts for a little over one-quarter of total world consumption but nearly two-fifths of world imports. Of the suppliers, only the Middle East services all the major consuming regions to a significant degree.

The overall picture can be seen in Figure 3.5, which shows countries' share of total world imports and the principal suppliers of those imports, that is, the major oil exporting countries. Inter-area movements of oil accounted for about three-fifths (58.6 per cent) of total world oil consumption in 2003, with the remainder consumed in the country and/or region it was produced. For example, the United States' own production was equivalent to 37 per cent of US consumption; Europe's and Eurasia's own production was 86 per cent of consumption (largely on account of Russia's exports to Europe); and the Asia Pacific region's production was only 35 per cent of consumption.[23]

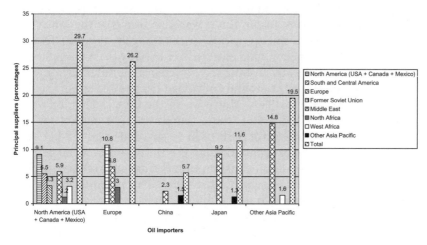

Figure 3.5. Major oil importers and principal suppliers
Source: calculated from data in *BP Statistical Review of World Energy 2004*,
at *http://www.bp.com.*

All of these changes in the distribution of production, reserves, consumption and inter-country/regional trade in the world oil industry have taken place against the backdrop of this industry's massive overall expansion throughout the twentieth century: between 1913 and 1948 the annual growth rate of production was about 6.5 per cent; and from 1948 to 1973 (during the post-war boom) the growth rate was 7.5 per cent annually. However, the ending of the post-war boom ushered in a fundamental shift in the pattern of demand. In 1979 production was only 12 per cent higher than in 1973, and by 1985 it was 12 per cent lower than in 1979; by 1991–2 production had just recovered to the 1979 level; since then the industry has seen a steady but lower increase of around 2 per cent annually, falling to just over 1 per cent in times of recessions such as the period after the 1997/8 financial crises in Asia and elsewhere. In a similar manner to these changes in the demand for oil, total energy demand faltered during the recessions of the 1970s and early 1980s and then recovered, and now expands at an energy ratio (the amount of energy used per unit of GDP) of less than one-to-one in the OECD bloc, and somewhat more than this in the developing world.

Overall, then, the price increases of oil in the 1970s and the perceived instability of the main source of supply, the Middle East, reduced the demand for oil and encouraged a search both for greater efficiency of energy use and for alternative sources of supply (whether non-OPEC oil or other fuels). But it was also true that the growth of energy demand (and energy ratios) was falling in the OECD bloc because of changing economic patterns, essentially from manufacturing to services and away from energy-intensive manufacturing. This trend pre-dated the oil crisis and continued despite the fall in the real price of oil in the mid-1980s. However, in the OECD bloc, and particularly in the United States, there remains a core market for oil: namely, the transport sector. (BP used to say that it got 75 per cent of its profits from 25 per cent of the barrel – the part that made petrol.) About 70 per cent of US oil consumption is transport-related, and of this some three-quarters is for road vehicles. This is reinforced by the tax system in the United States: while the pre-tax price of US petrol is *higher* than in most developed countries, 'the rest of the developed world imposes a tax over six times larger'. More generally, as Clyde Prestowitz has pointed out, oil use is built into the very fabric of the American way of life:

> By 1975 the [United States] was designed and built to favor cars and airplanes over trains and buses, private transportation over public. Most of us lived in large, widely spaced houses far from our jobs, recreation, or any place else we might go. The lifestyle that cheap energy had given us was no longer a choice: The very architecture of the country demanded it.

In Japan, by contrast, energy use per unit of GDP is less than half that of the United States, and in Europe it is about two-thirds. To put all this into perspective, says Prestowitz, 'if America had the same energy efficiency as the EU, it could not only do without oil imports from the Persian Gulf, it could do without oil imports period'.[24] This is certainly a considerable overstatement, since what determines the scale of US oil imports is mainly the energy efficiency of the transport sector, but the more general point about the absence of any serious concern about fuel efficiency in American domestic politics is well taken. Congress has thus far stymied all attempts seriously to address the question of energy efficiency in general, and oil efficiency in particular, notwithstanding routine, high-profile statements – from Presidents Nixon to George W. Bush – about the need to reduce US oil import dependence.[25]

Whether the demand for energy use in general, and for oil in particular, will once again achieve their earlier rates of expansion remains a basic and as yet unanswered question for the future of the geopolitics of oil. What is reasonably clear, however, is that the locus of demand for oil imports will continue to shift away from the United States' key allies in Europe and Japan and towards the Asia Pacific, especially to countries such as China and India.

OPEC and World Oil

This anticipated long-term dependence of the rest of the world on OPEC and the Middle East's oil is important because the oil market does not work like a normal market and because of the political and geopolitical instability of the Middle East. Despite the fact that structurally oil markets have been getting more competitive and more transparent since the 1970s, for most of the 1980s and 1990s there was a major imbalance between supply (and reserves) and demand, such that even when the world demand for oil did not absorb all the supply that was on offer, prices did not fall far enough to balance the market either through increased demand or through the loss of high-cost supply. The oil market was characterized by excess supply, and prices appeared to have a 'floor' beneath them which prevented them falling sufficiently to clear the market.

Precisely because of this price floor, much of the new capacity developed in the industry since the 1970s – in the non-OPEC areas of the North Sea, Alaska, Siberia and the new oil provinces of Mexico – was *higher* in cost than most of the existing capacity that was under-utilized, and most of the production 'shut-in' (that is, proven and available reserves which were not being used) during the 1980s and 1990s was of *lower* operating cost than a large amount of the production taking place elsewhere (see Figure 3.6). Moreover, during the 1980s and into the early 1990s, (additional) capacity in low-cost regions could have been expanded more cheaply than most of the post-OPEC, new developments; and yet total capacity in low-cost regions was only about half utilized in the 1980s and early 1990s and was in fact being run down.[26]

The legacy of these developments is still apparent in the tighter market conditions of recent times. Thus, while OPEC accounted for 77 per cent of world reserves and the Middle East for 63 per cent in 2003, their shares of world output were only roughly 40 per cent and 30 per cent, respectively. On the other side of the picture, the United States accounted for 9.2 per cent of world output in 2003 on the basis of a mere 2.7 per cent of the total reserves and Russia accounted for 11.4 per cent of total output on the basis of 6 per cent of world

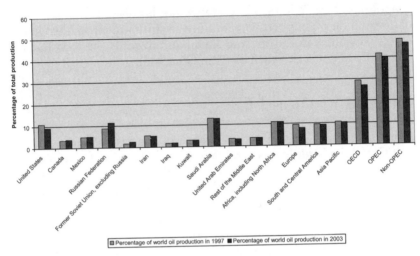

Figure 3.6. World oil production, 1997 and 2003
Source: BP Statistical Review of World Energy, 1998, 2004, at *http://www.*
bp.com.

reserves. Production in the United States peaked in 1970, eased off
at a slightly lower level for nearly two decades, and then began to fall
in the late 1980s. The (post-)Soviet industry continued to grow until
the early 1980s, then flattened and may now be rising again, though
this expansion is unlikely to continue beyond 2010. Together, the
United States and the Soviet Union had accounted for 40 per cent of
the growth of world oil production in the post-war period. Evidently,
future growth will have to come from the OPEC countries.

Why didn't the demand for oil match the supply? Why wasn't high-
cost oil displaced by low-cost supply? To understand why there was
continuing over-supply in the oil market we need to focus on why the
comparative costs of oil production are not properly reflected in crude
oil prices.[27] The single most important technical factor influencing
the cost of crude oil production is the productivity per well. But the
productivity per well is itself partly a function of price, through the
impact of price on the choice of technique; and so high-productivity
(low-cost) oil will not automatically displace low-productivity (high-
cost) oil at prices above the competitive level. Low-cost producers will
simply earn larger rents. In addition, since the marginal costs of oil
production are considerably smaller than the capital costs (finding oil
and sinking a well are costly, running an existing well is cheap), new
sources of low-cost oil will not generally displace existing high-cost

sources. Even given these facts, we still need to ask why low-cost producers were unable to increase production in order to increase their market share at lower oil prices. The simple answer is that they could not afford to do so.

In periods of over-supply (a characteristic of the oil market from the late 1970s through to the first couple of years of the new century), the key influences on the price of oil are the actions of swing producers, that is, those able and willing to alter output by relatively small amounts on a regular basis. These are, typically, the producers with large reserve/production ratios and with large production/population ratios. They are, in effect, Gulf OPEC in the widest sense – Saudi Arabia, the United Arab Emirates, Kuwait, and Iran and Iraq. It is certainly true that OPEC does not and cannot act as a cartel to rig the oil market. The only period when it attempted to do this (1982–5) was a signal failure. In fact, disarray within OPEC has been more or less a constant.[28] Even moments of Saudi–Iranian cooperation, in the late 1990s just as in the mid-1980s, have struggled to stabilize the market because no producer – not even the Saudis – has been able to afford to drive the price low enough for long enough to displace the higher-cost producers of oil and other energy sources. This is not because of their *costs of production*, which are in many cases several times lower than those in the high-cost areas, but because they are rentier states and economies and thus have socially determined target incomes that are more or less necessary to assure social stability and the legitimacy of their rule. And as long as higher-cost producers can survive in the market, OPEC (and Saudi Arabia in particular) cannot control the industry in conditions of excess supply.

There is also another set of considerations to be taken into account in assessing the production decisions of those low-cost producers with large reserves and high reserve/production ratios. To begin with, it is important to remember that the prices of oil products – for example, motor fuels – do not simply reflect the cost of crude oil and the technology which turns crude into products. What intervenes between cost and price, often in a massive way, are the taxes imposed on both the products of crude oil at the point of sale and the activities of those firms that transform crude into products. This means, in effect, that the rents generated in the oil sector accrue not only to the producers of crude but also to the private (generally multinational) firms involved and, most especially, the governments in the main *consuming* states. Struggles over the size and the division of the rents involve the actions of all three parties – the national oil companies of the producing states, multinationals and consuming governments.

Put another way, oil rents may be appropriated at any point in the chain from production to final sale of refined products, in the form of producer rents, industry surplus profits and government taxes. This is why some Gulf producers, notably Kuwait and Saudi Arabia, moved downstream in the industry and established a presence in Western (and then Asian) consumer markets. This gave them similar interests in pricing as (private) international oil firms, as they sought higher value added for their integrated petroleum concerns, rather than the highest possible prices for crude oil. (Financial investments in the developed economies, financed by profits from oil sales, further cemented this linkage.) Equally, an aggressively low price for crude in pursuit of market share at the expense of higher-cost (and non-OPEC) producers would in all probability have been met by tariffs to protect 'security of supply' (from high-cost sources outside OPEC) and, in any case, would not have been passed on to consumers as consuming states would have likely raised taxes on refined products.

In short, the oil market during the 1980s and 1990s was characterized by a situation where there was structural over-supply, in which the low-cost producers neither could afford to drive the high-cost elements from the market (because they were rentier states and economies), nor had any real incentive to do so (because of their downstream integration with the main consumer markets). It was this latter coincidence of interests between the production and marketing strategies of Saudi Arabia, Kuwait and the United Arab Emirates, multinational oil interests and the governments of the consuming nations that provided the economic basis of US–Saudi relations during much of the 1980s and 1990s.[29]

The United States and Middle East Oil

After the United States aligned itself with the conservative, monarchical states and against the nationalist regimes, it established a form of indirect control over Middle East oil that replaced British suzerainty, Britain having withdrawn 'East of Suez' between 1967 and 1971. 'Britain's role as the manager of Gulf security', says Avi Shlaim, 'had had three aspects':

> insulating the region from penetration by other great powers, preventing interstate conflicts such as those between Iraq and Kuwait, and helping local rulers foil military coups and combat subversion. The

secret of Britain's success lay in keeping a low profile and a small military presence and, above all, in limiting the supply of arms.[30]

The United States continued this policy with the crucial difference that it promoted, rather than limited, the supply of arms to regional allies. This policy built on the earlier inroads made by the United States in Saudi Arabia after 1945 and in Iran following the coup against Mossadegh in 1953. But it represented a military response to the political and geopolitical *failure* to craft a regional anti-Soviet alliance (something the United States attempted periodically from the days of the Baghdad Pact in 1955 to the efforts of the Carter administration in the early 1980s following the Soviet invasion of Afghanistan and the Iranian Revolution). During this period the major Western oil companies controlled production decisions, and US strategy for the Gulf rested on the 'twin pillar' policy of support for Iran and Saudi Arabia. As indicated above, this was the system of control that played a central role in providing the material basis of US hegemony during the long phase of rapid, catch-up growth among the leading capitalist economies. It was overthrown by the OPEC-related events of the two oil shocks (1973/4 and 1979) and the Iranian Revolution (1979). Two decades of unrelenting crisis followed – the 1973/4 price rise and the (temporary) Arab 'embargo' in response to the 1973 Arab–Israeli war; the post-OPEC nationalization of control over oil production decisions in the key Middle East and, especially, Gulf states; the communist accession to power in Afghanistan, the subsequent civil war, Soviet invasion and resistance of the mujahidin; the Iranian Revolution, followed very quickly by further major increases in the price of oil and the outbreak of the Iran–Iraq war of 1980–8; the Israeli invasion of Lebanon in 1982 at the same time as decisive Iranian counter-attacks against Iraq; and Iraq's invasion of Kuwait in 1990 and the subsequent first US-led war against Iraq of 1991.

However, despite these setbacks, the United States was able to fashion a new form of influence in the 1980s based on an increasingly close alliance with Saudi Arabia (and the Gulf states). The key elements of the new form of influence were as follows. In the first place, while US oil imports (including from the Middle East) were rising, the United States was much less dependent on Middle East oil than were Western Europe and Japan. European states pursued national, rather than EU-wide, policies towards the region that could not match US efforts. Japan had virtually no influence on the region. Geopolitically, the Soviet position was increasingly precarious. Large developing countries, such as China and India, were not yet significantly involved in a competitive search for energy resources. Secondly, although the Iranian Revolution was a major blow to US power in the region, the mutual ruin of the contending parties in the Iran–Iraq War (1980–8) nullified this loss somewhat, as did a growing involvement of Pakistan in regional security.

And finally, Saudi Arabia and the Gulf states, in effect, exchanged military security for cooperation on pricing and production decisions in OPEC, thereby reconciling their economic interests with those of the oil majors and the major consuming countries. The social and political structure of the Saudi state ruled out the development of large-scale domestic armed forces, for fear of creating a source of coup d'état against the ruling family, while the smaller Gulf states saw the role of the United States as a protection against their larger neighbours – Iran and Iraq, of course, but also Saudi Arabia. The Gulf states, especially Saudi Arabia, have an independent economic interest in retaining their long-run market shares, while seeking short-term adjustments of supply in order to influence prices so as to meet their budgetary needs, but in moments of crisis or tight supply they have generally sought to bring stability to the market. Although officially denied, it is widely believed that the United States made some arms sales and defence arrangements with Saudi Arabia conditional on its actions within OPEC.[31]

The creation of the Rapid Deployment Force (RDF) in 1977 and the promulgation of the Carter Doctrine (1980)[32] – to resist any attempt by a hostile power or powers to control the Gulf, if necessary by force – was one key statement of this new dispensation, and the first US-led war against Iraq (to reverse the invasion and occupation of Kuwait, 1990–1) was a direct outcome of it, given the actions of Saddam Hussein's regime. Notwithstanding the success of that war and the generally benign movements in the oil market during the 1990s (that is, security of supply and declining real oil prices), there were, however, a number of problems associated with this new form of control that became progressively harder to handle.

Moreover, by the 1990s, two further changes had massively altered the geopolitical landscape and the economic issues at stake. Geopolitically, the Cold War had ended with the dissolution of the communist systems such that the United States and its ideology of an increasingly open international capitalist order stood at the centre-stage of world development, unchecked by any organized bloc of state power. Elevation to the status of sole military superpower and the enfeeblement of the 'radical' Arab regimes in Iraq and Syria as well as the involution of the Iranian Revolution allowed the United States directly to deploy military force to the region on an unparalleled scale. Equally, the steady (if slow) ascendancy of markets and private property across the Middle East, as the protection afforded to statist, protected models of development by oil rents receded, worked in America's favour. Economically, however, the United States now had neither the preponderant resources, nor the political incentives, to offer concessions to its allies: it no longer needed capitalist allies to range against its communist adversary and it could no longer afford to tolerate discriminatory trade and investment practices on the part of its major trading partners. In the longer term, the United States faced the prospect of future geopolitical and geo-economic competition – that is, competition among states for influence or control over the course of international politics in pursuit of strategic advantage and economic gain – from China and India and perhaps from a resurgent Russia.

Specifically, the United States will increasingly need to source oil imports from the Middle East (and elsewhere) for its domestic market, just like the Europeans and the Japanese have done. Over time, China and India (and other Asian states) can be expected to draw on world market supplies in increasing quantities. If America will increasingly be compelled to source its domestic needs from the rest of the world's oil, then how can oil continue to function as a form of material redistribution for its allies? Does the end of the Cold War imply that former allies (as well as continuing adversaries – Russia, China) will now become just competitors and, therefore, that mutually advantageous forms of coordination will be increasingly difficult to engineer? What form of international oil industry, if any, might meet these new demands, and what might be the role of the United States in structuring this new international oil industry?

The reconsolidated strategy developed in the 1980s was based, geopolitically and economically, on the stability of the Washington–Riyadh axis, the 'dual containment' of Iran and Iraq and the effective exclusion from the region's geopolitics of other outside powers such as Russia, China, India and the European Union. But in truth this was little better than crisis management and a very high-risk strategy. It relied on Saudi Arabia and Pakistan as key regional allies; it had little support in Europe (even the closest ally, the UK, did not support the economic position towards Iran); it was actively opposed by Russia and China and then India; and it provoked opposition in the wider Arab and Muslim world.

In brief summary:

1. US needs for oil imports were growing, such that by 2020 as much as two-thirds of US oil consumption might need to be imported.
2. OPEC power was bound to increase, given the absence of a major shift away from oil in the major consuming regions, in a context where the big growth in world oil demand was most likely to be Asia, especially in China and India.
3. US strategy depended on the Washington–Riyadh axis holding, on the continuation of the dual containment of Iran and Iraq and on the exclusion of other outside powers from the region's geopolitics.
4. The US already faced opposition to its policies from the EU and Japan, especially regarding dual containment.
5. Russia, China and India actively opposed the policy and this opposition was bound to increase. (India was particularly annoyed by the fact that US policy after the events of 1979 – that is, in Iran and Afghanistan – had given Pakistan a much greater role in the region.) Russia was seeking to rebuild its influence in the region after the Soviet collapse, directly frustrating US policy towards Iraq and Iran. China was beginning to follow Russia's line in its own ways.

In addition, the policy of relying on a combination of the dual containment of Iran and Iraq and friendly relations with Saudi Arabia to stabilize the oil market was at odds with other elements of US international oil policy and its wider geopolitical interests. I first consider the changing geopolitical field before returning to the question of oil.

Reshaping the Greater Middle East

During the Cold War, US policies towards the Middle East and towards Afghanistan and Pakistan were largely unrelated. India's non-alignment and relations with the Soviet Union were reasons for close US–Pakistani relations, and in the 1960s the first U-2 spying missions over the Soviet Union had flown from bases in Peshawar. Still, the Chinese success in the war with India in 1962 also highlighted the importance to the West of India's position. And in the 1970s, while Kissinger did use Pakistani intermediaries as part of the opening to China, US–Pakistani relations deteriorated as a result of Pakistan's nuclear programme. Prior to 1979, in fact, relations were at a low ebb and US interests and involvement in Afghanistan were minimal.

The year 1979 marked a major turning point in US foreign policy towards the Middle East and Central Asia because of the two events which were to shape so much of politics and geopolitics in those regions as well as in the wider international system: namely, the Iranian Revolution in February and the Soviet invasion of Afghanistan in December. Taken together, these developments posed a major challenge to US strategy towards the USSR, to the wider Middle East and to relations with China, Pakistan and India. The Iranian Revolution represented the loss of a key regional ally as well as listening stations directed at the Soviet Union – though the latter were soon relocated to Pakistan. Afghanistan, of course, became the cockpit of an attempt to confront and weaken the Soviet empire, thereby further increasing Pakistan's importance as a key regional ally.

In Afghanistan, the rise to power of the pro-Soviet People's Democratic Party of Afghanistan (PDPA) in 1978 provoked a civil war as significant elements of the Muslim society resisted its secularizing and socialist measures, specifically its policies of compulsory female education and land reform. The decision of the United States to arm the mujahidin was taken, according to President Carter's National Security Adviser, Zbigniew Brzezinski, in the summer of 1979 in order to 'induce a Soviet military intervention'. Brzezinski later said that: 'The day that the Soviets officially crossed the border [24 December 1979], I wrote to President Carter, saying: "We now have the opportunity of giving to the USSR its Vietnam War." '[33] That said, according to Steve Coll:

[Brzezinski's] contemporary memos – particularly those written in the first days after the Soviet invasion – make clear that while [he] was determined to confront the Soviets in Afghanistan through covert action, he was also very worried that the Soviets would prevail. Those early memos show no hint of satisfaction that the Soviets had taken some sort of Afghan bait. Given this evidence and the enormous political and security costs that the invasion imposed on the Carter administration, any claim that Brzezinski lured the Soviets into Afghanistan warrants deep scepticism.[34]

Nevertheless, the opportunity to impose costs on the Soviet Union by arming and financing the mujahidin was real enough and too good to miss. This meant that relations with Pakistan would be crucial, for as US Secretary of State George Shultz noted in a memo to President Reagan in 1982, 'We must remember that without Zia's support, the Afghan resistance, key to making the Soviets pay a heavy price for their Afghan adventure, is effectively dead.'[35] For his part, Pakistan's military leader, General Zia, was concerned that Kabul's communist government would stir up Pushtun independence activists along the Afghan–Pakistan border. In 1979, Hafizullah Amin, the Afghan Prime Minister, had explicitly stated his desire for a 'Greater Afghanistan', declaring that the Duran line – the line the British had drawn through Pushtun lands to divide Afghanistan from its empire on the subcontinent – 'tore us apart'.

Prior to these events, as mentioned above, US–Pakistani relations had soured because of the latter's nuclear programme. By 1972, President Bhutto was aware of the Indian nuclear programme (though India did not test its bomb until 1974) and initiated a Pakistani response, which was pursued with urgency after 1974. In 1965 Pakistan had concluded an agreement, under international safeguards, with Canada for the Karachi Nuclear Power Plant, which was capable of producing plutonium. After 1974, Canada cut off all supplies of fuel and a potential deal with France came to nothing after strong American objections to Islamabad and Paris. In 1975, the major powers began to coordinate in the London Supplier's Group to cut out any countries, such as Pakistan, that had not signed the Nuclear Non-Proliferation Treaty. But all of this began to change in 1979, and US Secretary of State Alexander Haig told his Pakistani counterpart, Agha Shahi, in 1981 that 'we will not make your nuclear programme the centrepiece of our relations'.[36] By 1984/5 Pakistan had the bomb, though it did not test it and become a declared nuclear power until 1998 in response to Indian tests.

Meantime, the war in Afghanistan continued. Pakistan's Inter-Services Intelligence directorate (ISI) became the conduit for weapons and money to flow to the mujahidin, and Saudi and US money provided generous backing. In the spring of 1985, Mikhail Gorbachev assumed power in the Kremlin and the US National Security Agency learned that he was willing to give his generals one to two years to win the war and that by the autumn of 1986 he was planning to leave. The main priority for the United States was to accelerate the Soviet withdrawal and to continue support for the mujahidin's resistance to the communist government in Kabul. On 14 April 1988, the Afghan communist government, Pakistan, the USA and the USSR ratified the Geneva Accords. After this the CIA continued to support the mujahidin for as long as Moscow supported the government of President Najibullah, that is, until 1 January 1992. Notwithstanding this continued support, US geopolitical priorities now lay elsewhere. There had been a popular rebellion in Kashmir in 1989, and in 1990 the CIA had reported that Pakistan's nuclear programme had reached new and dangerous levels. That year saw Saddam Hussain's invasion of Kuwait and 1991 witnessed the end of communism and the final collapse of the Soviet Union. On 1 January 1992 Gorbachev cut off assistance to Najibullah and the CIA's legal authority for covert action in Afghanistan ended. 'There would not be an American ambassador or CIA station chief assigned directly to Afghanistan for nearly a decade,' says Steve Coll, that is, not 'until late in the autumn of 2001' after the fall of the Taliban.[37] In effect, US policy in Afghanistan became Pakistan's policy, or at least was subordinated to Pakistan's policy.

Following the Soviet withdrawal from Afghanistan, Pakistan's policy was to support Gulbuddin Hekmatyar's drive for Kabul as well as his attempt to eliminate all his rivals in the Afghan resistance. And while some State Department officials believed that other commanders – such as Massoud and Abdul Haq – might be included in a *shura* of independent Afghan leaders, outside ISI control, and sought to enlist the support of Saudi intelligence to this end, the CIA opposed the idea that the United States could manage Afghan politics. Hekmatyar had the support of officers from the ISI's Afghan bureau, members from the (Pakistani) Muslim Brotherhood's Jammat-e-Islami, officers from Saudi intelligence and Arab volunteers from many countries. If one reason for Pakistan's support for Hekmatyar was to have an ally in Kabul, another was ISI's reliance on training camps in Hekmatyar-controlled Afghan territory, and the Afghan and Arab volunteers produced by those camps, for its campaign to bleed Indian troops in Kashmir. In the mid-1990s, the ISI told the Pakistani President, Benazir Bhutto, that there simply were not enough native Kashmiri guerrillas to do the job.

Meantime, from 1994 onwards the Taliban movement was on the rise and (astonishingly) Benazir Bhutto thought that it might provide a means of expunging Iranian, Russian and Indian influence in Afghanistan, thereby opening trade routes for Pakistan to Central Asia. The ISI's relations with the Taliban were complicated, however, because Mullah Omar was determined to challenge Hekmatyar for leadership of the Pushtuns. According to Ahmed Rashid:

During 1995 the ISI continued to debate the issue of greater support for the Taliban. The debate centred around those largely Pushtun officers involved in covert operations on the ground, who wanted greater support for the Taliban, and other officers who were involved in longer term intelligence gathering and strategic planning, who wished to keep Pakistan's support to a minimum so as not to worsen tensions with Central Asia and Iran. The Pushtun grid in the army high command eventually played a major role in determining the military and ISI's decision to give greater support to the Taliban.[38]

By the spring of 1997, the ISI concluded that a Taliban *government* would be easier to deal with than a Taliban *movement* and that others would simply have to accept a *fait accompli*. In the eventuality, besides Pakistan, only Saudi Arabia and the United Arab Emirates were to recognize the Taliban as the government of Afghanistan.

US–Pakistani relations again deteriorated towards the end of the 1990s: India and Pakistan both tested nuclear weapons and became declared nuclear powers in 1998. By 2000, after Musharraf's military coup of October 1999, President Clinton was publicly lecturing Pakistan's people to the effect that their unelected leader's policies on Kashmir and nuclear weapons were making Pakistan 'even more isolated, draining more resources away from the needs of the people, moving even closer to a conflict [with India] no one can win'.[39] Then came 11 September 2001. In response, President George W. Bush declared that: 'We will make no distinction between those who planned these acts and those who harbor them.' Accordingly, US Secretary of State Colin Powell argued forcefully that it was time to make Pakistan and Afghanistan choose and President Musharraf took the historic decision to break with the Taliban. The Northern Alliance's drive against the Taliban, supported by CIA officers and US Special Forces, followed immediately and President Hamid Karzai took the oath of office in Kabul on 22 December 2001.

Al-Qaida and the West Asian Crisis

The immediate background to the rise of al-Qaida was the civil war in Afghanistan. Al-Qaida was created during US-, Saudi- and Pakistani-backed operations to finance and organize the mujahidin's resistance to communism in Afghanistan and to recruit (mainly Arab) Muslims from abroad to fight for that cause. Once the Taliban came to power in Kabul (1996), they formed a close alliance with Osama bin Laden's al-Qaida organization, indeed in some respects al-Qaida became the military arm of the Taliban. However, while the

Saudis had been willing to provide support for the fight against the PDPA and their Soviet backers, they were not prepared to accede to demands for a strict Islamism of the Saudi state and, in particular, the demand that the United States withdraw from the Arabian peninsula. This would have amounted to a transfer of control of the Saudi state from the monarchy to Islamist forces. And so, after helping to evict the Soviets from Afghanistan, al-Qaida turned its attention to its erstwhile Western backers, who were also engaged in the military support of the monarchical regime in Saudi Arabia. This confrontation with the United States was designed to radicalize the masses in the Arab states and the wider Muslim world against local states allied to the West. The result was explosive, as Fred Halliday explains:

> Three elements therefore came together: a reassertion of the most traditional strands in Islamic thinking, a brutalization and militarization of the Islamic groups themselves, and a free-floating transnational army of fighters drawing support from Pakistan, the Arab world, south-east Asia and Chechnya with its base in Afghanistan. In the context of the greater west Asian crisis, and the revolt against the states of the region, as well as their western backers, there now emerged an organized and militant challenge.[40]

The 'war on terror' (now the 'long war'), declared by President Bush in the aftermath of the attacks of 9/11, is shorthand for a complex set of problems that defy easy summary. Many analysts took issue with the use of the word 'war', because the perpetrators of the acts were not states but part of a transnational network, a cellular structure that crossed a number of territories on a clandestine basis, and because there was no obvious way in which the war aims could be specified and measured. Terrorism is, after all, a tactic – the continuation of politics by other means – and how can one fight a tactic? Gabriel Kolko, for example, describes al-Qaida terrorism as 'desperate and essentially random' and of no geo-strategic consequence.[41] Oliver Roy, by contrast, while agreeing that political Islam had largely failed in its challenge to local, authoritarian and secular states, argued that the tactic of embroiling the United States in a fight against militant Islam was real enough, even if its primary purpose was to radicalize the Muslim masses against their own regimes rather than the West.[42] Still others saw the actions of al-Qaida as an example of an 'asymmetrical conflict', that is, a conflict whose nature is determined by the marked lack of symmetry in the power of the contending forces.[43] Understood thus, al-Qaida terrorism was a mode of irregular warfare where the definition of 'irregularity rest[ed] on the legal status of the rival belligerents, not the character of the fighting', in which case the United States 'should consider [itself] at war with a rational adversary'.[44]

US policy reflected the uncertain character of this challenge. As early as 1995, President Clinton was worried about terrorist acquisition of weapons of mass destruction. In 1996 Osama bin Laden was expelled from Sudan and moved to Afghanistan. But the 'White House did not begin to push for covert operations against bin Laden beyond intelligence collection until the end of 1997, a year after he established himself openly in Mullah Omar's Kandahar'.[45] Even after the 7 August 1998 bombings of the US embassies in Nairobi and Dar es Salaam, Clinton still sought to trade diplomatic recognition of the Taliban for custody of bin Laden. As late as the summer of 1999, the State Department was not prepared to back Massoud's Northern Alliance, though it signalled that it did not oppose Russian and Iranian support. The Pentagon, and especially CENTCOM, had close links to Pakistan's army and argued that support for Massoud in the form of weapons or battlefield intelligence would be, in effect, to join India in an indirect war against Pakistan. And not even the attack in Yemen on the USS *Cole*, on 12 October 2000, convinced the US military of the need for commando operations in Afghanistan. In fact, notwithstanding Clinton's deployment of cruise missile strikes against Sudan and Afghanistan, Donald Rumsfeld's description of Clinton's policy towards asymmetrical warfare against US interests in the region as one of 'reflexive pullback' was very largely accurate.

Given all of this, US policy struggled with two questions: Who was the enemy? How dangerous was the threat? Ultimately, decision makers at the highest level concluded that Washington could not put counter-terrorism at the top of its agenda with Islamabad because of other concerns such as nuclear weapons, Kashmir and the stability of Pakistan. Remember that in 1998 both India and Pakistan conducted atomic tests, therewith becoming declared nuclear powers, and in 1999 Pakistan's forces crossed into Indian-controlled Kashmir, bringing the countries close to a major military conflict.

Notwithstanding Rumsfeld's estimate of Clinton's policies, the advent of the Bush administration did not mark a significant shift in American policy. Despite briefings from the outgoing Clinton administration and Richard Clarke's entreaties to use the Northern Alliance against the Taliban, Vice-President Dick Cheney, Secretary of Defense Donald Rumsfeld and National Security Advisor Condeleezza Rice did not make the issue a high priority – they were focused on China, Russia and missile defence. Islamabad was initially worried that the new administration in Washington would tilt to India: President Bush's campaign has raised large contributions from Indian-American business and some conservative intellectuals on his team did advocate a shift to India to balance against a rising China. But Zalmay Khalilzed, who was an influential figure on the National Security Council, argued that Pushtuns, including exiles and royalists like Hamid Karzai, not Massoud's Northern Alliance, had to be the basis of any anti-Taliban strategy. By the spring of 2001, however, Secretary of State Colin Powell and his deputy Richard Armitage recommended arming the Northern Alliance, and in July the deputies' committee 'recommended a comprehensive plan, not just to roll back al Qa'ida but to eliminate it. It was a plan to go on the offensive and destabilize the Taliban.'[46] Before that plan could get anywhere, of course, 9/11 had changed the geopolitical landscape dramatically. Or rather, and more accurately, it changed the political mood in Washington and thereby the ways in which an already shifting landscape was interpreted.

The term 'asymmetric conflict' originally came to prominence during the Vietnam war to refer to the way in which the militarily weaker party seeks to take the conflict to public opinion in the enemy's homeland as an attempt to undermine its will to prosecute the war. It was an adjunct of the theory of guerrilla war, which also relied on asymmetry (between forces able to move and mix among the rural population and combatants – local or foreign – who were largely confined to urban areas), as part of a national liberation struggle. As such, it is one very plausible reason why the United States, the dominant military party to that conflict, lost. The most likely rationale of the 9/11 attacks is that they too were, in part, an attempt to undermine the adversary's will, only this time the will of the United States to continue support for the monarchy in Saudi Arabia. Most importantly, however, these attacks (and others in places such as Yemen and Kenya) were directed at mobilizing the masses in the Muslim world itself, primarily against local regimes.

These jihadist-salafist movements of Central Asia, Afghanistan and Pakistan, according to Mariam Abou Zahab and Olivier Roy,

after having begun their existence within a purely national framework or with a single purpose, namely the liberation of Afghanistan – have come to form a transnational network with the United States as the special target. . . . In fact, events have unfolded exactly as if the

jihadists had continued the anti-imperialist, anti-colonial and Third
World tradition, which belonged till the 1980s to the lay extreme left
or to a nationalist left. The turning point, that is to say the islamisation
of anti-imperialism, was the Islamic revolution of 1979 in Iran.

But it is important to understand that the 'islamisation of anti-
imperialism' did not simply represent a change in the form of struggle
since it now operates in states that are politically speaking *post*-colo-
nial. In fact, these movements now faced a sharp choice. To the extent
that they promoted a real strategic Islamic internationalism that
sought to challenge the United States – as perhaps Mullah Omar did:
'Mullah Omar literally sacrificed his regime to protect Bin Laden' –
they lost any local support that they may have had. 'Afghan support
for the Americans was effective and conspicuous,' say Abou Zahab
and Roy, 'the Afghan Taliban fighters were routed, and the foreign
[Arab] volunteers were crushed. . . . There was little significant reaction in the Arab world, and only the feeblest of demonstrations were
mounted in Pakistan.'[47] On the other hand, to the degree that they
engage in local political struggles and attempt to maintain a genuine
social base in the societies in which they operate, their regional links
are merely tactical and accidental and their main opponents become
not only the local authoritarian regimes but also the local, secular
opposition.

The conjunction of secular, progressive opposition to local authoritarianism and anti-imperialist struggle has, therefore, been shattered:
internationally, militant Islam has come to represent a free-floating,
strategically ineffectual, form of terrorism; domestically, it represents
the most reactionary form of opposition to local authoritarianism.
One might almost say, if somewhat formulaically, that in the colonial
era local authoritarian rulers survived in power in large part because
they enjoyed the support of colonial powers. In these circumstances,
national liberation was an essential precondition for the conduct of
local progressive struggles. In the post-colonial epoch, by contrast,
dominant outside powers support local authoritarian forces because
they have more or less secure access to the means of rule and are
prepared to subordinate their foreign policies to the international
relations of the former. But, in these conditions, the alignments
between local political struggles and the orientations of outside
powers are altogether more contingent and variable. In many cases,
the strongest opposition to the role of outside powers is associated
with the most reactionary form of domestic politics. This has often
been the fate of militant Islam across many Muslim societies.

Whatever its precise political and strategic character, by its very nature, asymmetric conflict is extremely hard to deter. In particular, violent asymmetric conflict carried out by clandestine adversaries is almost impossible to prevent. The operation of the balance of power and the logic of deterrence presuppose conflicts of interest as well as a common recognition of certain shared objectives – namely, survival. The logic of deterrence is, says Thomas Schelling, 'as inapplicable to a situation of pure and complete antagonism of interest as it is to the case of pure and complete common interest'.[48] Faced with an adversary that has an absolute hostility, that is prepared to risk all, deterrence is largely irrelevant. As Gilbert Achcar has argued, in this situation 'the causes of "absolute hostility" must be reduced or eliminated, in such a way that a "common interest" emerges as a possibility'.[49]

One way of reducing the threat of al-Qaida would have been to address the issues that provoked its hostility in the first place, broadly US foreign policy in the Middle East and, in particular, its military support to the regime in Saudi Arabia. Another response was to try to eliminate al-Qaida. If the asymmetry of US power was producing absolute antagonists that could not be deterred, then why not use that very same power to destroy the adversary, even before it attacked, and engineer a new situation capable of producing some minimal common interests? This was the core of the doctrine of pre-emption, as some in Washington came to believe that *both* the destruction of the enemy *and* addressing the issues that provoked the hostility could be achieved by the one and the same military means.

Since al-Qaida was, in effect, the military arm of the Taliban, the latter was directly implicated in the attacks of 9/11. The precondition for treating the attacks as a criminal matter – that the state from which the attackers operated was prepared to uphold international law – arguably did not obtain. Christina Lamb reports Mullah Omar's bodyguard as follows: 'We laughed when we heard the Americans asking Mullah Omar to hand over Osama bin Laden. . . . The Americans are crazy. Afghanistan is not a state sponsoring terrorism but a terrorist-sponsored state. It is Osama bin Laden that can hand over Mullah Omar not vice versa.'[50] In any case, this was no part of Washington's agenda and, in truth, there was precious little international support for such a strategy. Nor were the war aims of the United States unlimited. They may not have been wholly clear, but destroying al-Qaida's ability to operate inside a state that itself repudiated all international responsibilities was not especially opaque.

And although the war against al-Qaida has not been fully success-ful, there is little doubt that its capacity for organized activity was dramatically curtailed by its eviction from Afghanistan; the Taliban government that had existed in symbiosis with al-Qaida and allowed its territory to be a base for transnational terrorism was routed; the jihadist-salafist elements in the Muslim world have received a decisive *geopolitical* setback (notwithstanding the post-invasion turmoil in Iraq); a new administration was established in Kabul that had some chance of ending the long-running Afghan civil war; Pakistan's (and especially the ISI's) sponsorship of militant Islam as a tool of foreign policy against India in Kashmir and beyond has been disciplined; and the United States was able to establish a (temporary?) military pres-ence in resource-rich Central Asia. There are no guarantees that any of these gains will prove to be durable, but from the point of view of the United States it is hard to see that it is a worse situation than that which existed prior to 9/11. In that sense, those who questioned whether it was a war that could be won were on shaky ground: it was a war, and from Washington's viewpoint a major battle has been won.

It was the first battle of what was announced in the Pentagon's 2006 quadrennial review as the 'long war', since the instability following the collapse of the Soviet empire in Central Asia and the defeat of the Taliban means that the United States faces what the US Department of Defense now describes as an 'arc of instability' running from the Middle East through Central Asia to Northeast Asia. This is the region that lies at the centre of Washington's planning. As Elizabeth Wishnick notes in a paper for the Strategic Studies Institute of the US Army War College, it is a region in which American policy aims at

> preventing the hostile domination of key areas and preserving a stable balance of power; maintaining access to key markets and strategic resources; addressing threats from territories of weak states and ungoverned areas; preventing the diffusion of weapons to non-state actors; sustaining coalitions; and preparing to intervene rapidly in unexpected crises.[51]

From Kabul to Baghdad

The second battlefield was, of course, Iraq. As far as Iraq was con-cerned, the question for the United States was whether continued deterrence made better sense than pre-emption. ('Regime change' had been Washington's and Congress's policy since 1998.) It is perhaps not surprising that the United States believed that what was done in

Afghanistan could also be done in Iraq, for all the differences between the two cases. Strategically, the only real difference was that the action in Afghanistan could be presented as a defensive response, whereas that in Iraq was clearly pre-emptive or, more accurately, preventive. Important though this difference may be, the underlying rationale was broadly similar: namely, state or nation building. In order to see why invasion was in some ways an attractive alternative, it is necessary to situate Iraq in relation to the broader role of the United States in the Middle East.

As we have seen, ever since the Iranian Revolution of 1979, US Middle East policy was based on a series of contradictory commitments which increasingly undermined its ability to play a directive role. Its hegemony increasingly relied on the regional deployment of military power. Yet, the lesson of the Iranian Revolution was that this was an unsustainable strategy in the long run and, in any case, key regional allies in Jordan, Turkey and Saudi Arabia were domestically uncomfortable with the effects of economic sanctions and sporadic military attacks against Iraq. Even leaving aside the tensions created by US support for the Israeli responses to Palestinian resistance to occupation, the policy comprised hostile relations with Iran, which at least on economic matters had little support in Europe or Russia; a failed attempt permanently to deal with the threat to regional stability posed by Iraq (because of a collapse of support from Russia, France and China on the Security Council); and military support for Saudi Arabia and the smaller Gulf states that was generating considerable opposition among many Arab Muslims (most of the 9/11 hijackers came from Saudi Arabia, though their radicalization and bases appear to have been in Europe). There was, in short, precious little basis on which the United States could construct even a minimal set of common interests with the region.

Between the end of the Gulf War of 1991 and 9/11, US policy towards Iraq had been one of containment and deterrence. This was based on two principles: UN-monitored disarmament and economic sanctions. By the late 1990s, these had stalled and demonstrably failed to achieve their objectives. The Russians and Serbs, for example, had been active in rebuilding Iraq's air defences; the French and Russian governments believed that sufficient disarmament had been achieved to allow a relaxation of the economic sanctions; and there was growing international criticism of the disastrous effects of sanctions, as implemented by Saddam Hussein, on the civilian population of Iraq.

In the light of the failure to find either the weapons or the links to al-Qaida that were the official justification for the war, it is as well to remember that the core neo-conservative case for the forcible removal of Saddam Hussein – that is, on the grounds that the United States' long-term position of dual containment of Iraq and Iran and support for the increasingly fragile and brittle polity in Saudi Arabia were unsustainable at acceptable political cost – was advanced explicitly on the basis that his regime probably did *not* have 'weapons of mass destruction'. This is what made it politically and militarily feasible to 'finish the job'. If Saddam Hussein ever regained such weapons in significant quantities and a realistic capability of using them, the opportunity would have passed.[52]

A new start in Iraq, however, might provide the beginnings of a strategy for dealing with what Halliday has called the 'west Asian crisis', a series of crises affecting the region that encompasses the Arab states of the Middle East, Iran, Afghanistan and Pakistan. Given the largely favourable outcome of events in Afghanistan noted above, the United States' overwhelming military power gave it the confidence to regard war as favourable to a messy combination of containment and deterrence. Reconstituting states that are able to operate successfully within, rather than against, the prevailing capitalist order of coordinated sovereignty was the prize. If Saddam could be removed from Iraq, US troops could be withdrawn from Saudi Arabia, thereby putting pressure on, but also giving space for, the monarchy to address its domestic opposition; Syria and Iran could be pressured into withdrawing support from radical Palestinian factions that undermined the ability of the 'moderate' leadership to commit meaningfully to peaceful negotiations with Israel; and a new round of the Palestinian–Israeli 'peace process' could begin. In this context, Iraq presented a golden opportunity.

The alternative, as viewed from Washington – that is, the attempt to control or protect strategically important sources of raw materials and, by extension, the regimes that facilitated access to them – was an expensive and risky policy of crisis management, rather than a strategy that was conducive to long-run US interest in an open international order. It was based on regimes that were liable, at best, to generate more opposition to US interests, and, at worst, to be overthrown by even less palatable forces. What made this particular region of crisis a candidate for this approach was, of course, its strategic and resource significance: the oil and gas resources of the Middle East and Central Asia are a vital economic interest for the dominant capitalist powers (and increasingly for China and India too). And what made the new approach something more than a reckless gamble was the overwhelming military preponderance of the United States after the end of the Cold War.

That, at least, was the theory. What this might mean in practice and how, or even if, it could be implemented was not at all clear. It was an attempt to impose a new dispensation of power, such that the resulting states and economies can be successfully coordinated with the rest of the capitalist world, rather than a prize to be won by the United States at the expense of rival core imperialisms. It was imperialism but it was not, primarily, inter-imperialist rivalry. (It was imperialism more in the manner of Marx and Luxemburg – that is, the variable political moment of incorporation into international markets – than the kind of inter-imperial rivalry discussed by Bukharin and Lenin.) Thus far, its bearers have been the military forces of the United States and the United Kingdom. Even if Afghanistan and Iraq are not a one-off enterprise (some kind of military action against Iran cannot be discounted), a composite response made possible by the events of 9/11 and the corresponding (yet probably temporary) shifts of public opinion in the United States itself, this turn of policy does not represent a wholly new departure, let alone a new doctrine for global order. The United States' definition of self-defence to include, in certain circumstances, pre-emptive attacks, or preventive war, may have shocked the pieties of the UN, but if this was an innovation at all, it was only one in the *declared* politics of military strategy consonant with a strand of US thinking that has existed since considerations of pre-emptive nuclear strikes against the Soviet Union in the early 1950s and the string of interventions in the South throughout the Cold War.

The Role of Oil in the New Middle East Strategy

Ever since the OPEC nationalizations of the 1970s, US policy towards the international oil industry outside America rested on a combination of support for its companies as the producers and distributors of traded oil and cooperative relations with swing producers – especially Saudi Arabia – to stabilize international markets. As Edward Porter has noted, this strategy 'to ensure development of necessary capacity' has 'served well to diversify as well as expand supply sources. This diversification consisted of both a growing non-OPEC market share (during periods of high price) and increasing intra-OPEC competition (during periods of lower price), both of which were promoted by a trade and investment strategy.'[53] (At the same time, successive administrations have developed the Strategic Petroleum Reserve as a hedge against extreme disruptions to the market.) To this end, policy has emphasized encouraging non-OPEC production by securing bilateral investment treaties, pressed for reforms of legal and administrative systems relating to property rights and contracts, and channelled executive agency resources to favoured projects (through institutions such as the Overseas Private Investment Corporation, the Export–Import Bank, the Trade Development Agency and the US Agency for International Development).

The security of supplies from the Gulf has been a long-standing source of concern for US geopolitics in the Middle East. After the fall of the Soviet Union and the collapse of the communist empire, a new set of security concerns emerged around the pipeline politics of Central Asia. In this new area of development, the aim has been to detach these resources, and the routes by which they reach international markets, from Russian monopoly control and to prevent any assertion of Iranian influence that would further increase the role of the Gulf as a conduit for the world's oil. For these reasons the United States, from Clinton's second term onwards, opposed a proposal to route Kazakhstan's resources through the Russian port of Novorossiyk on the Black Sea as well as a project aimed at linking Turkmenistan, Pakistan and Afghanistan. Instead, the US has successfully persuaded Azerbaijan, Georgia, Kazakhstan, Turkey and Uzbekistan to support its preferred option of a Baku–Tbilisi–Ceyhan (BTC) pipeline running from Azerbaijan through Georgia to Turkey. This was so despite the involvement of US oil companies – Chevron and Unocal, respectively – in the other proposals and despite the fact that the companies concerned reckoned these proposals to be better commercial prospects than the BTC option.

Indeed, the BTC option fitted into a geopolitical strategy that the United States had been pursuing in the region since it recognized the Central Asian states in 1991. As Wishnick has noted:

> Expanding U.S. military engagement with Central Asian states has been viewed as a key mechanism to promote their integration into Western politico-military institutions, encourage civilian control over militaries, and institutionalize cooperative relations with the United States military, while dissuading other regional powers – especially Russia, China, and Iran – from seeking to dominate the region.[54]

While the United States has, of course, pressed for a leading role for US companies in these developments, it has not done so at their behest. Rather, it is more accurate to say that, because of their technological leadership across all stages of the industry and their ready access to sources of finance, US companies are key enablers of US policy in regions of the world oil industry that are technologically backward and capital-poor.[55] Clearly, this policy received a boost from the events of 9/11. Perhaps because they feared antagonizing the United States or perhaps because they wanted a freer hand with their own problems – in Chechnya and with Uighur separatists – Russia and China extended considerable cooperation to the US military operation in Afghanistan. Russia acceded to a temporary US military presence in the region, allowed the use of its airspace, shared intelligence and supported the Northern Alliance, while China was active in helping to persuade its ally Pakistan to work with the Americans.[56]

Nevertheless, Central Asian oil (and gas) was never going to be a major alternative to dependence on the Middle East. Against this background, it is important to note that the policy of sanctions – against Libya, Iran and Iraq – ran directly counter to the logic of American policy since the 1970s and, even more importantly, was not working. Unilateral US sanctions against Iran involved non-US companies taking business that might otherwise have gone to US firms. Similarly, in Libya foreign oil companies were returning while American companies were excluded from business. Notwithstanding several Congressional efforts, the United States had little success in turning unilateral sanctions into multilateral ones by coercing third parties. Even the multilateral sanctions against Saddam Hussein were breaking down, such that from 1996 through to the build-up to the second US-led war, Iraq was the dominant source in the growth in supply of Gulf oil. In fact, between 1995 and 2001, the supply growth of Libya, Iran and Iraq was 44.6 per cent, while that of OPEC as a whole was only 14.5 per cent. More generally, there was a tightening of the oil market and a recognition that projected levels of future demand were significantly higher than current rates of addition to supply. Thus, creating a suitable investment climate for the major oil companies in areas of new and existing reserves became an increasing priority. The Cheney report of 2001 recommended that the United States 'make energy security a priority of our trade and foreign policy', a recommendation endorsed by President Bush.[57] In effect, that implied, *inter alia*, bringing the sanctioned states in from the cold, since taken together they accounted for very nearly *one-quarter of total world proven reserves* (24.5 per cent in 2003).

A change of regime in Baghdad might provide an opportunity to integrate Iraq's oil into international markets and to strengthen the US position in the Gulf order. Saudi Arabian oil reserves are currently around 263 billion (thousand million) barrels, but this figure is up from 165 bn in 1982. Iraq's current reserves are 115 bn (larger than those of the United Arab Emirates), despite the fact that its industry has been starved of investment over the period since the 1990/1 war (see Figure 3.7).

The US Department of Energy estimated that Iraq's reserves could rise to 220 bn barrels and that another 100 bn barrels may be undiscovered in the western desert. Iraq's oil, then, might provide both a major addition to world reserves and hence a means of reducing Saudi Arabia's central role as the sole effective swing producer. (Before the war in 2003, it was reported that French, Russian and Chinese companies had deals with Saddam Hussein's regime involving access to some 120 bn barrels of Iraqi reserves – that is, in excess of the currently declared total. Ahmed Chalabi, the Pentagon's original favourite to head a transitional authority in post-invasion, occupied Iraq, had said that the Iraqi National Congress would not regard itself as bound by these contracts.)

There is also an important point about the form of any Iraqi reintegration carried through under US auspices. Robert Vitalis has spoken of the 'closing of the Arabian oil frontier' to American control in the 1970s and 1980s, arguing that we have seen the end of the era of the 1940s and 1950s, 'when Aramco was in effect the kingdom's public works agency and oil ministry and America's private diplomatic and intelligence operation rolled into one'. So, the 'era of empire . . . is over for the US in the Gulf. . . . The overseas Arabian oil resource frontier

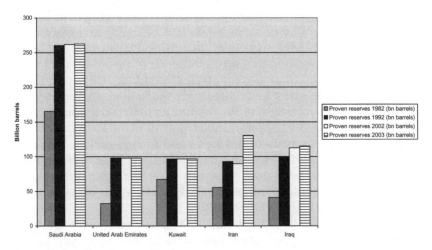

Figure 3.7. Expansion of proven and declared reserves, 1982–2003 (bn barrels)
Source: BP Statistical Review of World Energy, 2004.

is closed now that state has secured overarching control inside this zone.'[58] To the extent that a form of mutual dependence continues to exist between Washington and Riyadh based on an implicit exchange of military and oil security, this may be an exaggeration. But the basic point is sound. And it remains the case that Saudi Arabia and the other Gulf states are reluctant to open up their oil sectors to foreign direct investment, to equity interests in production. Still, the primary concern of the United States was not directly the *ownership* of Saudi oil, since the kingdom has little alternative but to sell it on world markets, but rather the *levels* of production and the political stability of the state and the wider geopolitical stability of the region. The large oil companies – that is, ExxonMobil and Chevron-Texaco of the United States, Royal Dutch-Shell and BP of the UK (and Holland) and Total of France – currently produce only some 35 per cent of their sales volume and have ownership rights to proven reserves of a mere 4.2 per cent of the world total. Nine out of the top ten of the world's oil companies ranked by reserves are national oil companies (see Table 3.2).

Table 3.2. Top twenty oil companies, by reserves, 2003

		State ownership %	Million barrels
Saudi Aramco	Saudi Arabia	100	259,400
NIOC	Iran	100	125,800
INOC	Iraq	100	115,000
KPC	Kuwait	100	99,000
PDV	Venezuela	100	77,800
Adnoc	UAE	100	55,200
Libya NOC	Libya	100	22,700
NNPC	Nigeria	100	21,200
Pemex	Mexico	100	16,000
Lukoil	Russia	8	16,000
Gazprom	Russia	73	13,600
Exxon Mobil	US	–	12,900
Yukos[a]	Russia	–	11,800
PetroChina	China	90	11,000
Qatar Petroleum	Qatar	100	11,000
Sonatrach	Algeria	100	10,500
BP	Britain	–	10,100
Petrobas	Brazil	32	9,800
Chevron Texaco[b]	US	–	8,600
Total	France	–	7,300

[a] Now in effect controlled by the government.
[b] Does not include recently acquired Unocal.
Source: 'Oil in troubled waters', © *The Economist*, 30 April 2005: 12.

In this context, Michael Renner concluded that: 'If a new regime in Baghdad rolls out the red carpet for the oil multinationals to return, it is possible that a broader wave of denationalization could sweep through the oil industry, reversing the historic changes of the early 1970s.'[59] Iran, Saudi Arabia and the other Gulf states would then be under huge pressure to follow Iraq's lead and allow foreign investment on outsiders' terms. If this was Cheney's agenda, the plan hasn't worked. Iraq has set up a Supreme Oil and Gas Council and is re-establishing the Iraqi National Oil Company. Moreover, after the occupation of Iraq, oil companies made it clear that they would not commit themselves to invest, partly because of the overall security situation, but also because they needed an Iraqi government with domestic and international legitimacy, otherwise 'there remained the strong possibility that any oil deals they might make could be deemed illegal by some future Iraqi government, and their assets in Iraq subject to expropriation'.[60] Meanwhile, in 2004 and again in 2005, the Saudi oil minister, Ali Naimi, restated the view that Saudi Arabia does not need foreign investors to develop its industry. On the other hand, whereas Saudi Aramco stated in February 2004 that its 'maximum sustainable capacity' would only be around 12 mb/d and that this could not be achieved until 2016, Daniel Yergin reported in 2006 that 'Saudi Arabia is on track to increase its capacity . . . to over 12 million barrels per day by 2009'.[61]

Even if the major US oil companies end up with a substantial role in Iraq, this will likely involve production sharing agreements (PSAs), in which the state-owned oil company retains legal title to the reserves and the foreign investor is remunerated by 'cost oil' – that is, oil sold at market prices to cover its costs – and by an agreed share of the remaining 'profit oil'. And given that the United States has been unable to impose a pliant regime in Baghdad, there is no reason why Iraq cannot bargain as toughly as any other oil-producing state in future PSA negotiations. The key point is that whoever gets to set the terms of future bargains between the national oil companies of the producer states and the international oil companies of the consuming countries, it remains the case that three-fifths (and rising) of the world's oil is traded on highly integrated markets across national borders and the rest moves on national or regional markets in which prices are aligned with international movements.

None of this is to question that US policy in the Middle East is very much concerned with oil supplies. The geopolitics of the Middle East matter so much to the United States because that is where most of the world's (proven) conventional oil is. But even if the drive to control Iraq's oil, rather than the wider geopolitical logic of shaping a Middle East consistent with American objectives, was a key determinant of the war against Iraq (and, in my view, the available evidence counts against such an interpretation), the form of control that the United States is now seeking to fashion is in any case one that is open to the capital, commodities and trade of many states and firms. To that extent, 'control' may be the wrong word: neither the agencies of the US state nor its oil companies control the world's oil in the sense of being able to direct the use of it. US policy cannot (yet?) be seen as an economically exclusive strategy, as part of a predatory form of hegemony.

A concern to open the region's oil to world markets and US companies has been a constant and growing issue of foreign policy ever since US firms interested in Saudi Arabian oil concessions persuaded President Roosevelt to make the kingdom a recipient of Lend-Lease in February 1943, a connection that was underscored – at least symbolically – by the President's meeting with the Saudi king, Ibn Saud, at Cairo on his return from the Yalta conference two years later. The earlier post-war oil diplomacy was exclusive and designed to contest British interests in the region. But it operated in a context where there was indeed a rival imperialism and the United States was concerned that the Middle East might be tied into the sterling bloc. The point is that the very success of the US in Saudi Arabia (and later in Iran) meant the *defeat* of British imperialism in the Middle East as part of the creation of a unified international capitalist economy under US hegemony. In this context, the producer states that have seized control over production do not constitute rival imperial powers and nor are they likely to ally with, say, China or Russia *against* the United States.

One alternative to these existing arrangements would be a network of more or less direct bilateral deals between state-owned or state-supported companies in the producing and consuming countries, thereby displacing essentially economic competition among firms in international markets by geopolitical competition among states. Elements of China's forays into Africa, the Middle East and Central Asia may have something of this character. The seizure of the commanding heights of the Russian oil and gas industry, carried out under President Putin between 2005 and 2007, might also represent a move in such a direction. Another possibility is a collective agreement over investment, production and pricing negotiated between the key consuming countries and the main producing states – not so much geopolitical competition as cooperation. There have been some influential voices in OPEC in the past and in the US Congress more recently raising this latter possibility, including the idea that the major powers may need to create an organization to deal directly with the key oil-producing states, but this kind of thinking has not had any influence on the Bush administration. Whether it will come to the fore as the G-8 begins to engage with questions of oil prices and energy security remains to be seen. If it does, the G-8 will have to expand to include, at least, China and India for it to produce any lasting results.

For the present, however, most of the world's oil does not flow according to directly political arrangements. Ownership and investment rights matter primarily because, for the United States as for other countries with significant oil companies, they are mechanisms by which the means of technologically more developed, capital-rich firms can be applied to the end of increasing output in the technologically less developed, resource-rich but capital-poor regions where the world's oil is very largely and increasingly located. Policy obviously plays a key, sometimes critical, role in creating the conditions for new investments, and large infrastructure projects always involve state activity – hence the importance of pipeline politics, for example – but for a country such as the United States the quantity of oil imports and even the identity of particular suppliers are not necessarily good indicators of strategic vulnerability.

In short, the United States is using its military power to fashion a geopolitical order that provides the political underpinning for its preferred model of the world economy: that is, a relatively open, liberal international order. US policy has aimed at creating an oil industry in which markets, dominated by large multinational firms, allocate capital and commodities. State power is deployed not just to protect present and future consumption needs of the United States and the profits of US 'oil capitalism', but also to guarantee the general preconditions for a world oil market. So, to the extent that the openness and stability of the international oil market are premised on American geopolitical and military commitments – and, in my view, that extent is very considerable – 'control' is an accurate description: the military power and geopolitical influence of the United States provide the necessary and sufficient conditions for the stable operation of the international oil market. This system has, of course, been designed to secure US interests. But it has equally served the interests of the other leading capitalist powers. And it may yet serve the interests of China, India, Brazil and others too.

Carry on Driving?

One objection to the analysis presented thus far is that the currently benign deployment of US power in relation to world oil – that is, benign according to the interest of the major oil-consuming countries – could rapidly turn threatening as ever-increasing demand runs up against limited and perhaps even falling supply in the years to come. For what it is worth, I think this scenario is extremely unlikely to materialize in the foreseeable future, but even if it were to, inter-imperialist or great power rivalry in a scramble to control the world's oil is far from an inevitable outcome. Even if conventional oil supplies soon become limited, it is likely that there are technologically available alternatives at reasonable cost; that competition and capital accumulation in the energy sector would then centre on production and innovation in these substitutes; and, therefore, that mercantilist, zero-sum rivalry over oil would not be the shape of the future.

If the United States cannot get control over the levels of Middle East oil production in the short to medium term, does it necessarily matter greatly? As yet, the 'virtual' centrality of Middle Eastern oil that would seem to follow from the underlying reserves and reserves to production ratios has not materialized since industry has always been able to find more oil elsewhere: between 1971 and 2005, 1,500 billion barrels have been added to booked reserves, while under 800 billion have been consumed. And Cambridge Energy Research Associates estimate that production capacity might increase by up to 15 mb/d by 2010 and by 20 to 25 per cent over the next decade. Indeed, it is precisely because a good deal of low-cost oil has been excluded from the world market by the oil-producing states that the price has been as high as it has and, therefore, higher-cost oil has still been profitable to produce.[62] Even if the costs of making new higher-cost oil available have risen, as may be indicated by the recent period of high prices, it might be argued that this underlying logic can continue for as long as Middle Eastern producers limit access to their reserves. But surely, there is not enough oil outside the Middle East for this to continue for much longer? Is not that why Cheney was so determined on war with Iraq?

The answer depends on understanding 'reserves' and the possibilities for substitution away from conventional oil. To begin with, published figures of 'proved reserves' – such as in the *BP Statistical Review of World Energy* – are defined as 'those quantities that geological and engineering information indicates with reasonable certainty can be recovered in the future from known reservoirs *under existing economic and operating conditions*.[63] But economic and technological conditions are never constant: 'Technological change improves our ability to find oil and exploit what we find less expensively, thus increasing estimated reserves. Price increases shift more of the resource into the reserve category.'[64] In other words, reserve figures do not represent the physical magnitude of a stock; they are an inventory that results from investment in exploration and development. Therefore, for a profit-maximizing firm, they are 'the forecast cumulative profitable output, not the total amount of oil that is believed to be in the ground'.[65] This means that, as Mark Jaccard explains, reserves represent an 'inventory that producers replenish from the resource base . . . to offset consumption. Their goal is to keep the size of the reserves relatively stable over time since small reserves could lead to unsatisfied demand and loss of market to competitors, while large reserves imply excess inventory with the attendant decline in net returns to investors.'[66] (State-owned oil companies certainly answer to a different set of shareholders than firms operating in competitive capital markets, but they face basically the same set of trade-offs.) It also means that price increases are not a signal of decreasing physical magnitudes: a price increase 'may help us see if a finite resource like oil is becoming scarcer – if the price increases from resource depletion exceed the rate at which discovery and technological change lower production cost – but it does not tell us about the absolute magnitude of the resource'.[67]

It is highly likely, in fact, that the current rise in prices represents the run-down of excess capacity in the system (from some 15 per cent of global demand in 1986 to perhaps 2 or 3 per cent in 2005), rapidly rising demand in emerging markets (especially China), inadequate refinery capacity world-wide (but especially in the United States), geopolitical risks (Venezuela, Iraq, Nigeria, Iran, etc.) and natural disasters (such as hurricanes). The truth is that until very recently the oil industry world-wide has been living off finds made in the 1950s and 1960s, capitalized and developed in the 1970s; and the OPEC producers have been scared to develop potentially excess capacity following the price collapse in the mid-1980s. A sustained increase in prices will begin to change all of this, and there are already signs that this is beginning to happen.

A second difficulty with understanding reserves is that estimates of proven reserves are notoriously unreliable and subject to manipulation for various economic and political reasons: most obviously, the allocation of production quotas in OPEC depends in part on a state's level of reserves. Some argue that the official reserve figures of the major Middle East states are seriously misleading. But despite scare stories – popularized in such books as Matthew Simmons's *Twilight in the Desert: The Coming Saudi Oil Shock and the World Economy* – the most likely reality is that the stated conventional reserves of Saudi Arabia, Iraq, Russia and maybe others *underestimate* the real picture.[68] Moreover, if we focus not on proven reserves of conventional oil but on ultimately recoverable reserves, including unconventional oil – that is, oil sands, heavy oil and oil shale – then, according to the US Geological Survey, not only does the Middle East lose its global centrality (having around one-third to one-half of the world's total oil), but also the peak of world production moves well beyond, say, 2030, when conventional oil output *may* reach a plateau. For example, Canada's oil sands, with currently proven reserves of 175 bn barrels (i.e. some two-thirds the size of total declared Saudi reserves), have production costs of around $15–20 per barrel. At $50 per barrel, deeper and more dispersed formations may be economically exploitable, raising reserves to as much as 314 bn barrels. Venezuela claims 1.2 *trillion* barrels of recoverable reserves of heavy oil in the Orinoco basin, oil that is unconventional only because with existing refineries it costs more to refine than lighter Middle East crudes.

It is against this background, finally, that we need to consider the possibilities of substitution away from conventional oil. The sticking point as far as conventional oil is concerned, as Rutledge rightly emphasizes, is the transport sector, and particularly the ever-expanding demand for individual, personal or family mobility via cars. Like Klare, Rutledge thinks the United States' 'addiction' to oil is dangerous and shows no signs of stopping:

> In 2003, motorization had ultimately driven America to war; but America was just carrying on driving. Addicted to oil, it remained unrepentantly the car country, rejoicing with the Pulitzer Prize-winning essayist Clarence Page that 'Cars are us in this big-car nation, and we are our cars . . . Cleaner Air? Fuel Efficiency? Maybe next century.'[69]

What is even worse, now the Chinese are joining the car culture! Where will all the fuel come from? The answer is that it doesn't have to come from conventional oil at all. Technologically speaking, it is feasible to manufacture fuel from other hydrocarbon sources than crude oil such as unconventional oil, or even natural gas or coal. The critical question is one of cost. Mark Jaccard estimates that substantial additions to conventional oil can be brought on stream at full production cost (which includes exploration, development and extraction) of less than $20 per barrel while unconventional oil from oil sands has a full production cost of about $25. Synthetic substitutes for refined petroleum products produced from natural gas and biomass are also economic when oil prices are in the $25 per barrel range. Finally, new investments in coal plants that produce refined petroleum products are profitable once oil is above $35 per barrel.

The Economist is somewhat less sanguine, reckoning that tar sands and gas- and coal-to-fuel technologies are economical around $40 per barrel and shale oil at $50 per barrel. Either way, these are figures substantially *below* the price of oil in 2005–7. The clear implication, then, is that if the major oil producers continue to be 'locked out of the Middle East' as those states continue to sit on their 'virtual' reserves, 'the new era of manufactured fuel will further delay the onset of peak [conventional oil] production'.[70] And as the major energy companies substitute away from conventional oil either to unconventional oil outside the Middle East or to manufacturing fuel from other sources, so the costs of these alternatives will set a ceiling to the sustainable long-run price of conventional oil – perhaps somewhere between $40 and $50 per barrel. As the resource base described in Table 3.3 shows, this gives plenty of time to develop electricity- and hydrogen-based alternatives for the transport sector.[71]

Table 3.3. Fossil fuel resources, 2000

Fossil fuel	Production in 2000 (exajoules – EJ)	Total reserves (EJ)	Total resource (EJ)	Reserve/ Production in 2000 (years)	Resource/ Production in 2000 (years)
Coal	100	21,000	200,000	210	2,000
Oil	163	11,000	32,000	67	196
Conventional		*6,000*	*12,000*		
Unconventional[a]		*5,000*	*20,000*		
Natural gas	95	15,000	49,500	158	521
Conventional		*5,500*	*16,500*		
Unconventional[b]		*9,500*	*33,000*		
Total	358	47,000	281,500	131	786

[a] Includes: oil sands, heavy oil and oil shale.
[b] Includes: coalbed methane and tight formation gas, but excludes geopressurized gas and gas hydrates.
Source: adapted from Mark Jaccard (2005), *Sustainable Fossil Fuels*, Cambridge: Cambridge University Press, p. 153, Table 5.1. © 2005 by Marc Jaccard. Reprinted with permission from Cambridge University Press.

Currently, there are certain limits to the ability of electricity to compete in some end uses, especially transport. Around two-thirds of the world's electricity is derived from fossil fuel plants with an average primary-to-secondary conversion efficiency of 35 per cent. By contrast, natural gas and oil, which for some uses are easy or easier to handle and transport, can convert with an efficiency of 75–90 per cent. There is also the battery problem: electricity is very difficult to store as compared with carbon fuels. Hydrogen can be produced from water by electricity or from hydrocarbons and water using the chemical energy released in burning. Hydrogen can serve as an energy source directly or it can be combined with oxygen to produce electricity and water in fuel cells at higher energy efficiency than direct combustion. As with electricity, a hydrogen-based economy faces several challenges 'related to hydrogen storage, refuelling infrastructure, safety of compressed hydrogen, and the cost trajectory of fuel cells'.[72] Over the long run, however, there is no reason why a shift from hydrocarbon fuels to some combination of electricity and hydrogen could not be engineered.

Nor need the cost be prohibitive. Tables 3.4 and 3.5 give Jaccard's cost estimates for (carbon-neutral) generation of electricity and for producing hydrogen using different inputs. For the purposes of comparison, current electricity generation costs are around 4 c/kWh and oil at $40 per barrel are equivalent to $7/GJ.

In other words, the input cost of alternatives to oil are some 25–50 per cent higher than oil at 2004 prices and, '[s]ince the cost of the commodity typically represents less than half of its final price, after transmission, distribution and taxes have been added, even a 50 per cent increase in the commodity cost would only result in a 25% increase in the final price seen by consumers' as compared with prices that were easily affordable at the time.[73]

Table 3.4. Comparative costs of (carbon-neutral) electricity generation (cents per kilowatt hour [c/kWh], in $US, 2000)

Pulverized coal – post-combustion sequestration	Coal – integrated gasification combined cycle	Natural gas – combined cycle gas turbine	Nuclear	Hydro	Wind	Biomass	Solar – photovoltaic
6–7.5	5.5–7	5.5–7	6–10	6–8	6–8	6–8	15–20

Assumed input prices are coal $1.5–3/gigajoules (GJ), natural gas $5–7/GJ, biomass $2–5/GJ.
Source: Mark Jaccard (2005), *Sustainable Fossil Fuels*, Cambridge: Cambridge University Press, p. 217, Table 7.1. © 2005 by Marc Jaccard. Reprinted with permission from Cambridge University Press.

Table 3.5. Projected hydrogen costs ($/GJ in $US, 2000)

Coal gasification	Natural gas steam methane reforming	Nuclear electrolysis	Wind/Hydro electrolysis	Biomass gasification
8–10	8–10	18–25	18–25	10–15

Assumed input prices are as above and electricity prices as above.
Source: Mark Jaccard (2005), Sustainable Fossil Fuels, Cambridge: Cambridge University Press, p. 220, Table 7.2. © 2005 by Marc Jaccard. Reprinted with permission from Cambridge University Press.

Conclusions

Whatever the medium-term outcome of the US drive to 'control' world oil, in the long run the depletion of conventional oil need matter little, as long as there are substitutes for the secondary energy it produces. The key question is whether the back-stop alternatives to conventional oil cost a lot more and whether they can be brought on stream in reasonable time. The answers are that the alternatives are not that costly and could be made available in a matter of several decades. The real danger for the world economy is not that it will run out of oil any time soon, let alone the technically viable substitutes, but that price and investment cycles in the international oil and energy industries make a smooth transition beyond conventional oil more difficult than it need be. The kinds of diversification and substitution briefly discussed above will take place only if there is a sustained period of higher-priced oil. If oil returns to the $20–30 per barrel range, then many of the alternatives noted above become uneconomic. As Jaccard shows in detail, currently available technology can produce the energy an expanding world economy needs for the coming century, and technologies exist to effect a gradual transition to a predominantly electricity- and hydrogen-based use of secondary energy, both sourced from non-conventional oil hydrocarbons.[74] And all of this could be done at a cost roughly equivalent to oil at $40–50 per barrel in 2004/5 prices, that is, substantially lower than the price the world economy was bearing in 2006/7. As the old joke has it: the stone age did not end because they ran out of stone; and the oil era could end before we run out of oil. And if the world economy does start to run out of conventional oil, there are plenty of alternative substitutes. The money will be made in developing the alternatives and capital accumulation and innovation will move on to new sources of energy – resource wars between the two 'hungry giants' need not be the shape of the future.[75]

4 AMERICAN POWER, THE FUTURE OF THE DOLLAR AND THE CHALLENGE OF CHINA

Introduction

The notion that the United States is, in Joseph Nye's well-known formulation, 'bound to lead' has not gone unchallenged.[1] There have been repeated warnings – from Paul Kennedy through to Emmanuel Todd – to the effect that imperial overstretch threatens to undermine US power, or that the unilateral assertion of military power is hastening what Charles Kupchan sees as 'the end of the American era' because unilateralism encourages balancing against the United States, as opposed to bandwagoning alongside it, and because military supremacy does not deliver political influence.[2] The two major powers that have been identified as potential challengers of, even rivals to, the United States are the European Union and China. The European Union is, to be sure, essentially a civilian power that has chosen a path of international alignment that is inextricably linked to transatlantic economic integration rather than rivalry. But its currency, the euro, is the only plausible rival to the dollar as a key currency in the foreseeable future. China is a rising power undergoing rapid industrialization and military modernization, it is a key consumer of oil that will become increasingly dependent on imports from the world market, and it currently plays an important role in financing the US current account deficit, thereby supporting the dollar. It is also, I will suggest, at the centre of a tectonic shift in the balance of economic power in the international economy. In the light of these circumstances, this chapter considers two key pitfalls in the pathway to a US-led cooperative international order – the future of the dollar in the context of the launch of the euro and the challenge posed by China in the context of what Angus Maddison has referred to as 'resurgent Asia'.[3]

I begin with the international role of the dollar. It is often said that the United States derives considerable benefits from the fact that its currency serves as the *de facto* key currency of the international economy. This is a complex area, but I try to establish what role the dollar serves and what are the costs and benefits to the United States that follow from this role. I also assess the possibility that the euro might replace the dollar, or at least come to rival it as a second key currency. I conclude that while the United States does derive some clear and important benefits from the international role of the dollar, its functioning as an international currency is no longer solely in the hands of the US Treasury. The future of international monetary affairs is now in the hands of Brussels and Frankfurt, Tokyo and Beijing, as well as in Washington and New York. The United States has already lost the unilateral power to ensure a dominant role for the dollar over the next several decades as much of that role rests on the revealed preference of international markets beyond its control as well as the acts of commission (and omission) of other financial centres. If the agencies of the US government (the Treasury and the Federal Reserve) misuse what considerable leverage they have left, then the United States will have no option but to accept the costs and live with the likely consequences of increased monetary autonomy in Europe and, in the longer term, in Asia.

The long-term future of Asian capitalism inevitably raises the potential challenge of China. This is the second issue addressed in what follows: can and should the United States seek a policy of containment towards China? Some realists (such as John Mearsheimer)[4] advocate just such a turn and some radical critics (such as David Harvey)[5] see this as the most likely axis of inter-imperialist rivalry. Unlike the competitive cooperation that is the clear implication of economic multi-polarity and interdependence in the fields of monetary and trade policy, even in relation to resources such as oil, the United States is now in a uni-polar world, militarily speaking. The central question for the United States is, therefore, how to combine its economic and military ambitions. One way in which the choices have been debated is in terms of whether to treat China as a 'strategic partner' in the project of managing a world-wide capitalist order, that is, to enlist it as a partner in the production of collective power, or to deal with it as a 'strategic competitor' that threatens that order, as a potential adversary in clashes of coercive power. Until now, and for a while yet, the obvious answer is to do both. As Kupchan points out, it is 'simply too early to pronounce China either a strategic partner or an implacable adversary. Furthermore, America can afford to adopt a wait-and-see attitude toward China.'[6] The important point to understand, however, is that at some point this will involve a strategic choice, in a situation in which the decisions of the United States and China, as well as those of Japan, Russia and India, are interdependent.

Treating China only as a strategic competitor would be tantamount to a new policy of containment. I argue that this makes little sense. On the one hand, it is not obvious that the United States possesses the ability to stall Chinese – or, more generally, Asian – industrialization to any significant degree. And, on the other hand, there is no evidence that Western Europe, Japan, Russia and India could be brought into a collective endeavour directed to such an end. If anything, US hostility to China's emerging status would likely drive China and Russia closer together, as its attempted dominance would look increasingly threatening to both. In short, the United States really has no option but to accommodate the rise of China's *economic* power while simultaneously seeking to maintain its qualitative military supremacy. Given that accommodating the rise of China's economic power will further reduce US economic autonomy in the expanding structure of coordinated interdependence, whatever the prospects for military supremacy, I argue that the United States' continuing role in the Northeast Asian strategic environment will require delicate balancing as well as a definition of US interests that can encompass the interests of the main regional powers.

International Money

Before discussing the international role of the dollar, we need to consider the role of (international) money in general. It is conventional to list the use value of money in terms of three related functions, after its role as a medium of exchange, unit of account and store of value. Money's role as a medium of exchange, as a circulating means of payment, presupposes its 'general acceptability to satisfy contractual obligations'; its role as a unit of account, as a valuation of diverse commodities, presupposes its ability to signal information quickly and reliably; and its role as a store of value, as a means of holding wealth, presupposes 'its ability to preserve its purchasing power'.[7] Crucial to all of these functions is generalized trust among independent producers that money can be used to settle debts. The sources of this trust are manifold, but what is equally important is that coordination on a given token as money reduces transaction costs. Moreover, 'the larger the size of the money's transactional network . . . the greater will be the economies of scale to be derived from its use': that is, there are increasing returns to the supply of money services, the transaction cost per transaction is a decreasing function of the volume of transactions and, therefore, money is a public good whose usefulness increases as the network of transactions that it facilitates expands.[8]

Money, then, is a special kind of increasing returns collective good, but one where the users can be made to pay by private providers because money balances (cash and demand deposits) carry no interest. Users of money are prepared to pay a price to the extent that they forgo earning interest on other assets. In turn, users will be prepared to do this to the degree that they are confident that these assets will not lose their value. As Paul De Grauwe explains:

> The supplier [of money] issues a liability, which is used as money, and purchases an asset (extends credit). The source of the profit of the issuer of money (the bank) is the margin between the interest rate earned on the asset and the interest paid on the liability. When the liability of the bank gains increasing acceptance as money, the users are willing to pay more for the service, i.e. they are willing to forgo a higher interest rate when holding this money. As a result, the interest margin between the assets and the liabilities of the bank can increase.[9]

How do suppliers of money services convince holders to trust them? Various ways have been employed historically, typically involving efforts to build reputations, but the most important has been to 'guarantee that the money can be converted at a fixed price into another asset of whose value the supplier has no control'.[10] Still, the credibility of these commitments has never been absolute. Eventually, with the nationalization of money by states and the development of central banking systems to manage the currency, the necessary trust came to depend in substantial part on the credibility of *inherently unenforceable* political commitments.

Since the issue of inherently unenforceable political commitments applies both to national monies and to the case of a single national money functioning as international money, it is worth pondering the reason for this predicament. There is a well-known economic 'theorem',[11] the Coase theorem, which says, roughly speaking, that as long as property rights are clearly defined and transaction costs are minimal, the allocation of property rights has no bearing on the efficiency of outcomes. By analogy, the Coase theorem of politics says that 'political and economic transactions create a strong tendency towards policies and institutions that achieve the best outcomes given the varying needs and requirements of societies, *irrespective of who, or which social group, has political power'*. Even given that there may be genuine uncertainty about the best policies and institutions to adopt, there are strong pressures against policies and institutions that are *known* to be inefficient. Against this panglossian vision, theories of social conflict assert that 'societies choose different policies, some very disastrous for their citizens, because those decisions are made by politicians or politically powerful social groups that are interested in maximizing their own payoffs, *not* aggregate output or social welfare'. While this might appear to be a case of mere theoretical possibility on the one side (the political Coase theorem), and obvious empirical reality, on the other (social conflict), accounts of social conflict need to be able to

> pinpoint what specific 'transaction costs' would systematically prevent the Political Coase Theorem from applying. In other words, why do politicians and powerful social groups not make a deal with the rest of society to choose the policies and institutions that maximize output (or social welfare), and then redistribute part of the gains to themselves?. . . . [The answer is that] Underlying the Coase Theorem is the ability to write enforceable contracts. . . . When it comes to contracts that the state or social groups controlling the state would like to write with others (e.g., the citizens), they will, by definition, be non-enforceable because groups controlling the state cannot *commit* not to using their power to renege on their promises or not to changing the terms of the contract. This implies that the allocation of political power creates an inherent commitment problem, undermining the potential to reach efficient outcomes.[12]

And what applies as between the state and its citizens applies even more so as between separate states. Still, despite the fact that in both cases there is no outside, or third, party with the coercive means to enforce agreements, so that binding contracts have to be self-enforcing, there are mechanisms that can mitigate the problem. Domestically, elected governments, based on repeated interaction between state and citizens, can develop commitments based on reputations, policed by the threat of ejection from office; internationally, states also deal with one another on a repeated basis and are able to change their 'contracts' conditional on the actions of the other party, subject to the existence of available alternatives. Within any given state, confidence in fiat money is nowadays assured by Central Bank monopoly control over the supply of the national currency (including a lender of last resort function), competitive private sector bank creation of deposit accounts, and regulations such as reserve requirements and deposit insurance schemes. 'By effectively imposing one currency on the whole country,' writes De Grauwe, governments ensure 'that the economies of scale in the supply of money [are] fully exploited. . . . The economies of scale in the money supply process have been made external to the banking firms.'[13] While this partial nationalization of banking has eliminated the worst instabilities of the competitive provision of private monies, it has made inflation an ever-present tendency in the system since the state can (in principle) coerce citizens to use an (in principle) non-convertible currency as the domestic medium of exchange and unit of account. Since there are no checks on the issue of the currency by the government, the function of money as store of value is hostage to the temptation of the monetary authorities to pursue inflationary policies. Historically, policies of domestic seigniorage, in which inflationary increases in the supply of money reduce the real value of money already in circulation and where government debt is not fully index-linked to the nominal price level, have been the default mechanisms of fiscally bankrupt states.

The Dollar as International Money

If we apply these considerations to the international level, we find that there is no accepted theory of the optimal number of currencies for a world of many states. The existence of one money, then, might seem to be optimal, maximizing the economies of scale inherent in the provision of money services, but competition between national monies is an important discipline against inflationary policies and unwarranted devaluations – that is, the exploitation of international seigniorage. Still, the optimal number is certainly very much less than the very many national monies currently in existence. What this means, in fact, is that the economies of scale inherent in the provision of money services are anything but 'fully exploited' at the level of the world economy as the national monies of states act to fragment a much wider and deeper potential world market for money. Given this fragmentation, if firms and banks (including Central Banks) in different countries are to trade and invest with one another and to lend and borrow from each other, then one or more national monies must circulate so that private (and public) actors can undertake international transactions.

While there could in principle be markets in foreign exchange for each currency against all others – that is, all national monies could function as international money – there are considerable economies in the use of one currency. If a foreign exchange market had to be made against each exchange rate, then there would be $N(N-1)/2$ such markets in an N-country world. With one currency serving as international money there are just $N-1$ markets. The collective benefits are therefore clear. Moreover, since reasonable price stability is itself a public good for capitalist economies, and since inflationary pressures are an ever-present danger in modern economies, the gains are even greater if a single currency can establish a credible reputation for price stability and thus serve as the nominal anchor for the system as a whole. In that event, as long as faster (slower) productivity growth in one part of the system is matched by faster (slower) wage increases, exchange rates will be stable. Alternatively, with given growth rates of nominal wages in different countries, the ratio of productivity growth in one country to another determines the rate of currency depreciation (or appreciation) required to maintain international competitiveness.

At the same time, however, the countries whose currencies function as international monies are able to capture some of the benefits that flow to providers of money services, as their financial and banking systems, including Central Banks, obtain larger spreads between their assets and liabilities. Such countries can also finance current account deficits in their own currency. Set against these benefits are some costs. On the one hand, others must be convinced in the stability of the international currency as a store of value. On the other hand, if the national currency is to function as international money, this means that there will be systematic foreign intervention in one's foreign exchange markets by others while one largely abstains from intervening oneself. These costs or constraints imply that the national monetary authority has to maintain international trust in the stability of the currency; be able to manage the dilemma that may arise between the provision of liquidity and the preservation of credibility; be ready to act as a lender of last resort in times of crisis; and maintain large, deep and open capital markets. For these reasons, the international circulation of a national currency is directly a high-order political issue. With these considerations in mind, let us now turn to the international role of the dollar.

The Dollar as Key Currency

Using the standard functions of money as a starting point, Benjamin Cohen has distinguished six roles for international money, as shown in Table 4.1.[14] It is not necessary for a single currency to perform all these functions, and in theory, and to some extent in practice, a range of national currencies can serve as international monies. However, historically speaking, only a few currencies have performed the full range of money functions in the international economy, and these are often called *key* currencies – sterling in the nineteenth and early twentieth centuries and the dollar since the end of the Second World War have been key currencies. Let us consider the various roles of the dollar as a key currency.

The role of the dollar as a vehicle currency itself refers to three things: settlements between non-bank firms, which are closely tied to its role as an invoice currency; the retail foreign exchange market in which firms deal with banks; and the inter-bank market. It is only in the latter that the dollar is *the* medium of exchange. The dollar plays

Table 4.1. International money

Functions of money	Role of an international currency	
	Private sector	Public sector
Medium of exchange (or means of payment)	*Vehicle currency* used to settle international trade and to discharge international financial obligations	*Intervention currency* used in foreign exchange markets and currency used for balance of payments financing
Unit of account (*numeraire*)	*Invoice (or quotation) currency* used to denominate international financial instruments and to invoice foreign exchange transactions	*Peg currency* used in expressing exchange rate relationships and as an anchor for other currencies
Store of value, including standard of deferred payment	*Banking (or investment) currency* used to denominate deposits, loans and bonds	*Reserve currency* used as international reserves by monetary authorities

no special role in the retail foreign exchange market and invoicing varies with the trade concerned. In standard manufactured goods, in which trade is organized largely by 'reference prices' published in trade journals, as well as non-standard manufactures traded through complex supply networks, there is a preference for invoicing in the exporter's currency or the currency of the larger country, though most invoicing in East Asia is in dollars. Where there are well-established, organized markets – for example, in raw materials and financial assets – the dollar dominates.

The dollar also dominates the intervention currencies because Central Banks typically intervene in the existing inter-bank foreign exchange market, where the dollar plays a central role. The move to floating exchange rates in the early 1970s as well as the inflation in the United States with which this was associated was for a while a disadvantage to the dollar's role as a store of value. Indeed, these instabilities encouraged some diversification to other currencies by Central Banks as a hedge against exchange rate movements. But because the use of non-dollar currencies for Central Bank intervention amounts to intervention in the foreign exchange markets of other countries (and is thus often resented), Central Banks prefer to intervene using dollars (the United States is long used to such intervention). Meanwhile, in the 1990s the United States re-established a reputation for low levels of domestic inflation. For these reasons, then, the dollar continues to play a disproportionate role as a reserve currency.

The predominant roles of the dollar as a vehicle and an invoicing currency also encourage the holding of dollars as a banking currency, and the dollar remains the main liquid asset, notwithstanding diversification into other monies. As Paul Krugman has pointed out, these roles reinforce one another: 'If the dollar is a good store of value, the costs of making markets against the dollar are lower, thus encouraging the vehicle role. Conversely, the medium-of-exchange role encourages both invoicing in dollars and holding dollars.'[15] So, the dollar does indeed dominate the structure of exchange in the world economy even as the underlying structure of payments that originally backed that dominance is less and less centred on the United States. Krugman elaborates the point as follows:

[There is a need for a] distinction between . . . the *structure of payments* and *the structure of exchange*. By the structure of payments we will mean the matrix of final demands for foreign exchange for the purposes of trade and investment. By the structure of exchange I mean the matrix of actual foreign exchange transactions. . . . If the choice of a currency as a vehicle is a response to the relative size of the markets in it, and if a currency's becoming a vehicle itself swells those markets, then the choice of vehicle may be self-justifying. This in turn suggests that once a country's currency gets established as the international medium of exchange, it will continue in that role, even if the country loses the position in the structure of payments that originally gave it that position.[16]

What, then, are the advantages that the United States derives from its national currency functioning as an international key currency? Three readily spring to mind: first, the economic benefits of international seigniorage; secondly, the ability to earn significantly greater returns on US assets than the United States has to pay for its liabilities; and, thirdly, the autonomy granted to the conduct of macroeconomic policy.

Consider first the issue of international seigniorage. Notwithstanding popular claims about the United States exchanging paper for real resources, seigniorage is, in reality, the least important of these advantages. The estimates vary but the real economic advantage that the United States derives from currency seigniorage abroad is probably 0.1–0.2 per cent of GDP. In absolute terms these are big figures, but relatively speaking they are trivial and, if they were all that dollar hegemony amounted to, the United States would not miss its passing, though it might (with others) regret the manner of that passing. 'The problem is *not* one of the United States having given the world paper in exchange for real goods and services', says Krugman, since 'very little of the "dollar" holding of the world is backed up by high-powered money; essentially it consists of short-term securities and bank deposits, many of the latter outside the United States. In principle then a change in the desired currency composition of liquid assets could be accommodated without any redistribution of wealth.'[17] (However, the shift from one key currency to another or others can be very destabilizing for the liquidity of international finance, so 'it is not a collapsed but a collapsing role of the dollar that we should worry about'.[18]) That said, the United States does benefit somewhat from valuation effects on its assets and liabilities. In the first place, 'US external assets tend to be more heavily in equities', which 'appreciate in nominal terms with inflation and stock market booms', whereas its external liabilities are 'more heavily in debt obligations', which are not affected by such changes. And secondly, 'the external liabilities of the United States are denominated in its own currency, whereas external assets are much more heavily denominated in foreign currency'.[19] This means that the secular devaluation of the dollar since 1973 marginally ameliorates the net international investment position. But once there is an alternative reserve currency – the euro – Jeffrey Frankel rightly asks, 'how many times can the US fool foreign investors?'[20]

Next, while seigniorage in the strict sense is not a key issue, the international role of the dollar is closely bound up with the role of New York as the world's banker. One key aspect of this, hard to quantify but undoubtedly important, is the way in which dollar-denominated financial markets serve to disseminate US business practices – corporate finance and governance in the broadest senses of these terms – as increasingly universal standards across the world, thereby giving a certain (if temporary) competitive edge to the international expansion of US firms. Another aspect, which can be quantified, is the ability of the US financial system to garner a disproportionate share of the world's short-term, liquid deposits and to lend these on a long-term basis in riskier, higher-return assets. The large, open, deep and transparent US capital markets are a natural place for foreigners to put the low-risk (low-yield) part of their portfolios, while US investors can be expected to put their high-risk (high-yield) investments overseas. 'The result', notes William Cline, 'will be a systematic excess of observed rates of return on US assets abroad over foreign assets in the United States (even though the risk-adjusted rates of return might be equal).'[21] Cline calculates that the interest rate differential between what the United States earns on its investments overseas and what it has to pay on its debts has been around 1.2 per cent per year over the last several decades.

It might be argued that this is the result of the fact that the United States has a comparative advantage in supplying financial services and innovation to the rest of the world and that the rest of the world is happy to pay for this, as Ricardo Hausmann and Frederico Sturzenegger have contended.[22] More likely, this interest rate differential is simply an artefact of the dollar's international role and would not survive a serious challenge by a rival such as the euro, as Menzie Chinn and Jeffrey Frankel suggest: 'Possibly this American role of the world's banker . . . would survive the loss of the dollar as the leading international currency,' they note, '[b]ut it seems possible that the loss of one would lead to the loss of the other.'[23]

Assessing and comparing the (changing) autonomy of macroeconomic policy, finally, is notoriously difficult as it presupposes both reliable models of how the economy works and an appropriate choice of relevant counterfactuals. Nevertheless, it is safe to say that for the advanced capitalist economies, the central conundrum of macro-economic policy autonomy derives from the fact that, given capital mobility, countries cannot readily maintain control over both their monetary policy and their exchange rate. Now, these countries are determined to retain control over monetary policy in order to be able to combat inflation and mitigate the worst effects of economic cycles and downturns. They have also long been determined to liberalize trade, investment and financial flows among themselves. The price they have been prepared to pay since the early 1970s is that of floating exchange rates, though they have regularly intervened in their own foreign exchange markets to 'correct' severe misalignments and to manage rapid, destabilizing changes. In fact, in cases of serious exchange rate misalignment in the past, the three major trading and investment blocs (the United States, Japan and Western Europe) attempted to coordinate the management of their exchange rates. For example, the Plaza Agreement (1985) and the Louvre Accord (1987) sought to devalue the US dollar against both the Deutschmark and the Japanese yen. (In practice, such arrangements worked by signalling policy changes, especially in relation to interest rate move-ments.) International discussion of the need for coordinated exchange rate realignments – this time between the dollar, the renminbi (and other Asian currencies) and the euro – surfaced again in 2006 and 2007.

From Fixed to Floating Exchange Rates

To sharpen our focus on the economic benefits and macroeconomic autonomy that the United States enjoys by virtue of the international role of the dollar, it is instructive to compare the world of floating exchange rates with that of the dollar standard that operated until the early 1970s. Between 1958 and 1971, the dollar standard (theoreti-cally linked to gold) system operated quite successfully and currency convertibility and stability provided an environment in which inter-national trade and investment could expand rapidly. However, the international monetary system of the long boom contained two serious design flaws. The first problem was that the system was unbal-anced. Effectively, it was a dollar standard. The founding idea was to rule out devaluation as a response to balance of payments deficits (except in the most persistent cases) and to finance temporary deficits from the IMF. Deficit countries were still expected to deflate their economies to restore equilibrium to their balance of payments. This created a system-wide problem: if countries deflated their economies to eradicate their payments deficits, the surplus countries would also see their surpluses fall. If surplus countries sought to recoup their position either by devaluation or by deflation, in turn, then the problem would reappear in the weaker economies. The system as a whole, therefore, had an inherent deflationary bias.

In practice, this bias was overcome because the largest economy in the world, the United States, was willing to run a persistent balance of payments deficit. The United States could do this because the reserve currency never had to intervene in its foreign exchange market and did not bear the burden of financing its balance of payments. 'The reserve country has the power to affect its own economy, as well as foreign economies, by using monetary policy,' Paul Krugman and Maurice Obstfeld explain, but: 'Other central banks are forced to relinquish monetary policy as a stabilization tool, and instead must passively "import" the monetary policy of the reserve centre because of their commitment to peg their currencies to the reserve currency.'[24]

Even so, as early as 1960 Robert Triffin pointed out that there were limits to how far this policy could consistently be maintained. By 1961, the value of overseas dollar holdings exceeded that of the US gold and foreign exchange reserves, thereby undermining long-term confidence in the role of the dollar as a store of value. For a while this did not matter too much: the United States benefited from having its currency circulate as international money; the inflationary impact of dollar surpluses on domestic inflation in Western Europe and Japan was limited; the new surplus countries (above all, West Germany and Japan) were reluctant to see their currencies serve as international monies alongside the US dollar; and the United States guaranteed the military security of Western Europe and Japan and could therefore expect a certain degree of cooperation in the international management of the dollar standard.

After a time, however, the United States found the system too much of a constraint on its national autonomy because the only way it could devalue its currency was if all the others agreed to peg theirs at the new (revalued) rates. After failing to gain widespread agreement on such a revaluation, in 1971, President Nixon unilaterally ended the system by abrogating the commitment to exchange dollars for gold and imposing a 10 per cent import tax until trading partners agreed to revalue their currencies against the dollar. Despite two years of negotiations over the nature of the international monetary order (1971–3), the fixed exchange rate regime was finished.

The second problem with the original design was that it made no provision for the re-emergence of private international financial markets:

> Until the beginning of the 1960s, domestic financial markets tended to be protected from external competition by capital and exchange restrictions introduced to limit the destabilizing impact of short-term cross-border flows of private capital . . . international capital transactions were still dominated by official operations effected outside of financial markets. . . . Private-sector finance was still dominated by traditional domestic banking activity and was subject to government controls.[25]

From the late 1960s onwards, however, private markets rapidly developed in payments services, capital flows and bank-based financial intermediation. The IMF had no responsibility for, or control over, these developments. The result was a significant erosion of the ability of governments to manage the exchange rate regime through buying and selling their foreign exchange reserves, since foreign exchange transactions in private markets soon overwhelmed public interventions. The state-led international monetary system overseen by the IMF was replaced by a market-led system. Indeed, it was repeated speculative attacks against the 1971–3 Smithsonian realignments – hailed by President Nixon at the time as 'the most significant monetary agreement in the history of the world' – that finally broke the back of the fixed exchange rate regime.

In principle, a shift to floating exchange rates removed the asymmetries of the previous system; the United States could now devalue unilaterally and other countries had no need to passively import US monetary policy. (However, the United States remained relatively insulated from financial market pressures on budget and current account deficits for lack of rival banking and reserve currencies.) Under both a fixed and a flexible exchange rate regime, the change in net foreign assets of an economy – that is, the net foreign assets of the private sector and the monetary authorities – is equal to the current account. So: the change in the net foreign assets (official) = current account minus the change in net foreign assets (private). In the fixed exchange rate regime, the change in the net foreign assets (official) was the residual variable which adjusted to accommodate whatever values appeared in the current account and the change in the net foreign assets of the private sector. This meant that in practice the threat of a run on official reserves caused governments to adopt macroeconomic policies that limited their current account deficits. By contrast, in a pure flexible exchange rate system the monetary authorities do not intervene in the foreign exchange market and so the change in the net foreign asset position of the official sector is zero. In this case, it is movements in the exchange rate that equilibrate the current account and the change in the net foreign asset position of the private sector.

There is, then, a trade-off involved in the choice between fixed and flexible exchange rate systems: in fixed systems, misalignments are small but tend to increase over time unless checked by *changes to policy*, and the country whose national money anchors the system, that is, serves as international money, has most of the freedom of manoeuvre in terms of monetary and fiscal policy as others have to subordinate domestic policies to the requirement of external balance; in flexible systems, misalignments are larger but tend to reverse themselves, and floating, together with capital mobility, has increased the range of policy choices available to many countries as the conditions for external balance are extended into an indeterminate future. Of course, that future is not completely indeterminate: there is an intertemporal budget constraint, a solvency constraint. As De Grauwe notes, the 'foreign debt which a country can issue today cannot be larger than the present value of all expected future current account surpluses and deficits'.[26] The point, however, is that the 'expected' is not known today.

So, with the move to floating exchange rates, other governments gained autonomy in the area of monetary policy such that long-run movements in their currencies tended to reflect their relative inflation performance (with relatively high-inflation economies seeing their currencies depreciate, and vice versa). However, monetary independence does not mean that economic shocks – including monetary shocks – are not transmitted from one country to another: 'there are still *real* links between countries, the mechanisms of transmission being (1) the capital market and (2) the terms of trade'. Because of these real linkages, there is potential scope for the Nash equilibrium, which arises when each country takes an independent decision, to be improved upon by concerted coordination. This is practically difficult but '[a]t certain times, such as a severe world recession, the message of the locomotive theory becomes relevant'.[27] That said, exchange rate coordination has been the exception and not the rule; perhaps with good reason. There are certainly costs associated when real exchange rates are misaligned: arbitrary changes in purchasing power; adjustment costs for firms and perhaps unemployment; misleading signals for investment; inflation; and protectionist pressures. And macroeconomic simulations suggest that there are potential gains from coordinated policies to manage significant current account imbalances. But the correlation of supply shocks across the regions of the world economy is generally low; even quite sustained misalignments do not appear to be as damaging for cross-border trade and investment as many originally feared because of the limited pass-through of international to domestic prices; and empirically calibrated models suggest that fixing exchange rates would *increase* the variance of other macroeconomic variables.[28] Most importantly, stabilizing exchange rates in a quasi-fixed regime would involve a significant compromise of domestic autonomy in monetary (and fiscal) policy.

In fact, the present international monetary system is, in reality, a non-system, as it does not have any 'uniform, world-wide rules of any real significance'. It can equilibrate in one of two ways. On the one hand:

> Countries other than the United States can manage their fiscal, monetary, and exchange rate policies so as to get the current account balances they want. The United States does not intervene in the foreign exchange market, and follows fiscal and monetary policies that are focused purely on domestic considerations. The US current account imbalance thus comes out as a residual.

On the other hand, countries other than the United States might not adopt current account targets and 'a price (interest rate) adjustment mechanism in the capital market equilibrates the system'.[29] In this case, given that US fiscal and monetary policies are very largely determined by domestic considerations, the United States still treats its current account as a residual variable.

The New Dollar Standard?

Until the mid-1990s, it seemed that domestic autonomy without current account targets, and hence fluctuating exchange rates mediated by interest rate differentials, defined the shape of the future. Since then, however, some analysts suggest that a new quasi-fixed dollar standard has emerged. To the extent that the dollar continues to have a privileged international role, the United States is much more able to fund its deficits in its own currency than are other countries. Indeed, many debtor countries face a situation where they cannot borrow abroad using the national currency (a condition dubbed 'original sin' by Barry Eichengreen, Ricardo Hausmann and Ugo Panizza[30]) and many creditor countries find that they cannot lend in their own currencies (a condition that Ronald McKinnon has termed 'conflicted virtue'[31]). In effect, outside of euro-land, the world appears to be back on a *de facto* dollar standard (Japan's place in the system is ambiguous). And with the re-emergence of large US current account deficits (around 6 to 7 per cent of GDP in 2005–7), this has once again prompted widespread debate about the functionality of this regime for the international economy as a whole as well as about the sustainability of the US position.

In considering this question, it is useful to recall some basic national income accounting identities as these apply to the world economy. On the product demand side, the national accounting identity for an open economy is:

$Y = C + I + G + X - M$ (where Y is national income, C Equation (1)
is consumption, I is investment, G is government
spending, X is exports and M is imports)

On the factor payments side, the identity is:

$Y = C + S_p + R$ (where S_p is private saving and   Equation (2)
R is government revenues or taxes)

Subtracting (2) from (1) and rearranging gives:

$$I - S_p - (R - G) = M - X \qquad \text{Equation (3)}$$

$R - G$ is government saving; and the fiscal deficit, D^f, is equal to government spending minus revenue ($G - R$), so equation (3) can be written as:

$$I - S_p + D^f = M - X \qquad \text{Equation (4)}$$

For any given economy, the sum of domestic absorption and exports is equal to GDP plus imports and this implies that any excess of investment over national savings is equal to the trade deficit (that is, the excess of imports over exports). Equation (4) simply makes clear that, for given levels of investment and private savings, an increase in the fiscal deficit must be associated with an increase in the trade deficit. The two deficits are not twins; they may move in different directions (because of other changes in investment and private saving), but they are certainly linked. Since, for the world economy as a whole, the trade balance is zero, this implies, *ex post*, that one country's surplus of investment over savings is another country's deficit. This is merely to clarify that any deficit, say, the US deficit, cannot be considered in isolation from another surplus, say, China's surplus. With this point in mind, I now examine the idea of the new dollar standard, or what some commentators refer to as a second Bretton Woods.

One side of the new dollar standard is the phenomenon of 'original sin'. In many developing countries, financial systems often lack fixed-interest bond markets and forward markets in foreign exchange against the dollar (and other currencies). If domestic commercial banks are unable (or not allowed) to take open positions in foreign exchange and if there are no liquid markets in domestic bonds, then *'foreign banks are unwilling to take open positions in the domestic currency*. Thus, with a tightly regulated domestic banking system and/or capital controls, a satisfactory free float is impossible.'[32] These countries cannot use the national currency to borrow abroad or even domestically for the long term. Debt-induced financial instability is, then, unavoidable as all domestic investment will either have a currency mismatch (projects that earn the national currency are financed by dollars) or a maturity mismatch (short-term loans for long-term projects). Note that the problem is not the *indebtedness* as such: given the stage of development these countries are at, it is appropriate that they take on debt to finance the necessary investment and cover the external balance. The problem is that the countries concerned cannot use their own currencies to do this. To compensate for this, governments seek to peg their currencies to the dollar, as most in Asia have done since the crises of 1997/8. Given the central role of the dollar internationally, exporters everywhere outside of euro-land price to the world market – and not just the US market – in dollars, and so any Central Bank that seeks to stabilize the purchasing power of its national currency has a strong incentive to peg against the dollar, provided inflation in the United States is low and reasonably stable.

The other side of the equation is the syndrome of conflicted virtue. In this case, creditor countries with similarly underdeveloped financial systems cannot *lend* internationally using the national currency; they can only lend using dollars (again euro-land is the exception: a net creditor to the world economy that can lend using its own currency). As countries generating surpluses, these countries face a problem of potential appreciation against the dollar and are compelled to make continuous interventions to prevent this, thereby amassing expanding foreign exchange reserves which are then switched into US Treasury bonds or similar low-risk, low-yielding instruments. One consequence of this is that 'the United States has a virtually unlimited line of dollar credit with the rest of the world'. Moreover, 'as long as the Federal Reserve Bank keeps ongoing price inflation very low, the dollar cannot be attacked in the usual sense' because dollar depreciation has no impact on the creditworthiness of US financial institutions (both their assets and their liabilities are denominated in dollars), nor does it affect the ability of the US Treasury to service its debts. The foreign exchange risk inherent in any market-based, decentralized system is 'shifted to creditor countries that, Europe aside, cannot lend to the US in their own currencies'.[33]

While this system is certainly open to abuse – the dollar dependence of debtors has given the US Treasury (often acting through the IMF) leverage over crisis-prone financial systems to effect premature liberalization to the benefit of US firms – it is also of benefit to both the United States and the major creditor countries. Clearly, the United States benefits from having 'a safe reserve asset, with assured international purchasing power', but it 'is also a great convenience to other countries'.[34] To see why this is the case, we need to consider the development strategies of the surplus-generating creditor countries. The central point to grasp, as Ronald McKinnon says, is that 'China is merely the leading edge of a more general, albeit somewhat hidden, East Asian export expansion into the United States – which in turn reflects very high savings rates by Asians collectively and abnormally low saving by Americans.'[35] With development strategies that are generating healthy export surpluses and, especially in China's case, with surplus labour ready to move into export industries, alongside very high savings rates because of underdeveloped financial systems, limited social protection and repressed domestic consumption, China and the five tigers – South Korea, Taiwan, Singapore, Malaysia and Thailand – have been content to pursue exchange rate protection, even if this means building up large, low-yielding dollar reserves.

US indifference towards the deficits, especially the current account deficit, is not just Republican politics, since there is no good economic reason to do anything until and unless the deficits produce higher inflation and/or interest rates in the United States. The steady devaluation of the dollar since President George W. Bush was elected has helped US exporters. And China is likely to move only very gradually to a full float of its currency as it has no interest in adding financial instability to its current problems. In any case, its current account surplus is not very large – surpluses with the EU and the United States are offset by deficits with Japan, Korea and Taiwan – and the accumulation of dollar reserves is largely driven by inward capital flows rather than (net) trade surpluses. Japan has no interest in repeating the experience of 1995, when yen revaluation choked a potential recovery. For Japan (and other Asian countries), buying dollars prevents the dollar–yen exchange rate from rising too abruptly. Equally, reinvesting those dollars in US Treasury bonds helps to keep US interest rates down and consumption up, thereby providing a market for Asian exports. Meanwhile, China worries about currency competition from other Asian economies, and these, in turn, from Japan through to India, have managed their exchange rates to match the renminbi (and the dollar) 'for fear of being "hollowed out" by China's burgeoning manufacturing prowess'.[36]

To what extent have these imbalances of savings and investment, surpluses and deficits, helped or hindered world growth? Overall, Cline estimates that 'the widening of the US current account deficit after 1992 contributed to an increase in demand for the rest of the world that reached the equivalent of about 2 per cent of rest-of-world GDP annually by 2004'. Since the US call on world capital markets has not contributed to an increase in interest rates world-wide, the net effect on foreign demand and growth of the US deficits has almost certainly been positive. Moreover, while a significant devaluation of the dollar as well as a substantial correction of the US fiscal deficit will be required to restore the United States to a sustainable path over the medium to longer term, thus far the financing of the deficits has not been especially onerous. Not only is the real economic burden much less than the accounting figures show, because of the valuation effects and asset and liabilities asymmetries noted above, but also the short-term prognosis, according to Cline, is that 'the accumulated burden from the past remains minor and it is [the] unfavourable prospects for the future that warrant the true concern'.[37] John Kitchen concurs on the basis of an estimate that the real cost of servicing US net international debt at the level typical of recent years is about 0.25 per cent of GDP.[38]

Might this system persist until all the surplus labour in Asia has been redeployed into the industrial sector, and until financial systems are well enough developed and domestic inflationary pressures sufficiently dampened to allow stable floating of currencies? Notwithstanding the benign scenario sketched thus far, there are several reasons to question the sustainability of these arrangements over the long run. In the first place, unlike the dollar standard of the Bretton Woods system, in which the United States borrowed short-term from

Europe to finance long-term investment in rebuilding the continent's war-torn capital stock, it now borrows to consume (investments in China aside). Wynne Godley and Alex Izurieta have argued that easy access to cheap credit artificially depresses an already dangerously low US savings ratio,[39] while McKinnon suggests that the current account deficit also depresses domestic manufacturing output 'by the amount of the trade deficit in manufactures'.[40] These considerations may help to explain why investment in the US economy has been directed mainly to real estate and the non-traded sector and the net flow of direct investment has been outwards, with inflows of shortening maturity from official, rather than private, sources. Secondly, bilateral US deficits with particular trading partners have become a target for Congressional efforts at protection. 'The leading indicator of American protection', says Fred Bergsten, is 'overvaluation of the dollar and its attendant external deficits.'[41]

On the creditor side of the equation there are two key problems: first, can the countries concerned sterilize their currency interventions and, thereby, prevent excessive domestic monetary growth and inflation? And, secondly, can they afford the reserve accumulation involved? The conventional wisdom – based on the Mundell–Flemming model – says that a country, with an open capital account, cannot pursue both an exchange rate target and monetary stability. However, there are experiences of successful sterilization over reasonably long periods, especially in 'repressed' financial systems. In any case, Wynne Godley and Marc Lavoie have argued that the Mundell–Flemming model is not well founded and that unlimited reserve acquisition need not feed through into an increase in the domestic money supply, the latter being entirely demand-determined.[42]

Be that as it may, secondly, there is a significant opportunity cost in holding low-yielding reserves in excess of those needed as an insurance against financial crises. In fact, if the countries concerned experience real appreciation of their currencies, then the returns may fall to zero or even turn negative. Dani Rodrik and, notably, Lawrence Summers (former Treasury Secretary in the Clinton administration) have argued that the ten leading holders of excess reserves are incurring an opportunity cost of between 1 and 2 per cent of their combined GDP. That is to say, if these reserves were invested at yields similar to those gained by US institutions over the last several decades, the growth rate of GDP would increase by 1 to 2 per cent. Even if this is a twofold overestimate of what more realistically might be realized, these still represent considerable losses. This may come to be too high a price to pay to maintain export competitiveness and to keep US consumption growing rapidly.[43] And in any case, as these economies develop further, they may need to focus more on domestic sources of growth in demand. Thus, Morris Goldstein notes that 'as domestic demand, economic growth, inflationary pressures, and domestic interest rates rise in the Asian creditor countries, the benefits of using large-scale exchange market intervention to maintain undervalued exchange rates fall while the costs [including the difference between the high returns foreigners get on inward investment and the low returns Asian Central Banks get on US Treasury securities] rise'.[44]

Overall, the figures do not really add up to a new Bretton Woods. As Cline points out, Japan cannot be considered a structural part of the surplus-generating periphery as it is not a labour-abundant economy. On the contrary, it is a labour-scarce economy because of an ageing population. In fact, the surpluses of the Asian periphery in total are only one half of the US current account deficit. More recently, the rise in the price of oil has had a major impact – net oil imports account for 35 per cent of the US trade balance. In 2006, the oil exporters' current account surpluses were $450 billion, compared with only $150 billion in 2000 (it is worth noting, *en passant*, that the Bank for International Settlements says that it cannot trace 70 per cent of the accumulated investable funds of the oil producers since 1999). The Gulf Cooperation Council economies – Saudi Arabia, Bahrain, Kuwait, Oman, Qatar and the United Arab Emirates – had a current account surplus of $227 billion in 2006. Developing Asia, including China, had surpluses of around $150–160 billion in 2005 and 2006.

Finally, there is the changed nature of the political and geopolitical context. The Bretton Woods framework was established in conditions of unchallenged US hegemony over the capitalist world in a context of pressing needs for post-war reconstruction and geopolitical unity in the face of the Soviet challenge. The world economy was more or less effectively uni-polar. Not only is the contemporary world economy multi-polar, but also there is no single axis of geopolitical competition that the United States can mobilize around to lead the rest of the capitalist world. As a result, on a broad range of issues – from negotiating trade and investment liberalization through to managing the international role of its currency – the United States neither acts alone, nor dictates the terms of the relevant international regimes.

The Fall of the Dollar?

Whereas the post-war dollar standard was, as John Grahl has argued, 'to a large extent an industrial phenomenon: the "dollar shortage" represented a universal hunger for US exports', today it is essentially financial and 'rests on the scale and liquidity of North American financial markets. . . . The capitalization of the two largest stock markets, NYSE and NASDAQ . . . [is] half the world total.'[45]

The dollar's primacy also rests on the size and liquidity of the bond markets of the US government: the reason US Treasury bills are reckoned to be the benchmark, risk-free assets is because the government owns the Federal Reserve Bank. The permissive cause, as we have seen, is the under-development of such markets – private and public – elsewhere, especially in emerging Asia, and the absence – until the launch of the euro – of an alternative currency.

In one sense, then, the international role of the dollar is simply what Benjamin Cohen describes as 'the revealed preference of the marketplace', a preference that Washington does well to accommodate.[46] But it is important to see what this is a preference for. Drawing on Hirschman's famous notion of voice, loyalty and exit, Grahl distinguishes between voice- and exit-based ways of mobilizing finance. In voice-based systems, the providers of finance maintain close links with the borrower, thereby overcoming the separation of principals and agents and of creditors and debtors. As such, voice-based systems are particularistic and opaque to outsiders. Moreover, to the extent that the separation of principals and agents, creditors and debtors, is overcome, the capital markets – that is, key institutions that drive competitive innovation – cease to function.

By contrast, the exit-based approach, Grahl explains,

> controls economic relations by the threat of departure – which depends on the existence of alternatives provided by the market. . . . it becomes easier as the corresponding asset-markets become deeper and more liquid. . . . [The form of a general shift towards exit-based systems has been] the deregulation and internationalization of dollar finance. . . . However crude the market-based mechanisms of dollar-based global finance, they have the decisive advantage of being reproducible. . . . The financial regimes to which they give rise can expand without limit to obtain a truly staggering scale. This, in turn, is based on the imposition of universal standards. . . . market-determined finance does have decisive advantages over the voice-based mechanisms of relatively closed industrial groups. Firstly, it is able to diversify risks over a vast number of companies and investment projects. Secondly, market-based disciplines can reduce agency and information costs.[47]

This means, of course, that the shift from a dollar based on industrial strength to one based on finance is bound up with a radically transformed role for finance in the world economy as a whole. This does not represent so much a shift from industrial to (merely) financial strength but rather a changed role of finance in spurring competition and innovation across all sectors. However, in considering the *future* of the present-day dollar-based system, it is also important to bear in mind that another key difference between the current system and the Bretton Woods arrangements is that there is now an alternative reserve currency: namely, the euro. The euro does not suffer from either original sin or conflicted virtue: there are very large private and official bond markets in euros and well-developed forward markets in foreign exchange. 'The world already enjoys a bipolar financial market,' says Bergsten, 'if not yet a bipolar international monetary system'.[48] Indeed, Europe's share of gross global capital flows increased from 55 to 72 per cent between 1995 and 2005, and in 2007 the capitalization of Europe's financial markets exceeded those in the United States for the first time in over a century.[49]

However, it remains the case that the official bond markets in euros are fragmented into different national markets. The international role of the euro is also hampered by the split of responsibilities between the European Central Bank and the national treasuries of the member states: the EU has no powers to tax and is legally prevented from incurring debts. Moreover, within euro-land the presence of uncoordinated national wage-setting arrangements exercises a deflationary pressure. If one country sets national wage increases below others (as Germany has been doing since 2000), it will reap a competitive advantage; the others will retaliate; and a deflationary pressure reducing consumption, investment and productivity will follow. (The solution is either to coordinate national wage increases or to liberalize labour markets so that there are no nationally set wage levels – hence the current conflict over the 'social model' in today's eurozone.) And, finally, the private capital markets also retain pronounced national characteristics despite rapid and continuing cross-border integration and EU-level harmonization.

Nevertheless, the project of monetary integration in Europe (which gained serious momentum after the break-up of the old dollar standard) has always been, in large part, about reducing dependence on the dollar. 'The current, very determined, efforts of the European Union to integrate member state financial systems, and to build huge, liquid markets in euro-denominated securities,' Grahl points out, 'should be seen in the context of this growing challenge' of the hegemony of international dollar finance.[50] If these efforts are successful, if the design faults of the euro can be rectified, and if the UK (and hence the City of London) were to join the euro, then it would pose a formidable challenge to the dollar. In that eventuality, as Chinn and Frankel have shown, under reasonable assumptions about the downward trajectory of the dollar, the euro could easily become the dominant international currency by 2020. 'Even if the Federal Reserve never succumbs to the temptation to inflate away the U.S. debt,' they note, 'the continuing U.S. current account deficit is always a possible source of downward pressure on the dollar.'[51] In this context, any attempt to misuse the dollar's continuing privileges by Washington would only hasten efforts to bolster the euro.

The future seems finely balanced. On the one hand, Maurice Obstfeld and Kenneth Rogoff, and Paul Krugman, have warned that a sharp adjustment of US net imports and significant exchange rate devaluation will be needed at some point to address the current account deficit, and that a hard landing is a real possibility.[52] On the other hand, those deficits are the counter to others' surpluses, and world financial markets are big, even in relation to US debts, and increasingly integrated. Gross global capital flows increased from roughly 5 to 15 per cent of world GDP between 1995 and 2005. In turn, this means that if foreign investors continue to diversify away from 'home bias' in their portfolios, then US current account deficits might be accommodated for the foreseeable future.[53]

In the early 1970s, Richard Nixon's Treasury Secretary, John Connally, said in response to European complaints about US policy towards the dollar: 'The dollar is our currency, but your problem.' This reflected the leverage that the United States then had over the key creditor countries, which were heavily reliant on US political and military leadership in their Cold War competition with the Soviet Union. At that time, the European and Japanese Central Banks were organized in a framework in which each agreed to hold dollars on condition that the others did likewise. Today, US leverage over where creditors put their money is much diminished. When he was US Treasury Secretary under President Clinton, Lawrence Summers was fond of saying that the fate of the dollar was still largely in US hands. That was and is true, but it means both that the United States can hold onto the international role of the dollar and that it can lose it. If there is a new Bretton Woods system in place, then we might be nearer to 1971 than 1958.

Resurgent Asia

Giovanni Arrighi has suggested that, faced with the challenge of a rising China and all that implies for increased competition over access

to world oil and the dependence of the United States on Asian surpluses to finance its deficits, US hegemony is increasingly being
reconfigured as a form of zero-sum dominance.[54] Similarly, David
Harvey sees incipient competition between China and the United
States as an ominous darkening of the international scene.[55] These
concerns are by no means confined to radical circles. China was
already a target on the radar of the neo-conservatives during the
Clinton interregnum. And the realist John Mearsheimer, reflecting
on the fact that China has the long-run potential not only to become
the regional hegemon in Northeast Asia but also to dwarf US economic and military power, argues that the policy of engagement
'is misguided'. Moreover, he says:

> It is clear that the most dangerous scenario the United States might
> face in the early twenty-first century is one in which China becomes a
> potential hegemon in Northeast Asia. . . . [If the rapid pace of China's
> economic growth is sustained] for sound strategic reasons, it would
> surely pursue regional hegemony. . . . What makes a future Chinese
> threat so worrisome is that it might be far more powerful and danger-
> ous than any of the potential hegemons that the United States con-
> fronted in the twentieth century. . . . [In this scenario] it is hard to see
> how the United States could prevent China from becoming a peer
> competitor. Moreover, China would likely be a more formidable super-
> power than the United States in the ensuing global competition
> between them. . . . [Fortunately for the United States] China is still far
> away from the point where it has enough latent power to make a run
> at regional hegemony. So it is not too late for the United States to
> reverse course and do what it can to slow the rise of China. In fact,
> the structural imperatives of the international system, which are pow-
> erful, will probably force the United States to abandon its policy of
> constructive engagement in the near future.[56]

This begs the question of whether the United States can slow China's
economic growth, and what price the international economy might
pay if it were to do so.

There is little doubt that rapid industrialization in 'resurgent Asia'
is creating a shift in the international economy with major implications for the relations between the older OECD economies and the
dynamic emerging markets and potential power-houses of China and
India. The investment bank Goldman Sachs predicts that by 2040 the
BRICs – that is, the acronym coined by the bank to describe the
emerging markets of Brazil, Russia, India and China – plus Mexico
will be larger in dollar terms than the G-7 economies, and China will
be the world's largest economy measured at market exchange rates.

Even the cautious and detailed work of L. Alan Winters and Shahid Yusuf sponsored by the World Bank estimates that China and India's share of the growth of world exports and services (18.1 per cent) will exceed that of the United States and Japan (16.2 per cent) over the period 2005–20.[57]

To be sure, after America and Germany overtook Britain in the late nineteenth century, catch-up has always been *relative*, as the leading regions of the world economy do not stay still while others converge on their levels of productivity and per capita living standards. Indeed, the pursuit of innovation has become part of the routine, competitive working of firms in the more advanced capitalist economies. Competition to innovate, rather than competition over price, is the defining feature of advanced capitalist development, characterized by large firms operating in oligopolistic market structures with well-developed financial systems and adequate means of protecting intellectual property rights.[58] In fact, throughout the period of consolidated industrial capitalist development in the advanced centres, from the 1870s through to the slowdown of the 1970s and beyond, the long-run rate of growth of labour productivity in the most advanced regions of the world economy averaged around 2 per cent per annum (typically in the range 1.5 to 2.5 per cent).

If we focus on the generation of productivity increases through innovation, then the United States remains at the centre of any story about the growth prospects for industrial capitalism: after the water-powered mechanization of industry and the steam-powered mechanization of industry and transport in Britain during the late eighteenth and early nineteenth centuries, virtually all the significant technological innovations of industrial capitalism, through to the current digital, IT, networked phase, have been very largely 'made in America'. Whether it is IT and the knowledge economy, or the financialization of economic activity based on the deregulation and internationalization of dollar-based finance, the United States is still firmly established at the leading edge of world-wide economic development. Of total R&D expenditure in the OECD bloc in the late 1990s, 85 per cent was in seven countries and the US share was 43 per cent of the total – as much as the rest of the G-7 countries combined. Of the top 100 firms in the new economy, as ranked by *Business Week*, seventy-five were in the United States and only six in Europe. In this respect, it remains the case that the United States has an 'innovation complex – those thousands of entrepreneurs, venture capitalists and engineers – unmatched anywhere in the world'; its universities are 'magnets for the world's talent and sources of much of its intellectual innovation'.[59]

As to the dynamics of catch-up in the developing world, in those parts of the world economy operating at substantially lower levels of social and technological development, growth can take place as regions that were previously effectively outside the reach of world markets pursue catch-up growth in relation to those at the (intermittently advancing) leading edge of technological development. Much has been made in what is known as endogenous growth theory of the ways in which innovation is an internal aspect of capital accumulation and growth in the economy as a whole. And this is indeed an important part of the reason for the fortunes of the advanced capitalist countries. But if we consider the long-run history of industrial capitalist development, then it is not just technology but also labour supplies that have been 'endogenous' to historical capitalism as its reach into other societies, pre-capitalist and now state socialist, has expanded. When this has happened, not only have resources been reallocated from lower to higher levels of productivity but also, and more importantly, capital accumulation has enabled follower economies to adopt more advanced technologies and thereby achieve much higher rates of growth than had been possible for the technological originators. Understood in these terms, the current pattern of North–South relations might be interpreted as involving a generalization of catch-up from Japan, through the newly industrializing economies (NIEs) and Southeast Asia, to China and perhaps India. The predictions of Goldman Sachs noted above assume that Brazil, Russia and Mexico at least will also be able to take advantage of this process.

Despite the downturn in the world economy since the 1970s and the ramifications of the debt crises of many developing countries in the 1980s and 1990s, it is becoming increasingly clear that the Japanese experience was but the first in a series of inter-connected developments across the Asian theatre, in which successful industrialization in one country raised real wages and thus prepared the way for the spread of industry to other economies. Japan's take-off into sustained per capita growth and conditional convergence on US levels of productivity began in the mid-1950s; the NIEs of Hong Kong, South Korea, Singapore and Taiwan embarked on a similar trajectory in the late 1960s; the ASEAN-4 of Indonesia, Malaysia, Thailand and (more problematically) the Philippines began to follow suit in the early 1970s; China started on its new path in 1979; and India joined in during the early 1980s.

The compound result of these successive waves of Asian industrialization is that the region now accounts for over 35 per cent of world output, over one-quarter of world exports and, since recovering from the 1997/8 crises, has contributed close to 50 per cent of world growth. Moreover, the Asian pole of the world economy is becoming increasingly integrated on a regional basis (levels of interregional trade are comparable to those in NAFTA, if somewhat lower than those in Europe) and there has been a rapid integration of production processes into regionally organized supply chains. From 1970 to 2005, Asia 'enjoyed both faster physical capital accumulation and faster TFP [total factor productivity] growth than other developing economies; in contrast, Asia's catch-up with advanced economies largely reflected capital accumulation'.[60] While some of the latter can be accounted for by sectoral shifts in output from lower- to higher-productivity activities, the greater part of Asia's catch-up on US levels has been the result of stronger productivity growth in both industry and services. In addition, between 1965 and 1990 East Asia's working-age population grew nearly four times faster than its dependent population, and this may account for as much as one-third of its growth during this period. The triad of the world economy is no longer the United States, Western Europe and Japan but NAFTA, the EU and an emerging Asia that includes China and potentially India as well.

How long can this process continue? Many factors will impinge on this, but the basic economic mechanism is that, until it reaches levels of labour productivity associated with the (constantly advancing) technological frontier, catch-up growth is essentially demand-driven. This means that, at the level of the world economy as a whole, where one country's exports are another's imports, it is capital accumulation (investment) that is the most dynamic element of aggregate demand, output and employment.[61] As long as there are labour supplies to be mobilized in pursuit of catch-up growth, savings and investment can drive the process forward. Clearly, the entry of China and India into world markets represents a huge new incorporation of low-cost labour into the development of historical capitalism as a whole, allowing investment-driven aggregate demand to play a central role in the shaping of economic activity. This opens up the *potential* for a major conjunctural shift in the balance of capital accumulation world-wide.

To the extent that much of the rural labour in China and other countries is underemployed, that is, to the extent that labour can migrate to the higher-productivity industrial sector without significantly reducing agricultural output, the world economy faces a source of low-cost labour supply for several decades to come. China has about half (47 per cent in 2006) of its labour force in agriculture operating at a productivity level barely one-eighth of that in industry and one-quarter of that in services. It has a unique combination of a huge population, over 60 per cent of which still lives in the country-side (a much higher share than in Japan at a similar stage of development), and an economy that is very open to trade and investment: China's average tariffs have fallen from 41 per cent in 1992 to 6 per cent after it joined the World Trade Organization in 2001, the sum of its exports and imports as a share of GDP is around 75 per cent (cf. a figure of less than 30 per cent for the United States and a peak of 32 per cent for Japan), joint ventures with foreign firms produce over one-quarter of industrial output, and the stock of total investment owned by foreigners is 36 per cent of GDP (cf. 2 per cent in Japan). 'In 2000,' Martin Wolf reports, 'inward direct investment financed 11 per cent of [China's] gross fixed capital formation, while foreign affiliates generated 31 per cent of China's manufacturing sales and, more astonishingly, 50 per cent of its exports.'[62] Not for nothing did *The Economist* argue that 'China's catch-up in income and its integration into the world economy could be the single biggest driver of growth over the coming decades.'[63] Recent research at the World Bank concurs: 'even though China is not the dominant force in the world economy, the shock she is administering to it is unprecedented'.[64]

In fact, China's entry into the international capitalist economy, alongside that of India and the former Soviet Union, has effectively doubled the size of the world's labour force. And while China's productive investment is similar to that of other earlier Asian growth experiences, Andrew Glyn points out that

> it is playing out on a massive canvas and with vastly larger supplies of surplus labour than were available to its Asian predecessors in the catch-up process. . . . Total employment in China is estimated at around 750 million, or about one and a half times that of the whole of the OECD. . . . Dwarfing in significance even the rise in density, international entanglement and fragility of financial markets is the growth of China, India and other developing countries. . . . Since the mid 1990s the majority of world GDP has been produced outside the old OECD countries and their share is declining. The centre of capital accumulation, the driving force of the system, is shifting away from the old core countries.[65]

Similarly, India's reform programme, which assumed a new urgency after the financial crisis of 1991 and in the wake of the collapse of diplomatic, strategic and trade support from the Soviet Union, is being driven forward both by pressing domestic considerations of social development and by the need to manage the strategic challenge of a rising China. India (per capita GDP ~ $3,000 purchasing power parity [PPP]) currently lags China's development record (per capita GDP ~ $5,000 PPP) by some considerable margin: its GDP is about half the size; its exports one-sixth of China's; foreign direct investment is an order of magnitude lower and the economy is more closed; adult illiteracy is much higher; and its growth rate has been much lower. That said, since the financial crisis in 1991, India has undergone a significant liberalization of its foreign trade and investment regime. In the longer term, its opportunities for catch-up in income and its integration into the world economy are on a similar scale to those of China: a World Bank study of the potential for China and India to reshape the global industrial geography notes that India 'has the labour resources, a growing base of human capital, the domestic market potential, and the nascent industrial strength to become an industrial powerhouse comparable to China today'.[66]

Since 1979, China has been the fastest-growing economy in the world: in the quarter-century or so since the launching of the four 'modernizations', China has had 'the fastest rate of total GDP growth (9.4 per cent), of per capita GDP growth (8.1 per cent) and of per worker growth (7.7 per cent)'.[67] Its transition has been one of a 'take-off' into sustained and high rates of per capita growth combined with the continued dominance of the Chinese Communist Party (CCP) over the state and the broad direction of social development. Most especially, China's entry into world markets has been characterized by a fruitful embrace of foreign investment and technology alongside productive flows of domestic resources from lower to higher levels of productivity – both between agriculture and industry and between lower and higher levels of skill and technology within the industrial sector – and from plan- to market-oriented output.

Viewed in the Soviet mirror, several features serve to define the Chinese experience to date. In the first place, while the modern state is the successor to the Chinese empire, and notwithstanding the unresolved final status of Taiwan and various 'internal' problems with national and ethnic minorities, China does not confront a legacy of modern imperial rule and control over geopolitical and political satellites of the kind that contributed to the disintegration of the Soviet Union in the 1980s. While the fragmentation of China's territory is not inconceivable, it is not on the current historical agenda and nor is it clear what the West would gain by such an outcome. Secondly, China began its reforms not only before the Soviet Union, but also from a very different starting point, developmentally speaking. When China embarked on reform, 71 per cent of employment was in agriculture and 19 per cent in industry (including construction and transport); in Russia (in 1985) the comparable figures were 14 per cent and 52 per cent, respectively. The subsidies to the state industrial sector in China were, therefore, a relatively small burden for the economy; in the context of world market prices, they were, by contrast, the central incubus of the Soviet system. In addition, whereas rural and urban living standards were broadly comparable in Russia, in China urban living standards were some two and a half times higher than rural levels, so there was a strong incentive for workers to move out of agriculture into (higher-productivity) industry.

This combination of relative political stability and difference of developmental starting point – an expression of the historical unevenness of industrialization in the state socialist world – meant that China could afford to undertake reform, first in agriculture and then in 'private' industry (joint ventures with foreign investment and township and village enterprises [TVEs]), while maintaining planning and output in the planned, state-owned sector. China's reforms began in the rural, agricultural sector based on de-collectivization (villages retained legal ownership but contracted land out) and a two-tier output and pricing framework (1979–82); they continued with the opening to foreign trade and investment, gradually introduced in the 1980s, with currency markets emerging in the late 1980s; and the reform of urban industry began in 1984 (again using a two-tier framework). In China's case, the relative failure of market-based reform in the state-owned enterprise sector was cushioned by the scope for the growth of a capitalist sector that was not directly controlled by the state, so that the economy as a whole was set on a path described by Barry Naughton as 'growing out of the plan'.[68] Thus far, China's experience has been a virtuous circle of reform, with continued absolute growth even in the state-owned sector.

And while the current Chinese experience represents an exit from a state socialist model of economic development, China's ability to combine this transition with a state-orchestrated form of catch-up capitalist industrialization is quite different from the Soviet/Russian case. This latter aspect of China's development, in fact, has much in common with the other examples of catch-up growth that have been in evidence in (capitalist) Asia from the 1950s onwards. This has meant that China has been able to become a part, perhaps now the dominant part, of a general shift in the historical geography of industrial capitalism to emerging Asia. China is also distinctive in several other respects. We noted above the degree of trade and investment openness of the economy and while its early reform-based growth, centred on the agricultural sector, was an internal affair, 'from the mid-1980s on . . . China's growth was fuelled and sustained by the opportunities that the world market offered'.[69] One aspect of this is that 'China has somehow managed to latch on to advanced, high-productivity products that one would not normally expect a poor, labour abundant country like China to produce, let alone export. . . . What stands out is that China sells products that are associated with a productivity level that is much higher than a country at China's level of income.'[70] Connected to this is the fact that, unlike much of the rest of Asia, China's growth has been based not only on rapid capital accumulation, but also on impressive growth of total factor productivity (TFP). Bosworth and Collins estimate that China's annual growth rate of TFP in the period 1993–2004 was 4 per cent (cf. 2.3 per cent for India) and its industrial TFP has grown at 6.2 per cent (cf. 1.1 per cent for India).[71]

In this respect, while much has been made of India's service sector and IT industries, and TFP in services has grown at 3.9 per cent a year since 1993, a detailed study of its prospects concluded that: 'With the exception of the business services processing and software industries, it is far from obvious that India is positioned to make a mark in the global market with its services industry at least during the next ten years.'[72] The clear implication is that in order for India to realize its potential and to follow in China's wake, it will have to build a development strategy around industry. China has shown that a large country open to trade and investment, with a determined and resourceful state, can build substantial industrial capacity across a wide range of sectors in a relatively short space of time. Whether India is able to follow in this path remains to be seen. That said, India's per capita growth rate has risen from 1.5 per cent in the period 1950–80 to 3.7 per cent in the 1980s, 4.1 per cent in the 1990s and 5.3 per cent in the new century.

Perhaps the key point to grasp in all of this is that far more important than either the imports of resources, capital and technology from world markets, or the dramatic successes in exporting to and amassing financial surpluses on world markets, has been the fact that what the economies of 'resurgent Asia' – China most of all – have really imported has been a 'market structure', in the sense of accepting the 'world market's requirements regarding prices and quality' as the principal mechanism of validating growth-oriented policies. It is, as Daniel Cohen rightly observes, the world market that plays the 'fundamental role . . . in the validation of the chosen strategies'.[73] It might be thought that the scale of Chinese development and the potential role of its vast domestic market changes this assessment. But this would be a mistake. China's economy is characterized by a fast-integrating set of nationally organized markets, with a common set of central institutions, but it is also a set of provinces whose trade with one another operates, in key respects, through the 'imported' structures of the world market. Indeed, as Alwyn Young has suggested,[74] for some purposes it is more helpful to think of China as twenty-five economies of 50 million people all trading with one another and the world market. As we saw above, China's economy is extraordinarily open to the world economy by almost any measure.

To be sure, there is no sign that conditional convergence on US levels of productivity is also bringing about convergence on US patterns of social and political development. Economic convergence does not necessarily imply social and political homogeneity: the forms of property relations through which enterprises are controlled, as well as the wider patterns of social and political development associated with these, often bear scant resemblance to the Anglo-American forms of corporate and market organization, let alone representative political systems. The fact that Asian capitalism uses world markets as the test or reference point for the success of its strategies does not indicate that its particular patterns of development, forged by means of a combination of prior historical experience and catch-up in the context of unevenness, will converge on those of the Anglo-American world.

On the contrary, thus far China's transition has been essentially social and economic, not political. It has been led throughout by the CCP and its military apparatus, the People's Liberation Army (PLA), both of which are determined to hold onto monopoly forms of control over the means of state power and to negotiate the terms of their engagements with international markets and other states on a centralized basis. Unlike the Soviet/Russian experience, in which political decentralization and party-free elections for regional government eroded central control, the CCP has retained the ability to reward and punish local and regional officials. So whereas the collapse of the party-state in Russia produced a hypertrophy of Soviet organization of the economy (barter relations, workers' veto power over restructuring of production), where monetization and price reform with soft budget constraints led to inflation and asset diversion, resulting in a period of mafia-like contract enforcement followed by the authoritarian stabilization and recentralization imposed under

President Putin, in China the party-state has remained firmly in control. The effect has been to maintain hard budget constraints on the economy even as aspects of property relations migrate from the public to the private sector. Since the domestic legitimacy of the Chinese government now rests squarely on national unity and economic performance – communist ideology and mobilization no longer play a significant role – the question of whether China can manage the social and political stresses of economic modernization with as much facility as it has its economic development to date remains to be seen.

Overall, there is little doubt that continued strong economic growth and rapid advances in productivity in China, India and elsewhere will produce strong export competition as costs fall and imports into Northern countries will become cheaper, so that real incomes will rise in both North and South. That is to say, the costs of competition are more than offset by the benefits of cheaper imports and stronger world growth. In fact, the biggest challenges will be faced not by the advanced Northern economies but by the middle-income countries elsewhere in Asia and in Latin America. For as Winters and Yusuf point out: 'These are the countries into whose product space China in particular looks likely to expand; they are the members of production networks that may be threatened by China's move into component manufacture; and they are the recipients of foreign direct investment designed to create export platforms for the multinational corporations.'[75]

But for Japan, North America and Western Europe, the picture is, for the most part, very different, as they

> have little to fear over the next decade and a half from Chinese and Indian competition in the high-technology and high-skill sectors in manufacturing and services, especially when those sectors rely on highly educated and experienced workforces, accumulated tacit knowledge, and innovation supported by heavy investment in research and development. Indeed, they have much to gain from specialization in these areas. The high income countries have not been competitive in the manufacture of garments, shoes, and consumer electronics for a long time, and so they have been strong gainers from the price reductions that the Giants [China and India] have engendered and will continue to engender.[76]

Moreover, faced with ageing populations, the advanced capitalist economies may also benefit from Asian savings. If one models the demographic and fiscal paths of the developed world – that is, the

United States, the eurozone and Japan – without their interactions with China, it is highly likely that the tax increases needed to finance existing welfare commitments to ageing populations will lead to a fall in the level of capital per unit of human capital and hence a fall in real wages as compared to the present. Of course, real wages might continue to rise because of offsetting technical change. But if China and the other Asian labour-abundant economies are added to the model, and even if Asian savings and consumption patterns converge on those of the developed world as they get richer, Asian savings can finance capital accumulation both at home and abroad, so that the real wage per unit of human capital can continue to rise in the developed world over and above that which would follow from technical change alone.[77]

For much of the last century, the central story of capitalist growth was one of the United States forging ahead of its European and Japanese rivals, aided to a considerable extent by the course of the two world wars, followed by the conditional convergence of Western Europe and Japan during the long boom that followed post-war reconstruction and the construction of a high degree of political and geopolitical unity in the developed world, roughly from the late 1940s to the early 1970s. But in the light of the developments reviewed above, a key aspect of the future may lie elsewhere. The combination of industrialization in Northeast Asia and the prospect of sustained growth in South Asia suggests that forces of convergence – due to trade; human capital formation; the provision of social overhead capital; changes of policies and institutions; the onset of diminishing returns in the North and the flows of resources, especially capital to parts of the South – may be beginning to assert themselves in the most populous regions of the world economy.

All of these changes are fraught with danger. Rising inequalities and competitive pressures in the developed countries could provoke a backlash against ever-increasing liberalization of trade and investment. A slump in China (similar to that which befell Japan during the lost decade of the 1990s) could have damaging effects in Northeast Asia and the wider world economy. The global current account imbalances and the capital flows needed to finance them, in particular the US deficits and the position of the dollar, could become unsustainable. However, there is nothing inevitable about any of these, and the major centres of decision making – in Washington, Brussels, Beijing and Tokyo – are not without considerable powers to manage seriously adverse developments, if they can effect a modicum of coordination among themselves.

Containing China?

What is hard to reckon, in my view, is not so much the idea that the United States might be prepared to forgo the absolute gains promised by these developments in pursuit of relative advantage vis-à-vis China, but the notion that it could seek to 'contain' them. These shifts are an important part of what Glyn has appropriately termed 'capitalism unleashed',[78] and the state that has been at the epicentre of promoting the coming tectonic shifts in the international economy is, of course, none other than the United States. China and the wider field of emerging Asian capitalist development is not Soviet Russia. The Soviet Union was not only a military and geopolitical rival to the United States but also a regime that sought to detach its territory, and with it its property, natural resources and labour force, from the world market. Moreover, it encouraged and supported other countries to do likewise. China's transition, as well as that of emerging Asia as a whole, represents an expansion and deepening of interdependence and integration in the world market.

Nevertheless, in marked contrast to economic multi-polarity, the states-system is now effectively uni-polar in terms of military power. The only sense in which the world is uni-polar, the meaning of the epiphet 'hyperpower', is in the military sphere. How far the United States can sustain the uni-polar moment is much debated, but it is certainly with us for the foreseeable future. William Odom and Robert Dujarric present the purely quantitative comparative data on military spending and manpower as in Table 4.2.

And the United States appears to be moving further ahead. According to the International Institute for Strategic Studies, in 2005/6 US military expenditure was $561 billion out of a world total of $1,097 billion, or 51 per cent of the total. Moreover, these quantitative

Table 4.2. US military power in comparative perspective

	% world military expenditure	% world active-duty personnel
United States	40	7
NATO	59	18
Asia-Pacific allies of USA	7	5
USA and all allies	66	23
Others	34	77

Source: adapted from William Odom and Robert Dujarric (2004), *America's Inadvertent Empire*, p. 66, Table 3.3 (New Haven: Yale University Press). © 2004 by William E. Odom and Robert Dujarric. Reprinted with permission from Yale University Press.

assessments probably considerably understate the true picture, not only because it does not take account of the higher productivity of US military expenditure as compared with that of its likely rivals, but also because it does not indicate the qualitative superiority of the US strategic position. Many recent commentators on American power – Michael Mann, Christian Reus-Smit and even John Mearsheimer – have argued that US military power is, in effect, limited vis-à-vis Russia and China since these states have an effective nuclear deterrent. In fact, it is not clear that this is the case, though both Russia and China can confidently be expected to pursue such a capability as a matter of national priority. In the case of Russia, according to Keir Lieber and Daryl Press, its strategic bombers are 'now located at only two bases and thus vulnerable to surprise attack, rarely conduct training exercises, and their warheads are stored off-base'; its 'mobile ICBMS [inter-continental ballistic missiles] rarely patrol'; '[m]ost of the time, all nine of Russia's ballistic missile submarines are sitting in port, where they make easy targets'; and '[n]either Soviet nor Russian satellites have ever been capable of reliably detecting missiles launched from U.S. submarines' and Russia's 'ground-based radar . . . has a gaping hole in its coverage that lies to the east of the country, toward the Pacific Ocean'. The conclusion is stark: 'Russia's leaders can no longer count on a survivable nuclear deterrent. And unless they reverse course rapidly, Russia's vulnerability will only increase over time.'[79] There were clear signs in 2007 that President Putin was using the windfall oil and gas rents of Russia to address some of these vulnerabilities.

China's current predicament is apparently even more precarious. China does not have any modern submarine-based, inter-continental nuclear missiles or any long-range strategic bombers. According to US government assessments, say Lieber and Press:

> China's entire intercontinental nuclear arsenal consists of 18 stationary single-warhead ICBMS. These are not ready to launch on warning: their warheads are kept in storage and the missiles themselves are unfueled. . . . It appears that China would have no warning at all of a U.S. submarine-launched missile attack or a strike using hundreds of stealthy nuclear-armed cruise missiles. . . . the odds that Beijing will acquire a survivable nuclear deterrent in the next decade are slim.[80]

Given this assessment, and on the basis of a review of current US weapons programmes, it is perhaps not surprising that Lieber and

Press conclude that '[t]he current and future U.S. nuclear force . . . seems designed to carry out a preemptive disarming strike against Russia or China'; and that 'Washington's pursuit of nuclear primacy helps explain its missile defence strategy'. The rationale for these conclusions is that against a sizeable retaliatory (second) strike, missile defence makes little sense; as an insurance against a few surviving missiles after a largely successful first strike, it is prudent: 'the sort of missile defenses that the United States might plausibly deploy would be valuable primarily in an offensive context, not a defensive one – as an adjunct to a U.S. first-strike capability, not as a standalone shield'.[81] Missile defence also makes sense if, like the US military, one believes that missile-based warfare is likely to be an increasingly important component of future regular warfare. If this is so, it becomes the logical complement of air defence.

But the meaning of uni-polarity, that is, what it implies for political struggles to shape the future of the international order, is far less clear, for we must reckon with the *costs* of exercising military power in order to achieve political influence. Uni-polarity undoubtedly confers advantages on the United States that it did not possess during the Cold War, at least not after the Soviet Union attained a rough strategic parity in the early 1970s, but the collapse of bi-polarity and, perhaps more importantly, the absence of a clear ideological division defining the fault lines of international politics renders the purpose of military power more opaque and makes the cost–benefit calculus involved in its exercise immeasurably more complicated. Who is to be deterred from doing what? Who is to be compelled to do what? And how can deterrence and compellance reassure allies when there is no longer a single axis of strategic political competition?

There is an argument to the effect that military uni-polarity enforces cooperation among the core capitalist countries. Such an account emphasizes the role of political power in shaping the international capitalist order, specifically the military power of the United States. As the consensual basis of US leadership declines – either because of the end of the Cold War or because of a reduced ability to operate as a pole of attraction – its hegemony can be expected to take an increasingly unilateral and predatory form, thereby prompting reactions in other power centres. Indeed, Peter Gowan's view is that 'US policies are tending to conflict with the collective interests of major capitalist centres'.[82] Mearsheimer's (offensive) realist recommendation that the United States choose containment over engagement similarly rests on considerations of military power and relative advantage.[83]

On the other hand, if inter-capitalist relations are, for the most part, capable of generating positive-sum gains, and if a coordinated interdependence provides benefits to all, even if the United States has greater bargaining power within that order than any other single state, then the role of US military power is much more ambiguous. In these circumstances, while US military power can always be used unilaterally, it will only serve as a means of hegemony when it is used to protect and advance the common interests of the coordinated liberal order. Perhaps more importantly, it is wholly unclear how military power can be used (at acceptable cost) to 'contain' what is at root an epochal shift in the social geography of international capital accumulation in a post-colonial world of many states, of which the rise of China's relative power is but one – albeit key – part. It is hard to see how the United States can use military power to halt the course of capitalist development on an international scale – after all, two world wars did not stop the long-run emergence of German and Japanese industrial power.

Militarily speaking, the uni-polar moment offers a temptation to attempt to freeze the current position of US superiority for the fore-seeable future, to maintain its coercive military edge over all other powers. This is what the modernization of the nuclear triad, the Revolution in Military Affairs and the National Missile Defense programme are all about. At present, US military strategy aims to prevent the emergence of any regional power capable of matching its military might. Over and above the nuclear supremacy noted above, one element of that strategy is continued investment in technological innovation in military affairs as well as the maintenance of forces on land, at sea, and in the air and space that are so far in advance of those of other powers that potential rivals see little point in attempting to compete with the United States. As of now, neither Russia nor China, let along Europe, is seeking to compete with the United States in any of these domains, and none is currently capable of doing so. The most they can do is to seek to restore (Russia) or develop (China) a nuclear deterrent against direct attack. This is likely to be the case for a generation or more.

The other element of military preponderance is open access, by means of markets and corporations, armoured by forward-basing and military cooperation agreements, to key strategic resources – most especially, oil – that underpin economic and military power. China and India have a growing dependence on Middle Eastern oil as well as Central Asian gas, and the largest expansion of oil and gas consumption over the next several decades will be in Asia. On current

trends, an increasing proportion of world oil exports will be accounted
for by the Persian Gulf region, over one-half and perhaps as much as
two-thirds by 2020. Maintaining influence in the Middle East, and
countering the influence of Russia, China and Iran in Central Asia,
are thus becoming increasingly important elements in US thinking.
Of course, this is, in effect, an extension of the Carter Doctrine of
1980, attuned to new circumstances.[84]

The danger, from a US point of view, which is well recognized in
Washington, is that attempts to maintain and extend its dominance
in these ways will provoke two kinds of reaction: first, new attempts
to acquire weapons of mass destruction as an insurance against US
power (the lesson of the Kosovo war, according to the Indian government, was don't oppose the United States without nuclear weapons),
as well as increasing incentives to trade the necessary materials on
the black market; and, secondly, popular antagonism to the United
States, and hence a fertile soil for terrorist networks, as a result of US
support for local, authoritarian regimes that facilitate access to
resources and bases. In this respect, it is important to underscore the
continued importance for the United States of access for forces on
the ground, as Odom and Dujarric state: 'Withdrawal to the sea, to
the air, or to space is withdrawal pure and simple.'[85]

That is to say, the political and geopolitical influence that comes
from US military power, across the Eurasian theatre, depends upon
the presence of US forces on the ground. There are two reasons for
this. First, military commitments only work if they are politically
credible, that is, if the potential antagonist has good reason to believe
that its adversary will deliver on its stated intentions. And the only
way of reliably signalling that one is serious about one's intentions is
to put nationals in harm's way, in effect to use one's forces as hostages.
Secondly, if conflict does break out, then only forces on the ground
can compel an enemy: as Mearsheimer has rightly insisted, naval and
air power are primarily useful as adjuncts to land-based forces. There
may be five dimensions to strategy – land, sea, air, space and cyber-
space – but most people can only inhabit one, and so the 'sole way to
control them is to command the land on which they live'.[86]

The United States and the Asian Powers

In contrast to the partial transcendence of inter-imperialist rivalries
and balance of power considerations within the transatlantic order,
the other potential powers – Russia and Japan; China, India and
Pakistan – consider one another, or at least potential coalitions of

others, as possible future threats to their security. Japan is integrated into the Atlantic order but, in other respects, these states treat one another as military-strategic rivals, even as they engage in forms of economic cooperation. Notwithstanding growing economic integration between and among these countries, each is either tempted, or threatened, by competition for regional dominance; all are currently increasing their military capabilities against one another as well as their smaller neighbours; and there are no regional or continental forms of cooperation that are durable enough to encompass and contain these differences. Questions of coercive power assume a much greater salience in this region and between its powers and the United States than in the transatlantic arena.

This is a complex area for US policy, since its Cold War alignments, directed at containment of the Soviet Union, no longer make sense; important legacies of the Cold War – most notably the division of Korea and the problem of the North – remain unresolved; and the underlying balance of power in the region is being rapidly reshaped by the knock-on effects of the collapse of Soviet power and the dynamics of Asian and, most recently, especially Chinese capitalist development. The operative principle for maintaining international order in this region is likely to remain the strategic management of the balance of power. What remains to be seen is whether (Leninist) inter-imperialist rivalries, or strategic great power rivalries, will develop in this region, or whether it can be incorporated into the coordinated interdependence of the OECD world. I will explore this by considering some of the relations between the United States, Japan, China, Russia and India.

The mainstay of US policy in Northeast Asia has been the alliance with Japan. For the foreseeable future, the US–Japanese alliance looks secure. Japan and China are engaged in several territorial disputes in the China Sea relating to undersea oil and gas deposits; the missiles that China targets against Taiwan can reach Japan, and any US defence of Taiwan could not be conducted without use of its bases in Japan; Japan now regards Taiwan as a security concern that it shares with the United States; and the United States and Japan are conducting missile tests together to establish the viability of ballistic missile defences. Japan is increasing its military commitment to the alliance but remains firmly under the protection (and hence also guardianship) of the United States. The alternative to this, including a substantial withdrawal of US forces from their bases in Japan, is very likely a nuclear-armed Japan (given its technological capabilities and its civil nuclear programme, Japan is, in effect, a recessed nuclear power), which would almost certainly prompt other countries in the region to acquire nuclear weapons.

China and Russia; Pakistan and India

In the era of the Cold War, China's external strategy focused on maintaining its political and territorial integrity in the bi-polar, superpower system. Initially, China pursued an alliance with the Soviet Union against the United States; this was followed in the 1960s by an abortive attempt to unite revolutionary forces in the Third World against both superpowers; and finally, once China concluded that the Soviet Union was less interested in the cause of 'international communism' (that is, an alliance with China) than it was in achieving a traditional great power status, it made a limited rapprochement with the United States, directed against the Soviet Union.

The collapse of Soviet power, together with the rapid and increasingly market-oriented industrialization of the Chinese economy, has brought about a new orientation in China's foreign policy, based on an attempt, first, to maintain the international preconditions for its internal development and, second, to reduce the ability of the United States (or others) to frustrate its international ambitions. Accordingly, China has embraced multilateralism as a means of countering US primacy, seeking – thus far with little success – to dissuade Japan and Australia from developing strengthened bilateral ties with the United States, ties which would be, in effect, directed against China. This is, however, a conditional and partial embrace of multilateralism since 'Beijing still views national military power as the primary guarantee of "comprehensive security"'.[87] China's pursuit of multilateralism is intended to forestall others balancing against it, with or without the United States.

As the successor state to the Soviet Union, Russia has had to make the most dramatic adjustment to the post-Cold War world. Russian foreign policy is still in a state of considerable flux and one can only hazard an interpretation of its long-run national strategic priorities. These are, I tentatively suggest, as follows: first, to manage the military, especially nuclear, balance with the United States in a way that ensures the continuing viability of Russia's deterrent forces; second, to stabilize its 'near abroad' by making independence among some of the former republics of the Soviet Union so painful that returning to the Russian embrace becomes the least costly option; third, to seek external assistance for its economic reconstruction, especially foreign investment in key sectors such as oil and gas and membership of the

World Trade Organization; fourth, to use its energy resources as a source of strategic influence over the European Union and others; and, fifth, to cooperate with the other permanent members of the Security Council – the United States, China, France and the UK – in selectively containing the proliferation of weapons of mass destruction and in the campaign against 'international terrorism'. These have not been clearly articulated, let alone consistently pursued, and there are several obvious tensions between some of them. But for precisely similar reasons to China, Russia has an interest in working mutilaterally on many issues.

In short, both China and Russia, perhaps like France and Germany in Europe, envisage a long and complicated struggle between American efforts to preserve its uni-polar moment and their desire to hasten the transition to a multi-polar world, in which the major powers fashion some kind of agreed regional division of labour among themselves, while working in concert on truly global issues. However, until such a situation evolves, neither has anything to gain from directly antagonizing the United States. Nor are they likely to forge an alliance hostile to US interests. China and Russia share a long border that constitutes a zone of potential instability and there is scant prospect that either will trust the other to guarantee its security. Moreover, it is far from clear how they could gain from establishing closer links with one another than they have with Washington. On the other hand, aggressive, unilateral action by the United States – especially in the Middle East and Central Asia – is likely to enforce a greater degree of (reactive) cooperation between China and Russia.

It is true that both can make life difficult for the United States in several respects: both have a veto on the Security Council; both can export nuclear and missile technology, effectively undermining the nuclear non-proliferation regime; both can limit their support for the 'war on terror' to areas of direct mutual concern; and both can be uncooperative on the settlement of various regional issues – for example, Iraq and North Korea. However, aside from frustrating unilateral American efforts, they have no interests in staging a direct confrontation with the United States. One critical unresolved question for both Russia and China concerns the question of nuclear proliferation. Whereas the United States has a clear interest in attempting to prolong its military dominance by preventing the emergence of new, regional nuclear powers, the logic for China and Russia is less clear. They cannot aspire to a uni-polar moment of their own; rather, the best they can achieve is regional dominance and international recognition of great power status in a multi-polar world. Accordingly, the prospect of a series of secondary, nuclear powers poses a quite different kind of challenge to their future power than it does to the United States. And without their cooperation, it is unlikely that the United States will be able to prevent further proliferation.

There are four strategic aspects to this question that are worth elaborating a little. First, as the state with the most powerful conventional forces, the United States has a greater interest in forestalling nuclear proliferation, thereby ensuring that its conventional dominance is not checked by the uncertainties inherent in confronting a conventionally weak but nuclear-armed power. Secondly, to permit weaker states access to nuclear weapons would reverse the equation of nuclear weapons with the defence of the geopolitical status quo that has obtained more or less since 1945, and, as Stephen Walt argues, this would 'send a powerful signal that these weapons were in fact an effective instrument of expansion or aggression. The consequences for world politics would be tremendous: Incentives to proliferate would grow apace, revisionist powers would be quick to repeat their efforts to intimidate others.'[88] Thirdly, while the emergence of a second tier of nuclear-armed regional powers might serve to stabilize the states-system by means of a generalization of the logic of deterrence, this would only apply once these powers had established secure second-strike capabilities. Leaving aside the question of whether the logic of deterrence is as secure as this notion presupposes, in the interim 'small, nascent nuclear forces [are] much more likely to promote instability by tempting opponents to pre-emptive measures' and 'war as a result of miscalculation would become much more likely'.[89]

Such measures may be 'pre-emptive', that is, conducted for fear that the adversary has aggressive intent, or they may be simply 'preventive', that is, designed to forestall a change in the balance of power, irrespective of presumed intent. Despite much sapient commentary to the effect that the former may, in certain circumstances, be legitimate and that the latter is not, this is a lawyerly discussion with scant purchase either on the general nature of political decision making in conditions of anarchy or on the particular realities of contemporary geopolitics. 'Prevention can be seen', as Lawrence Freedman rightly notes, 'as pre-emption in slow motion, more anticipatory or forward thinking.'[90] The stand-off between the triangle of the United States, Iran and the UN Security Council is being played for very high stakes in this regard and, accordingly, its outcome might be an important indication of future developments.

The fourth strategic aspect to the question of secondary nuclear proliferation is the notion that fissile material, as well as a capability to produce rudimentary nuclear devices, might fall into the hands of non-state actors. This is far from fanciful in cases of state collapse or the violent overthrow of existing regimes. The chances of this happening would only increase with an expanding number of nascent nuclear powers in parts of the world where stable state formation and national development is anything but guaranteed. The issue is not that 'rogue' states will pass on such material to irregular combatants, but that in conditions of state collapse, centralized, hierarchical control over the military and, *a fortiori*, key military assets would simply evaporate. (The case of Pakistan surely shows that this is not an idle speculation.) The idea, canvassed by Graham Allison among others, that the United States should offer a grand bargain to aspiring nuclear powers as a means of defusing these related strategic liabilities is, in effect, a plea to forswear the current and real political and geopolitical use of military uni-polarity in return for promises of future restraint on the part of others.[91] It is perhaps not surprising that this view has found little favour in Washington, still less in the Pentagon.

After 11 September 2001, Pakistan found itself on the wrong side of a renewed assertion of American power in West Asia. The United States demanded not only that Islamabad break relations with the Taliban and cooperate fully in the war against al-Qaida, but also that it must rein in the insurgents in Indian-controlled Kashmir and begin a peace process with New Delhi. As Owen Bennett Jones points out, 'before Musharraf's decision, in January 2002, to ban Jaish-e-Mohammed [a Kashmiri-based Islamist group seeking independence from Indian control] and Lashkar-e-Toiba [the 'Army of the Pure', a Pakistan-based group operating in Kashmir and Jammu], backing the insurgency was a major element of Pakistani state policy'.[92] Moreover, after the exposure of covert exchanges of nuclear technology with Iran, Libya and North Korea in 2003, Washington insisted that Pakistan end A.Q. Khan's clandestine network and share relevant intelligence with the CIA. For its part, the United States lifted sanctions – imposed on both India and Pakistan after their nuclear tests in 1998 – and renewed packages of economic and military assistance.

At the same time, US relations with India have markedly improved. Partly as a result of growing economic ties and partly as a result of the need to build better relations throughout Asia due to the growth of Chinese power, Washington has shifted its posture towards New Delhi. This began with engaged and active diplomacy under the

Clinton administration. But most dramatically, in July 2005, a US–Indian accord seemed to give India's nuclear programme a special status. Under the proposed deal, India would separate its civilian and military nuclear programmes, placing the former under international safeguards overseen by the International Atomic Energy Agency (IAEA), thereby gaining access to US civilian nuclear technology while keeping its military programme intact and outside the disciplines of the Non-Proliferation Treaty. Concluding the deal on 2 March 2006, both President Bush and the Indian prime minister, Manmohan Singh, described it as 'historic'. As of early 2008, the fortunes of this deal were still unclear, but if successfully cemented, it would, in effect, recognize India as the sixth official nuclear power.

What is the logical course of action for the United States faced with this strategic environment? As yet, forms of capitalism organized along broadly liberal lines, let alone liberal-democratic norms of politics, have not sunk deep roots in China and Russia – nor is there much indication that they will in the foreseeable future. China's economic strategy conforms to the norms of a liberal international capitalist order not primarily because of the domestic character of its markets and property arrangements, though these are changing in very significant ways, but because its strategy is oriented towards and validated by success on international markets. Moscow's energy policies have yet to align themselves with even the international norms of a liberal order. Correspondingly, the level and depth of economic cooperation and coordination among the United States, China and Russia do not match those found in the transatlantic arena. However, China has now joined the World Trade Organization and Russia has expressed an ambition to do likewise. China's surpluses currently play a key role in supporting the dollar. Assuming that China and Russia integrate smoothly into the existing institutional framework of the capitalist world, hegemony cannot rest on the kinds of economic preponderance that the United States enjoyed in respect of its European and Japanese allies on the eve of the Second World War. US coercive economic power can only continue to decline in this scenario. More likely, in fact, China and Russia's integration will dampen the liberal character of that order.

As with Western Europe and Japan after the Second World War, US policy must aim at the maximum reproduction of the economic aspects of Americanism outside the United States, and at keeping the US economy at the leading edge of productivity and technological development (even as its share of world income declines). Its economic power in relation to these other centres of capital accumulation and innovation will increasingly come from the coordination of the US economy with these economic competitors. Economically speaking, the US has no option but to follow the logic of interdependence rather than rivalry. Inter-imperialist rivalry has become a negative-sum game, a default option of last resort in the economics of the capitalist world.

At the same time, India and Pakistan require careful management given the antagonism between these two states and the potential instability of Pakistan. Whatever the future of state and nation building in Afghanistan, Pakistan will continue to face relentless US pressure in the 'long war'. By the same token, this is a source of significant political disquiet and opposition within Pakistan. Especially after President Musharraf went back on his commitment to give up his 'army uniform' in December 2004, the Muttahida Majlis-e Amal, a parliamentary coalition of Islamist parties that had been the mainstay of political support for his regime, turned against him. Continued US pressure to take action against madrassas and to ramp up actions along the northern border with Afghanistan against Taliban and al-Qaida elements have only worsened the domestic situation. In 2006 and 2007 this resulted in growing militancy within Pakistan and attempts to shore up a secular alternative by bringing ex-President Benazir Bhutto back into the fold. This was thwarted by her assassination in December 2007, and the subsequent elections of February 2008, which saw the defeat of President Musharaff's party, did nothing to change the underlying situation. It is very likely that Pakistan will remain a key fault-line state in the US struggle to reorder the Middle East and the wider West Asian region.

Strategic 'Partners' or 'Competitors'?

As to the longer-term game, the United States does have some considerable support, since neither Japan, nor Russia, nor India can regard an unchecked rise of Chinese power in the region with equanimity. As noted, the US position vis-à-vis Japan looks secure and relations with India are hugely improved. Reflecting US primacy, these powers are likely to undertake regional balancing alongside the United States, even as they are unlikely to bandwagon with it against China. However, there are also factors limiting closer US–Russian relations. On the Russian side, a permanent US presence in Central Asia would amount to a significant loss of influence. For the United States, at least, Russian membership of NATO would undermine that organization's already much diminished strategic purpose. As long as Russia maintains an interest in dominating its 'near abroad', including the resource-rich and strategically crucial regions of Central Asia, the United States is unlikely to welcome Russia fully into a collective security arrangement. Moreover, Russian membership of NATO would have destabilizing consequences elsewhere. It would either dilute the military character of the alliance to such an extent that it would become, in effect, a mini-Security Council, or if it remained a coherent alliance, what would it be directed against? It would become a mini-Security Council minus China.

As Henry Kissinger has pointed out, when Russia's domestic politics looked benign by Western lights, this would amount to an 'anti-Asian – especially anti-Chinese – alliance of the Western industrial democracies'.[93] Apart, perhaps, from Russia, who could gain from this? In any case, President Putin's authoritarian stabilization of Russia and the state's seizure of the commanding heights in the oil and gas industries make present-day Russia a problematic partner for the United States and the European Union.

The obvious role for the United States, therefore, is as the external – though not, strictly speaking, offshore – balancer to the rivalries and balance of power among these states. While some analysts recommend a strategy of offshore balancing for the United States – that is, a policy that refrains from 'large-scale, quasi-permanent military engagements overseas' (currently in Europe, Japan and South Korea and perhaps in a future Iraq) – in which forces would only be deployed when a change in the regional balance posed 'specific threats to U.S. vital interest',[94] this is to assume that the political and geopolitical influence that the United States derives from the forward commitment of military power to the European and Asian theatres is not a vital interest. Moreover, given what has already been said about the political importance of land forces, both as signs of commitment and as the *sine qua non* of an ability to turn military power into political outcome, the specific recommendations of advocates of offshore balancing – for example, Walt recommends that the United States drastically reduce its military presence in Europe, deploy its military forces in Asia primarily as air and naval forces and return to a balance of power policy in the Middle East aimed at denying dominance to others[95] – might easily be read as signs of strategic retreat as opposed to strategic restraint.

That said, given a gradual evolution from external to offshore balancing, conditional on the behaviour of regional powers, it is possible that the current readjustment of the balance of power in Asia, as well as the armament of many major states in the region against one another, can be peacefully managed, with the United States using its forward military deployments around the edges of the region as a sign of its intentions and as a means of deterring local attempts to disrupt the regional balance. For this strategy to be successful, however, the United States will need the cooperation of the major states in the region if faced with a serious attempt to disrupt the status quo. This policy might founder if several states within the region began to balance against the United States, but this looks very unlikely any time soon. For now this strategy presupposes the continued ability to forward base US armed forces and hence attention to the interests of its allies. It also presupposes that domestic considerations in the United States do not force a dramatic shift from external to offshore balancing. This cannot be taken for granted, for, as Fred Halliday rightly notes, one effect of the Revolution in Military Affairs is to 'highlight the gap between the US capability and that of allies', thereby giving ammunition to the idea of 'decoupling US defence from what for many, especially the Republican Right, has been an unusual, transitory commitment to the security of European states'.[96]

In the longer term, both economic integration within the region and changing assessments of the costs and benefits of seeking security through a finely balanced and nuclear-armed balance of power, might bring about greater political cooperation, mutual security guarantees and a diminishing concern with the military-strategic balance of power. If stably managed, this might allow China, Russia and India to join Japan alongside the West as members of a global Concert of powers – Russia is already a member of the G-8 – for the international economy. China and the United States also subsist in what Lawrence Summers has eloquently described as a 'financial balance of terror'.[97]

Alternatively, the delicate balancing act might break down. The removal of US forces currently guaranteeing the security of the South against the North on the Korean peninsula, for example, might raise serious questions about the future of US bases in Japan. More generally, a widespread withdrawal of the forward deployment of US forces from the Pacific Rim, while not threatening the homeland security of the United States, would dramatically change the strategic and political calculus among the major Asian powers. The United States would no longer be able to play the role of an external balancer in these circumstances, for even if the global reach of US military power enables it to conduct operations anywhere in the world from the territory and airspace of the United States and its key allies (as well as international waters), it is only a military presence on the ground that can effectively signal a clear political commitment to a determined adversary. This kind of strategic withdrawal by the United States would open up the prospect of major geopolitical realignments as the regional powers sought to balance against one another – Russia and India balancing against China, Pakistan and Iran perhaps? And what, then, of Japan? This would be uncharted territory.

For the present, however, the United States is a global power operating to sustain the regional balance and this suits the regional powers well, since all fear each other more than they do the United States. The strategic imperative for the United States is to continue to manage this regional balance and to forestall the emergence of either a threatening regional hegemon or an alliance of regional powers seeking to exclude the United States from the regional balance. In short, the military balance of power remains a fundamental basis of international order in Asia.

Conclusions

Given the nuclear revolution and the end of colonial rule, the direct and indirect utility of military dominance to compel adversaries is much diminished compared with the widespread use of great power military force prior to the Second World War, though the wars in Afghanistan and Iraq demonstrate its continuing importance in imperial settings. But outside of a catastrophic deterioration in inter-capitalist relations, wars against China and Russia are not feasible, even for the United States, and even as the United States seeks to maintain its military uni-polarity. What about the indirect uses of military power to deter enemies and reassure allies? Some Washington neo-conservatives argued that uni-polarity means that the United States has no need to act strategically. Some Marxist theorists of super-imperialism appear to agree. In Walt's summary, these arguments say that:

> So long as the United States maintains a healthy economic advantage and a global military presence that is second to none, other states will not dare to balance against it. Potential rivals will be unwilling to invite the 'focused enmity' of the United States and key U.S. allies like Japan and Germany will prefer to free-ride on U.S. protection rather than trying to create stronger military forces of their own.[98]

This is a prescription of perpetual dominance for perpetual leadership, but is it realistic? Or, rather, given that it is realistic, militarily speaking, how is the coercive power based on military primacy to be turned to economic and political advantage? Seeking primacy vis-à-vis an adversary that threatened your potential allies – as the Soviet Union did during the Cold War, even posing a threat to China after the early 1960s – made eminent sense, as leadership over those allies followed as a by-product. But seeking military primacy over a range of powers – Western Europe, Russia, China, India, etc. – when the strategic alignments among them are varied and changeable, and when all subsist in a world market that can only be governed by a significant degree of common endeavour, does not translate into political leadership.

A comparison with the position during the Cold War is instructive in this regard. The United States' NATO allies (and Japan) were willing to defer to its geopolitical leadership of the capitalist world on many issues because they reckoned that its military containment of the Soviet Union served their collective interests. By the same token, however, if US military power were to be enlisted in purposes that are not recognized as based on a collective interest, if it comes to be seen as serving the self-interest of the United States alone, then it will cease to generate the consensual leadership that has served it so well in the past. The collapse of the Soviet Union and with it the advent of the uni-polar moment massively frees the hand for the use of US military power, as many commentators have rightly insisted, but, for the same reason, it correspondingly reduces the role of that power as a lever of integration within the capitalist world unless it serves genuinely common interests. For example, if the modernization of the nuclear triad, the Revolution in Military Affairs and a successful National Missile Defense programme were effectively to decouple the security of the United States from the balance of power in Europe and Asia, that is, if the United States were able to retreat from its continental commitments and seek security in more unilateral ways, then it would be unable to command the geopolitical leadership of the capitalist world that it has treasured since 1945. In short, the price of that leadership is a forward commitment to maintaining stability in Europe and Asia. But that stability has to be one that genuinely accommodates the interests of Europe and Asia, not one that merely serves the self-interest of the United States.

The key aim for the United States is, as Walt has rightly argued, to keep the rest of the world 'off-balance', to stop other powers (individually or collectively) balancing against it. Because Walt sees this question largely in military-strategic terms, he recommends an off-shore balancing role as the best means of achieving this aim. I have suggested above that the United States is more likely – at least for the foreseeable future – to continue to act as an external balancer, and the political influence that derives from this is all the more important given the additional need to coordinate so as to prevent mutually damaging economic rivalries from developing. For in the field of international economic relations it is, and will increasingly be, the case that the key to US power includes both the specific assets of the territorial United States and the reproduction of 'Americanism' outside in the rest of the capitalist world, and the coordination of the one with the other. This system has, of course, been designed to secure US interests. But it has equally served the interests of the other leading capitalist powers. Increasingly, the United States will lose the ability to determine the shape of this coordination on a unilateral basis. Just as other centres of capital have needed to coordinate with the United States, so the US market will increasingly need to coordinate with the most dynamic poles in the rest of the world. The United States still has a greater ability to determine the nature of this coordination than others – this is what constitutes its specifically directive role within the hierarchy of capitalist powers – but this nonetheless presupposes collective benefits to all deriving from that coordination.

CONCLUSION

The Prospects for a Liberal International Order

'The long-term strategic alternatives for America', wrote Zbigniew Brzezinski, 'are either to engage in a gradual, carefully managed transformation of its own supremacy into a self-sustaining international system, or to rely primarily on its national power to insulate itself from the international anarchy that would follow a disengagement.'[1] Brzezinski's diagnosis is entirely consistent with the project for a liberal international order that was embodied in modernization theory – an American ideology of world-wide 'transformation of its own supremacy into a self-sustaining international system'. The question for the future is whether, after what Walter Russell Mead calls the 'bipartisan age of narcissism and hubris' that characterized US foreign policy between the fall of the Berlin Wall and the events of 11 September 2001,[2] and after the reorientation of foreign policy under the Bush administration, America can find new ways of continuing that project, or whether perpetual military innovation and unilateral exercises of coercive power will become additional forces for international disorder.

We have seen that what began as a specifically American project of post-war reconstruction and Cold War inter-capitalist unification has become a constitutive form through which significant aspects of the world-wide international capitalist order of many states are rule-governed and institutionalized. Clearly, power, including coercive power (in its military and other forms), has mattered greatly for this ordering of the international. And there is a substantial body of work that shows how the pacification of international order, imposed by US power after the Second World War – first in relation to the capitalist world and then, since the fall of communism and the Soviet Union, across the world – fosters interdependence. To the extent that a preponderant power is able to impose stability, investors and traders become more confident of the enforcement of contracts across jurisdictions; states become less worried by dependence and (potential) vulnerability when they don't expect patterns of interdependence to be ruptured; and powers are more able to focus on absolute than relative gains when they anticipate a peaceful future.

That said, I have urged two basic sets of considerations against realist and Leninist interpretations of these developments. In the first place, I have argued that the more or less steady international expansion of the scope and depth of the liberal economic order has been the result not simply of US coercive power but also of the positive-sum forms of collective empowerment derived from the incipient world-wide spread of Americanism and from coordinated economic interdependence. It is important to understand the collective benefits derived from the role of the United States as the leading source of innovation for key agents in the international economy as a whole – that is, the more or less continuous generation of technologies, practices and institutions that thrive in liberal markets (in short, Americanism) – as well as the positive-sum gains achieved by coordinating the United States, on the one side, and Americanism in the rest of the capitalist world, on the other. It is also important to register the degree to which even economies – such as China's or Russia's – which are configured in radically different ways to the property regimes and political systems of the West can and have benefited from international integration into this order. These latter aspects of American power are the material realities behind what Mead has described as 'harmonic convergence'; 'harmonic convergence', he says, '*was* the American project'.[3] And these realities of material interdependence are as much a part of the structure of the international system as are anarchy, coercive power and inequality.

To that extent, I agree with G. John Ikenberry that this 'order itself – built on the complex fusion of capitalist and democratic systems that cut across the advanced industrial world – is no longer supported by American power and leadership'. Or, rather, it is no longer *just* supported by American power and leadership. 'The order has taken on a life of its own. If we live in an era of "global empire",' says Ikenberry, 'it is not essentially an American empire but rather an empire of capitalist democracy.' This order 'is now a reality to which America itself must accommodate'.[4] Ikenberry's 'must' is surely normative as there are no guarantees that the United States will, in fact, continue in this manner. For, as I have also stressed, the distribution of economic power in this order is changing in dramatic ways and the Asian, and especially the Chinese, centres of accumulation and innovation are not especially well integrated into US-led forms of control. Moreover, there is no sign that the catch-up development of China or Russia, for example, will produce societies that are as open to political and geopolitical integration into this order as Western Europe and Japan were after the Second World War.

In this respect, we should recall that the uneven development of industrial capitalism on an international basis has always been a combined process, regularly throwing up new forms of hybrid society, routinely confounding expectations of linear and homogeneous development across a diverse range of societies and historical conditions – the 'empire of capitalist democracy' not only contains vibrant forms of authoritarian capitalism but also remains fractured on the geopolitical plane. It may be the case that the diffusion of industrial power has now both diminished US economic hegemony and made rival bids for hegemony unrealistic. It is probably also the case that the authoritarian capitalisms in China and Russia are more dependent on world markets than the older OECD economies and that they have more to gain (lose) from increased (diminished) economic integration. But these facts do not guarantee that a smooth and steady expansion of the empire of capitalist democracy is the wave of the future. Rival forms of capitalist development, conflicts between liberal and authoritarian political forms and geopolitical differences are still very much in evidence.

That said, I have stressed, secondly, the political and geo-strategic limits of military power in the contemporary international system, in which the sovereign nation-state is the dominant political form, where the mass of the population has been mobilized into national political fields, and in which there is no single, defining axis of geo-strategic competition. In conditions where the means of state building and industrial development are widely diffused, there are very substantial costs involved in any attempt to translate military power into coercive political advantage. And even the indirect use of military power to deter enemies and reassure allies is a complicated game. However, even if aspects of the militarism of the neo-conservative moment and the reckless reliance on military force of the Bush administration in the Middle East are likely to prove transient, the popular – even populist – elements of US foreign policy that marked the break with the conventions of the transatlantic-oriented elites is probably set to stay: as Mead perceptively remarks, because 'foreign policy is going to be expensive and demanding [it] can't be conducted over the heads or against the basic instincts of the American people'.[5]

The grounds for anticipating a continuation of the American project are that the United States has been the principal architect and beneficiary of the post-war reconstruction and subsequent development of the liberal capitalist international economic order, and that if it now attempts to use the uni-polar moment to abandon strategic restraint and pursue its interests at the expense of the other major centres of economic power, it will squander its remaining international political leadership. Indeed, in relation to resurgent Asia in particular, even the Bush administration has had some notable successes in more collective forms of engagement: better relations with both Japan and China; improved diplomacy with both India and Pakistan; and constructive discussions with China – especially after the appointment of Hank Paulson to Treasury Secretary – over questions of economic reform and international imbalances. Even in relation to European NATO and the European Union, there is some evidence that Washington may yet come to realize that Europe's military-strategic decline and weakness is as much a *problem* as an opportunity for the United States. In the long term, Charles Maier is surely right to suggest that 'the new wealth of Asia, the even partial union of Europe, and the slow, perilous diffusion of nuclear arsenals will set limits to the current interregnal imperium'.[6]

However, there are no guarantees that common interests will be realized, for the project of a liberal capitalist international order does not cancel the fundamentally anarchic character of geopolitics and the uneven distribution of coercive power among the major political actors. That said, understood as means to international order, liberal modes of international economic regulation do not aim to cancel the plurality of polities, or even the formal anarchy, of a system of sovereign states. Considered in its international dimensions, liberalism is not a set of proposals to supersede the historically given conditions of geopolitics, nor is it tied to claims that the consequent balance of power can be abolished by virtue of appeal to a harmony of interests.[7] Rather, the liberal project for international order aims to empower a world-wide civil society – especially a world-wide economy – in and against the powers of states and the system of states. It is an attempt to manage or mitigate questions of geopolitics and coercive power by subordinating as much of state activity and inter-state relations as is possible to the 'laws' of the market and the rights of property, on the assumption that, *au fond*, these laws serve the mutual interest.

The paradox of American power, then, is that its post-war international economic strategy has been broadly liberal – including a formal, *de jure* accommodation to liberal forms of sovereignty in an ever more post-colonial world of many states – albeit a highly selective and asymmetric form of liberalism, while its military policies have always striven for supremacy and a unilateral freedom of action. As we have seen, the United States now subsists in an economically multi-polar world, while confronting that order with military uni-polarity. To the extent that America's uni-polar moment can be sustained, this is likely to be a reasonably stable international order, notwithstanding imperialist adventures to pacify and discipline peripheral threats in strategically important regions. But military uni-polarity will only serve a collective function for the international economy to the extent that the United States is capable of exercising strategic restraint, thereby lessening the incentives of others to frustrate its purposes, and to the degree that it is able to define its interests in ways that accommodate the interests of other major centres of power in Europe and Asia.

Thus far, despite the provocations of the Bush administration, active balancing against the United States is not much in evidence. Yet nor is there any real evidence of new bandwagoning alongside it as opposed to attempts to draw on US primacy for purposes of regional balancing. But there are genuine indications of what has been called *soft* balancing. Soft balancing, as characterized by Stephen Walt, 'does not seek or expect to alter the overall distribution of capabilities. Instead . . . soft balancing is the *conscious coordination of diplomatic action in order to obtain outcomes contrary to U.S. preferences.*'[8] In terms of the analysis developed here, just as countries can coordinate *with* the United States, so they can coordinate *against* it; policy interdependence provides the terrain on which soft balancing takes place. Pertinent examples might include: the actions of France, Germany and Russia in the period between the first UN Security Council resolution (November 2002), directed against Iraq's presumed weapons programmes, and the US invasion of 2003; the common negotiating positions adopted by Brazil, China, India and South Africa in the World Trade Organization during the Doha round; the diplomatic engagements of Russia and China, Russia and Iran, China and the European Union, and China and Saudi Arabia – all of which signal the possibility of alignments that are not centred on Washington; and measures to hedge against the future such as the European Union's intermittent attempts to foster a more autonomous defence capability.

As to the longer term, Barry Buzan has argued that bids for super-power status on the part of the other major powers are limited by domestic constraints and the legitimacy that derives from the fact that the US-led international order accommodates a range of interests.[9] As far as Europe and transatlantic integration is concerned, I think this is substantially correct. China is another matter. Buzan notes that some aspects of China's social purposes and its international align-ments – territorial claims; nationalist mobilization, especially vis-à-vis Japan; persistence of an authoritarian polity; declared willingness to use force in certain circumstances (Taiwan); and explicit opposi-tion to US hegemony – are evidence that it may be a revisionist power, while others – the market orientation of its reforms and its World Trade Organization membership – suggest a more accommodating posture. The pressures on the side of accommodation, I suggest, are above all twofold: first, the fact of China's dependence for the foresee-able future on the world market and externally generated sources of technological innovation; and, secondly, China's predicament of military-strategic vulnerability.

As to the first of these, even if China's total GDP begins to rival that of the United States in the next several decades, its levels of per capita GDP and its productivity levels will continue to lag those of the US economy for a very long time. The prospects for China's stra-tegic position are much harder to predict, but it would not be surpris-ing if China were able to establish a credible nuclear deterrent over the next several decades and, at least, find means of checking US conventional supremacy in the East Asian region. And it is far less clear that the Chinese state would face the same kind of domestic constraints on a bid for a much more extensive regional and interna-tional role as would likely hamper any comparable EU initiatives. If this is so, then the United States will need to play the China card with subtlety and care, especially if, as I have suggested, the containment of China is not really an option, if only because the underlying issue is not only the rise of China as a *power* but also the ongoing processes of accumulation and development of industrial capitalism in emerg-ing Asia.

'Outside the scattered "black holes" of ethnic/religious conflict, many of them amid failing states and economies,' says Michael Mann, 'the world is not actually very dangerous. . . . Dangers loom *because* of American militarism.'[10] I think this line of interpretation is fundamentally mistaken. It is in error, in large part, because the con-juncture of contemporary geopolitics is anything other than benign. The current conjuncture is radically different from the post-war predicament in several key respects. In the first instance, there is no longer a single axis of strategic and ideological competition around which the United States can mobilize an alliance: the threat of WMD terrorism is real enough but it is not a strategic threat comparable to that posed by communism and Soviet power. The attempt to mobilize and brigade the rest of the world around the Manichaean divisions of the 'war on terror' have been a transparent failure and have done not a little to erode the legitimacy of US international political leadership.

Secondly, the *economic* uni-polar moment that the United States enjoyed vis-à-vis its capitalist allies after 1945 has given way to multi-polarity; and the international economy is undergoing a fundamental rebalancing in power and momentum towards emerging Asia, a region in which US power is not institutionalized to the degree that it is in the transatlantic arena. No other economy is going to overtake the US economy in terms of innovation and levels of productivity for the foreseeable future – the United States is not facing the predicament of Britain in the late nineteenth century (being overtaken by Germany and America) – but economic multi-polarity is now a permanent condition. And the Asian pole of that order is not under American control in the way that the transatlantic order is: there is no Asian counterpart to the EU and European NATO; the military alliance with Japan and the more recent rapprochement with India are not on a par with US–NATO integration (though that has been tested to the limit in Afghanistan); the degree of economic integration between the major Asian economies and the United States is less than across the Atlantic; and China will soon be a more important market than the United States for much of the region.

Thirdly, there are a range of new threats – the dangers of nuclear proliferation; the potential access of non-state actors to WMDs; the existence of weak and failing states across a broad swathe of strategically important and resource-rich territory from North Africa through the Middle East to Central Asia and beyond; the challenges posed by rising regional powers such as China and India; the troubled identity and orientation of what Brzezinski has called 'pivot' states such as Turkey, Ukraine and Iran;[11] and the transnational and global consequences of potential ecological and demographic crises – that can only be addressed collectively, if they can be addressed at all.

In short, the international system faces a series of changes and challenges that together make the prospects for a peaceful and stable future uncertain – to this extent the neo-conservative diagnosis was not in error. And while the Bush doctrine was seriously flawed as a grand strategy for the United States, and although elements of US policy – in particular the Iraq adventure – have been conducted with a reckless inattention to detail and consequences, the idea that dangers loom simply because of American militarism is a dangerous conceit that obscures the very real problems of managing coming geopolitical developments in a less brutal and unilateral manner. American militarism, we can agree, is not the answer, but the current conjuncture of world development is potentially very uncertain and constructive US engagement in managing it will be essential.

The fundamental *policy* question for the medium term, in my view, is whether the United States decides to keep faith with the project for a liberal international order or turns its back on it. At present, the United States is the only state that can violate the rules of this order with relative impunity and, given that no administration will willingly surrender military (and possibly now nuclear) supremacy – the Clinton administration was already committed, in the words of the 1998 National Security Strategy, to ensuring that US 'forces continue to have unchallenged superiority in the twenty-first century' – this means that keeping faith implies *self*-restraint. To be sure, unilateral actions can be checked by their consequences – Iraq may yet prove a salutary lesson in this respect – and, in the longer term, by others balancing against it. But if the United States can learn the virtues of self-restraint on a consistent basis, conditional on the similar restraint of others if and when they achieve a real capability to break the rules, it is likely to achieve far more for its own interests than if it pushes others into opposing positions. The day may yet come when the United States is compelled to respond to the power and geo-strategic initiatives of China, or the European Union, or even a resurgent Russia. For the foreseeable future, however, the choice to back or break with such elements of liberal international order as there are is still one that must be made in America, if it is to be made at all.

Yet the challenge is immense, for as Mead rightly says, responding constructively to this choice would involve something that the US political system has never yet been able to do: namely, to 'develop a coherent, politically sustainable strategy for American world leadership in *peacetime*'.[12] The obstacles are several. One the one hand, the compact between what Mead has called the Jacksonian school of American foreign policy, which embraces a populist, nationalist emphasis on the physical security of the United States, and the Hamiltonian alliance of the federal state and big business will not be easily undone. On the other hand, the Wilsonian impulses to spread US values and mores abroad, while never far from the surface in US politics, have been discredited and chastened by the neo-conservative blunders in the Middle East and the aftermath of the invasion of Iraq. And the Jeffersonian concern to avoid any foreign entanglements that might threaten liberties and democracy at home, which remains an attractive and resilient feature of American civil society and political culture, does not really speak to the choices that US foreign policy now faces. Forging an international leadership from this inheritance will be no easy task.

NOTES

Introduction: The American Project for a Liberal International Order

1 Quoted in Ferguson 2004: 80.
2 Quoted in Prestowitz 2003: 177.
3 Quoted in Wight 1986: 178.
4 Todd 2003: 7, original emphasis; cf. Brzezinski 1997 and 2004.
5 Buzan 2004: 157.
6 Crockatt 1993: 77.
7 Bull 1995 [1977]: 51.
8 The degree to which mutually recognized constitutive rules – in particular, various forms of sovereignty rules – have formed part of the structure of the international system is, of course, historically variable. The key issue at stake in the English school/constructivist debates is essentially one about the origins and importance of such rules. The real question is not for or against social constructionism as such; rather, the issues are: first, John Searle's (1995) question, *how* does social construction operate, secondly, as Ian Hacking (1999) asks, the social construction of *what*; and, thirdly, Stephen Krasner's (1999) pair of questions, how far does state-political action conform to the rules or norms of sovereignty, and how resilient are those rules across changing international environments?

Chapter 1   The American Ideology: Modernization Theory and the Neo-Conservatives

1 Letter to Arnold Ruge, 1843, available at *www.marxists.org/archive/ marx/works/1843/letters/43_09-alt.htm*.
2 Alexander 1995: 84.
3 Alexander 1995: 84.

4 That liberal imperialism is actual shows that it is possible, and that it is possible says that it is also real. But is the reality of the conjunction of liberalism and imperialism causal yet contingent or constitutive? Is it the case that unless liberalism is genuinely universal, it is merely the more or less extended licence of some exercised at the expense of others? For what it is worth, I don't think this is the case, but I don't have the space to argue the point here.

5 Alexander 1995: 33.

6 Before we proceed, it might be helpful to clarify a terminological issue that is liable to give rise to confusion. The phrase 'modernization theory' has been used in several different ways: first, some (e.g. Alexander) use it as virtually a synonym for what others refer to as the theory of 'industrial society', or at least that version of the theory dominant in the United States during the 1950s and 1960s, such that the work of modernization theory becomes more or less coterminous with non-Marxist, modern sociology; second, others (e.g. Giddens 1982) use it to refer to the work produced by the (Western) theorists of industrial society as they encountered the rest of the world after the Second World War, an intellectual and political engagement formed in the shadow of post-war reconstruction and the Cold War; and third, still others (e.g. Cammack 1997) use it to refer to a particularly naïve and optimistic set of schemas produced by that encounter, distinguishing the simplistic and general version from the more concrete and realistic 'doctrine for political development' adumbrated in the political development literature. My own view is that, depending on the purposes at hand, all and none of these distinctions can be drawn. Given the focus on global politics in what follows, I will primarily speak of modernization theory in the second sense distinguished above.

7 Alexander 1995: 11.

8 See Kumar 1978 for a detailed examination of this tradition of social and political thought.

9 Brubaker 1984 is the best study of Weber's varied attempts to grapple with the problems of rationality and rationalization.

10 Eisenstadt 1987: vii, emphasis added.

11 Eisenstadt 1987: vii. Eisenstadt is here recommending a movement from the former to the latter conception.

12 Ahmad 1992: 106.

13 This is precisely the identification that Huntington (1993 and 1996) would later question.

14 Leffler 1994.

15 Pollard 1985.

16 Smith 1981.

17 Wood 1986.

18 See Jackson 1990. Jackson, however, radically underestimates the role of the Cold War as well as indigenous nationalist movements in underwriting the new sovereignty regime.

19 Tilly 1990.
20 Krueger 1993: 48.
21 Gaddis 1982: 200.
22 Kuklick 2006.
23 Gaddis 1982: 208.
24 Rostow 1960: 174, 7.
25 Rostow 1960: 173.
26 Rostow 1971: 26.
27 Rostow 1971: 26.
28 Rostow 1971: 27.
29 Rostow 1971: 53.
30 Rostow 1971: 100, 98.
31 Rostow 1960: 174.
32 Rostow 1960: 174.
33 Rostow 1960: 8.
34 Rostow 1971: 100.
35 Rostow pre-empted Huntington (1968) by at least a decade.
36 Rostow 1971: 193–4.
37 Rostow 1971: 96.
38 Rostow 1971: 96.
39 Rostow 1971: 211.
40 Rostow 1971: 217–8, see also 226–7; and Rostow 1960: Ch.8.
41 Rostow 1960: 126, 128.
42 Rostow 1954: 88.
43 Rostow 1954: 244, 245.
44 Rostow 1960: 163, 166.
45 Kolko 1986: 321; see also Gaddis 1982: Ch.7.
46 Kennan 1952 [1947]: 112, 114.
47 Von Laue 1964: 15–16, 223. Note the antecedents of Fukuyama (1989 and 1992): 'the need for identification between rulers and ruled' = the desire for recognition; and 'the need for industrialization' = the demands or constraints of modern science and technology.
48 Von Laue 1964: 222.
49 Rostow 1971: 332.
50 Rostow 1990: x–xi.
51 Rostow 1990: xxiv.
52 Rostow 1990: xxxviii.
53 Rostow 1960: 90.
54 Rostow 1971: 314.
55 Perhaps the principal difficulty involved in assessing the contemporary status of modernization theory is that its various themes are now discussed in isolation from one another, resulting from the proliferation of competing alternative theories. In part this reflects the continuing separation of thinking about the 'international' from more general theories in the social sciences – something that, to his credit, Rostow never fell for. To some extent, it also reflects no more than the process

of specialization consequent upon an expanding division of intellectual and academic labour. But it also attests to a widely held scepticism about the possibility of all-encompassing critical theories of the kind offered by world systems theory. If one of the central problems of modernization theory was its false universalism, then it is not surprising that rival conceptions now eschew grand statements and opt instead for more particular claims.

56 Fukuyama 1989 and 1992.
57 Rosenberg 2001.
58 Rostow 1971: 331.
59 Smith 1985.
60 Fukuyama 1989 and 1992.
61 Kennedy 1988.
62 Mearsheimer 2001.
63 Huntington 1993 and 1996.
64 Friedman 1999.
65 Kaplan 1994.
66 Kissinger 2002: 25–6.
67 Buzan 2004: 80.
68 Reus-Smit 2004: 3.
69 Halper and Clarke 2004: 178.
70 Tertrais 2005: 10.
71 Discriminate deterrence had already proposed four new, additional weapons programmes as 'especially urgent': stealth systems for aircraft, missiles and satellites; 'smart' guided weapons with non-nuclear warheads and accurate guidance over long ranges; ballistic missile defences; and space-based capabilities for wartime operations.
72 Nasar 1998: 114.
73 The 'executive committee' of the US oil industry, the American Petroleum Institute, for example, argued for the lifting of economic sanctions against Iraq, Iran and Libya and, *sotto voce*, for a deal with Baghdad.
74 Lieven 2004: 11. See also Prestowitz 2003.
75 The issue of non-state actors gaining access to weapons of mass destruction had surfaced on the radar of the Clinton administration in early 1995. Indeed, according to Steve Coll (2004: 318), Clinton was particularly exercised by this matter.
76 Cooper 2004: 63, 65. It is perhaps significant for reckoning the strategic thinking of UK Prime Minister Tony Blair that Cooper was at one time a close adviser.
77 Cooper 2004: 24; see also R. Harvey 2003.
78 Kagan 2003.
79 *New York Times*, 8 March 1992; see also *www.pbs.org* (emphasis added).
80 Wohlforth 1999.
81 This is perhaps the key area of disagreement, theoretically speaking, between neo-conservatism and the nationalist right of Dick Cheney and Donald Rumsfeld.

82 Quoted in Reus-Smit 2004: 15.
83 See the characteristically astute remarks of Kissinger 2002: 27, 30.
84 Fukuyama 2006: 139.
85 See Daalder and Lindsay 2003.
86 Halper and Clarke's (2004: 19) statement that the liberal imperialism of the neo-conservatives is focused almost exclusively on 'the Middle East and military power, most of all the use of military power in the Middle East', is only a slight exaggeration.
87 Lieven (2004: 176) sees it as a form of 'national autism, an inability either to listen to others or to understand their reactions to U.S. behavior'.
88 Mann 2003: 24.
89 Todd 2003.
90 'Let arms cede to the toga', Tertrais 2005: 40.
91 Kupchan 2003: 215.
92 Ikenberry 2004a: 47; see also Kupchan 2003.
93 Ikenberry 2004b.
94 Buzan 2004: 148.
95 Ferguson 2004: 165.
96 Mann 2003: 82, 83.
97 Ignatieff 2003.
98 Kolko 2002.
99 Friedman 2003.
100 Bacevich 2002.
101 Clark 2003: 174, 186.
102 Ferguson 2004: 290, 211, 213.
103 Mann 2003: 97.
104 *Pro tem*, it is also the British way.
105 Halliday 2005: 214.
106 Todd 2003: 143–4.
107 Quoted in Lieven 2004: 6. As Lieven also suggests (172, 218), the Middle East 'is the great exception to [the] rule of the ultimate Realist domination of U.S. foreign policy' because, in his view, of an inflamed nationalism: 'The resulting influences on American thinking and policy sometimes stand quite outside any Realist – or indeed rational – framework of thought.' The consequence is that because of oil, Israel and nationalism, 'the United States appears hopelessly and permanently bound to an unstable, violent and hostile region', which is quite unlike 'all its other international military involvements', where 'the United States was able either to pacify an area [Western Europe, Japan, South Korea] or to withdraw from it [Indochina], or both'. This is fine as far as it goes, as long as we see that Lieven is here using 'realism' to indicate a measuring of means against ends, a more or less rational reckoning of costs and benefits. But, surely, it is the entanglement with the region rather than the inflamed nationalism *per se* that is the critical problem.

For it is the continued resistance of the Middle East to integration into a broadly liberal, coordinated international capitalist order and with this the inability of the United States to institutionalize a durable economic and political presence in the region that underpins the recurrent, even routine, reliance on coercive, often military, means.

Chapter 2   America's Transatlantic Empire: Where in the World Is America?

1 Alexander (1995: 8–9) does not recommend a 'return to . . . modernization theories of society as such', but he does contend that 'contemporary social theory must be much more sensitive to the apparent reconvergence of the world's regimes and that, as a result, we must try to incorporate some broad sense of the universal and shared elements of development into a critical, undogmatic, and reflexive theory of social change'.
2 Huntington 1996: 66.
3 Anderson 2002a: 23.
4 Quoted in Prestowitz 2003: 35.
5 Prestowitz 2003: 35.
6 Hardt and Negri 2000: xii.
7 Hardt and Negri 2000: 321.
8 Hardt and Negri 2000: xi.
9 Lieven 2000: xiv.
10 Quoted in Odom and Dujarric 2004: 50.
11 Ikenberry 2004b.
12 Emmott 2002; see also Emmott 2003.
13 Stedman Jones 1972: 217.
14 Lewis 1994: 152.
15 Fox 1944.
16 Anderson 2002b.
17 Gramsci 1971: 317.
18 Gramsci 1971: 318.
19 Gramsci 1971: 293.
20 Bright and Meyer 2002: 86.
21 Hardt and Negri 2000: 169.
22 Hardt and Negri 2000: 177.
23 See Tuck 1999.
24 Mill 2002 [1859]: 487.
25 Pagden 2001: 92.
26 Hardt and Negri 2000: 182.
27 O'Connor 1970: 118.
28 Meiksins Wood 2002: 23.
29 Maier 2006: 7.
30 Odom and Dujarric 2004: 48–9.

31 Chomsky 2003: 43, quoting Bacevich 2002: 215, original emphasis.
32 Chomsky 2003: 209.
33 Gill 2004: 42.
34 Chomsky 2003: 208.
35 Rogers 2000.
36 Chomsky (2003: 70), for example, sees the Cold War as 'in significant respects a "North–South" conflict writ large', while all those who argued that the Soviet Union was in some sense state-capitalist effectively see it in inter-imperial terms.
37 Todd 2003: 99, 109.
38 Todd 2003: 173.
39 Gill 2004: 25.
40 Todd 2003: 3; see also Meiksins Wood 2003.
41 Anderson 2002a: 23, 24.
42 D. Harvey 2003: 73, 201, 206.
43 Bacevich 2002: 215, emphasis removed.
44 Chomsky 2003: 156.
45 Meiksins Wood 2003: 167.
46 Hardt and Negri 2000; and Meiksins Wood 2003: 168.
47 Mearsheimer 2001.
48 Meiksins Wood 2003: 165.
49 Chomsky 2003: 165.
50 Peter Gowan is probably the best exponent of the first alternative, Ellen Meiksins Wood of the second, and Noam Chomsky of the third.
51 D. Harvey 2003: 103.
52 Marx 1973 [1858]: 539, 542; also quoted in Albo 2003 – a key contribution.
53 Hirschman, quoted in Baldwin 1989: 178.
54 Baldwin 1989: 174.
55 Gruber 2000: 7, 50.
56 Barzel 2002.
57 Olson 2000: 61, emphasis added.
58 Grieco 1993: 127.
59 Waltz 1979: 105–6, original emphasis.
60 Waltz 1979: 131. As an illustration, Robert Reich (1990), later to become Secretary of State for Labor in the Clinton administration, conducted an informal poll and asked a series of business and financial leaders, civil servants and politicians which of the following scenarios they favoured. Scenario 1: by 2000, US national income increases by 25 per cent and Japan's by 75 per cent. Scenario 2: by 2000, US income increases by 10 per cent and Japan's by 10.3 per cent. Reich reported that nearly everyone he spoke to (except the economists) preferred the second alternative.
61 Powell 1994; see also Snidal 1993.
62 Gruber 2000: 24, original emphasis.
63 Grieco 1993: 129.

64 Schelling 1960: 4–5.
65 Lundestad 1998: 4.
66 Milward 1992.
67 NATO's first Secretary General, Lord Ismay, said the alliance had been created to keep the 'Russians out, the Germans down and the Americans in'.
68 Lawrence 1996: 17.
69 Meier 1998: 252.
70 Hufbauer 1990.
71 Grahl 2004: 285.
72 Lawrence 1996: 59.
73 Crafts 2000: 24.
74 Glyn 2006: 8.
75 Crafts 2000: 37.
76 Glyn 2006: 79.
77 Glyn 2006: 61.
78 Grahl 2004: 297.
79 Todd 2003: 172.
80 See DePorte 1979.
81 Kagan 2002: 23, 25, 26.
82 Odom and Dujarric 2004: 37, 63, 60–1. However, despite the implications of Odom's and Dujarric's title, there is nothing 'inadvertent' about this empire.
83 Gowan 2004: 492, 498.
84 As Jon Elster (1985: 406) has noted, 'there are two ways in which group interest can shape political policies: by serving as a maximand for the policy choices or as a constraint on them'.
85 For an important discussion of the differences between exchange, conflict and coordination theories of social order in general and an investigation of liberalism, constitutionalism and democracy in these terms, see Hardin 1999.
86 See Axelrod 1984.

Chapter 3   American Oil, World Oil: Resources, Conflicts, Control and Scarcity

1 Klare 2003: 180.
2 Klare 2003: 181.
3 Klare 2003: 7, 72.
4 Rutledge 2005.
5 Rutledge 2005: 65. In fact Rutledge goes so far as to suggest that the administration was prepared to conduct the Iraq adventure as a net loss, since the large social costs are paid for by all taxpayers whereas the smaller benefits accrue to private companies.
6 A point that is well made by Goel 2004.

7 There is now something of a consensus on this across the political spectrum. On the left, see, for example, Callinicos 2003; Gowan 2002; and D. Harvey 2003; and, on the right, Soros 2004. There are dissenting voices: Halper and Clarke (2004) assert that the neo-conservatives who influenced policy after 9/11 had little interest in economics and that oil was not a major part of their thinking about Iraq.

8 Rutledge 2005: 205–6.

9 Rutledge 2005: 2.

10 Porter 2001.

11 On the role of oil in relation to US hegemony in the post-war, Cold War epoch, see Bromley 1991.

12 D. Harvey 2003: 85.

13 O'Brien 2003: 118.

14 Prestowitz 2003: 87.

15 Rutledge 2005: 19.

16 The Red Line Agreement (of July 1928) was a production-sharing deal among the companies that formed the consortium, the Turkish (later Iraq) Petroleum Company, operating in the area defined by the former Ottoman Empire – it was later extended to other parts of the Middle East. The Achnacarry (or 'As Is') Agreement (of August 1928) was a complementary agreement – originally concluded among Exxon, BP and Royal Dutch/Shell, though later extended to the other major companies – over marketing and pricing.

17 'Prorationing' was the officially sanctioned, organized sharing of demand among independent producers introduced to cope with oversupply and falling prices in the inter-war period.

18 Enrico Mattei, the head of Italy's state-owned Ente Nazionale Idrocarburi (ENI), is credited with coining the term 'Sette Sorrelle', the Seven Sisters, to describe these companies (minus CFP). But CFP was in both the consortium that controlled Iranian oil after the Shah's coup against Mossadegh and the Iraq Petroleum Company – it was ignored because it didn't fit in with Mattei's characterization of an 'Anglo-Saxon' cartel.

19 See, especially, Blair 1976.

20 Shaffer 1983.

21 International Energy Agency 2004.

22 To be sure, many industry experts believe these kinds of increases in output to be infeasible and many economists question the assumptions underling the specific predictions about increasing demand, but these are the policy statements of the US government and the principal coordinating body of the main oil-consuming nations.

23 These are only approximate measures of import dependence as even net importing regions like the United States also export some of their production, largely in order to balance the quality of the oil needed for refining.

24 Prestowitz 2003: 82, 91, 83.

25 Thus, President Nixon's televised address of 7 November 1973: 'Let us unite in committing the resources of this nation to a major new endeavor, an endeavor that in this bicentennial era we can appropriately call "Project Independence." . . . Let us set as our national goal, in the spirit of Apollo, with the determination of the Manhattan Project, that by the end of this decade we will have developed the potential to meet our own energy needs without depending on any foreign enemy – I mean, energy – sources. . . . We have an energy crisis, but there is no crisis of the American spirit' (quoted in Skeet 1988: 117).

26 See, especially, Hartshorn 1993.

27 See Roncaglia 1985.

28 See, in particular, Skeet 1988 and Terzian 1985.

29 I have described and analysed these development in more detail in Bromley 1991.

30 Shlaim 1995: 36.

31 Hartshorn's (1993: 22) authoritative account notes that Vice-President George H. Bush, during the Reagan era, intervened with the Saudis during the mid-1980s, when Saudi policy was pushing oil prices too low for US concerns – driving high-cost US producers out of the market – 'arguably his single most effective political act while Vice-President'. On the links between pricing and military decisions, see Kupchan 1987 and, in particular, McNaugher 1985.

32 The RDF, later under US Central Command, was established to intervene in cases of regional conflict that threatened the security of supply of Gulf oil, but after the Soviet invasion of Afghanistan in December 1979, its official, primary mission was to protect the Iranian oilfields against a Soviet attack.

33 Quoted from an interview with *Nouvel Observateur*, 15–21 January 1998, in Johnson 2002: xiii.

34 Coll 2004: 593.

35 Quoted in Coll 2004: 62.

36 Quoted in Bennett Jones 2003: 200.

37 Coll 2004: 239.

38 Rashid 1998: 86.

39 Quoted in Usher 2006.

40 Halliday 2002: 45.

41 Kolko 2002: 9.

42 Roy 2004.

43 Achcar 2002.

44 Gray 2005: 214–15, 228.

45 Coll 2004: 343.

46 Woodward 2003: 35.

47 Abou Zahab and Roy 2004: 4, 74.

48 Schelling 1960: 11.

49 Achcar 2002: 69.

50 Lamb 2002: 27.

51 Wishnick 2004: 6.
52 The real case is set out most powerfully in Pollack 2002.
53 Porter 2001: 7.
54 Wishnick 2002.
55 See the important analysis by Goel 2004.
56 According to Bob Woodward (2003), President Bush assured President Putin that US bases in the region would not be permanent.
57 National Energy Policy Development Group 2001: Chapter 8: 3–4.
58 Vitalis 1997: 16; for a more detailed discussion, see Bromley 1998.
59 Renner 2003.
60 Rutledge 2005: 194.
61 Yergin 2006: 75.
62 See Hartshorn 1993.
63 *BP Statistical Review of World Energy 2005*: 4, emphasis added.
64 Jaccard 2005: 155.
65 Adelman 2004: 18.
66 Jaccard 2005: 154.
67 Jaccard 2005: 14.
68 See Simmons 2005 and Maugeri 2006.
69 Rutledge 2005: 201.
70 *The Economist* 2006: 82.
71 Of course, this doesn't solve the global warming problem, for as Jaccard (2005: 222) also observes: 'None of the major ways of producing oil and its refined petroleum products (from conventional oil, unconventional oil, coal or natural gas) ha[s] a cost of production in excess of $40/barrel. . . . This suggests that consumption of refined petroleum products must be constrained by policy; it is not resource depletion and the resulting high prices that will save the world from oil-related pollution.'
72 Jaccard 2005: 67.
73 Jaccard 2005: 238.
74 With the development of carbon capture and storage technologies, these things could even be done with very low carbon emissions into the atmosphere.
75 The phrase 'hungry giants' was used by Raymond Vernon (1983) to describe competition between the United States and Japan for energy resources. China has replaced Japan in current scare-mongering.

Chapter 4   American Power, the Future of the Dollar and the Challenge of China

1 Nye 1990.
2 Kennedy 1988, Todd 2003 and Kupchan 2003.
3 Maddison 2006: 142–9.
4 Mearsheimer 2001.

5 D. Harvey 2003.
6 Kupchan 2003: 275.
7 B. Cohen 1998: 11.
8 B. Cohen 1998: 13.
9 De Grauwe 1989: 3–4.
10 De Grauwe 1989: 2.
11 It is not, strictly speaking, a theorem since, according to Cooter (1987: 67), attempts to formalize it 'encounter obstacles which suggest that it is probably false or a mere tautology'.
12 Acemoglu 2002: 1, 2, 3, original emphasis.
13 De Grauwe 1989: 6. Prior to the emergence of modern central banking systems, private banks appropriated the gains from increasing returns and competition between banks often led to serious monetary crisis. In some developing countries with 'repressed' financial systems the supply of money is fully under state control: the state, through the central bank, has a monopoly over the issue of both the currency *and* deposit accounts. It is well known that conventional economic theory – in particular, the general theory of equilibrium due to Arrow and Debreu – has difficulty incorporating any role for money because with complete information and perfect foresight, as well as trust in the institutions of property and contract, there would be no need of 'outside' money as the economy could be run on 'perfect individual credit' endogenously creating 'inside' money, in which all assets had matching liabilities. 'Outside' money is money that forms an asset for those who hold it but is not a liability for other agents in the economy. Although fiat money is legally a liability of the government, it is, in effect, outside money, since private agents cannot force the state to redeem or honour its liabilities. To be sure, the *de jure* right of the state to issue and control the national currency in a regime of fiat money is limited *de facto* given that when the 'price of government enforced credit arrangements become[s] too high, alternative means are sought' by private agents. At the other end of the spectrum, in a 'sell-all economy', in which 'all individuals are required to send all assets to market, maintaining only their ownership claims', then 'there is no credit . . . and the transformation of ownership bundles is achieved via a minimal financial structure, the single, simultaneous move, price-formation market. All trades require cash. This amounts to the complete monetization of wealth, which equals the volume of transactions.' To be sure, these models are simply theoretical extremes, violently abstracted from the realities of actual capitalist economies. Nevertheless, they serve to illustrate the 'essence of the monetary problem', which is the 'need for individual trust or for substitutes', where the 'economic value of trust in exchange' depends on the potential gains from trade and the institutional nature of the trading process. See Quint and Shubik 2004: 35, 29, 36.
14 See Cohen 1971.
15 Krugman 1992: 173.

16 Krugman 1992: 170–3, original emphasis.
17 Krugman 1992: 192, original emphasis. As Krugman (1992: 182) notes: 'In principle . . . a change in the desired currency composition of liquid assets can be accommodated without any redistribution of wealth. Banks could convert their depositors' Eurodollar deposits into [euro-denominated] deposits at the current exchange rate; the Federal Reserve could buy up Treasury bills while selling [euro-]denominated securities. The currency transformation need not involve capital gains and losses to anyone.'
18 Krugman 1992: 182.
19 Cline 2005: 34, 46.
20 Frankel 2006: 11.
21 Cline 2005: 49.
22 Hausmann and Sturzenegger 2006.
23 Chinn and Frankel 2005: 7–8.
24 Krugman and Obstfeld 1997: 514.
25 Padoa-Schioppa and Saccomanni 1994: 238.
26 De Grauwe 1989: 138.
27 Corden 1994: 187, 242, original emphasis.
28 See Eichengreen 1994 and Rogoff 2002.
29 Corden 1994: 166–7.
30 Eichengreen, Hausmann and Panizza 2003.
31 McKinnon 2005a.
32 McKinnon and Schnabl 2004: 343, original emphasis.
33 McKinnon 2003: 3, 5, 6.
34 McKinnon 2001: 11.
35 McKinnon 2005b: 4.
36 Dumas and Choyleva 2006: 3. The importance of these connections is illustrated by the fact that even a real appreciation of the renminbi against the dollar of 40 per cent would amount to a trade-weighted appreciation of about only 8 per cent if China's trading partners also revalued their currencies. In order to effect such changes, the countries concerned would have to find a way of coordinating themselves out of the Prisoners' Dilemmas they face.
37 Cline 2005: 220, 66.
38 Kitchen 2006.
39 Godley 2003 and Izurieta 2005.
40 McKinnon 2005a: 7.
41 Bergsten 2004: 82.
42 Godley and Lavoie 2004.
43 Summers 2006.
44 Goldstein 2004: 42.
45 Grahl 2004: 291. This is probably a slight exaggeration: Merrill Lynch put the figure at 44 per cent in 2004.
46 B. Cohen 1998: 156.
47 Grahl 2001: 29, 30, 37.

48 Bergsten 2002: 2.
49 Milesi-Ferretti 2007 and Wade 2007.
50 Grahl 2004: 292.
51 Chinn and Frankel 2005: 22.
52 Obstfeld and Rogoff 2005 and Krugman 2007.
53 Cooper 2005.
54 Arrighi 2005.
55 D. Harvey 2003.
56 Mearsheimer 2001: 401–2.
57 Winters and Yusuf 2006: 15, Table 1.3.
58 Baumol 2002.
59 Odom and Dujarric 2004: 128, 161.
60 IMF 2006: Ch.3: 4.
61 Glyn 2005.
62 Wolf 2004: 144.
63 *The Economist* 2004: 4.
64 Winters and Yusuf 2006: 7.
65 Glyn 2005: 15, 36.
66 Yusuf, Nabeshima and Perkins 2006: 34.
67 Hausmann, Lim and Spence 2006: 1.
68 Naughton 1995.
69 Rodrik 2006: 1.
70 Rodrik 2006: 4, 23.
71 Bosworth and Collins 2007.
72 Yusuf, Nabeshima and Perkins 2006: 38.
73 D. Cohen 1998: 26.
74 Young 1995.
75 Winters and Yusuf 2006: 21.
76 Winters and Yusuf 2006: 22.
77 Fehr, Jokisch and Kotlikoff 2005.
78 Glyn 2006.
79 Lieber and Press 2006: 47–8.
80 Lieber and Press 2006: 49.
81 Lieber and Press 2006: 52.
82 Gowan 2002: 22.
83 Mearsheimer 2001.
84 See Chapter 3.
85 Odom and Dujarric 2004: 92.
86 Gray 2005: 201.
87 Goldstein 2001: 844.
88 Walt 2005: 159.
89 Fukuyama 2006: 33 and Walt 2005: 159.
90 Freedman 2004: 86.
91 Allison 2005, but see also Walt 2005.
92 Bennett Jones 2003: 103.

93 Kissinger 2002: 79.
94 Walt 2005: 241.
95 Walt 2005.
96 Halliday 2001: 57.
97 Summers 2004.
98 Walt 2000: 11–12.

Conclusion: The Prospects for a Liberal International Order

1 Brzezinski 2004: 18.
2 Mead 2005: 4.
3 Mead 2005: 54, original emphasis.
4 Ikenberry 2006: 8, 3.
5 Mead 2005: 127.
6 Maier 2006: 15.
7 The *locus classicus* of this thoroughly misconceived charge is Waltz 1959.
8 Walt 2005: 126, original emphasis.
9 Buzan 2004: Chapter 4.
10 Mann 2003: 266, original emphasis.
11 Brzezinski 1997: Chapter 1.
12 Mead 2002: 321, emphasis added.

BIBLIOGRAPHY

Mariam Abou Zahab and Olivier Roy (2004) *Islamist Networks*, London: Hurst & Company.

Daron Acemoglu (2002) 'Why Not a Political Coase Theorem?', NBER Working Paper No. 9377, available at *http://www.nber.org/papers/w9377.*

Gilbert Achcar (2002) *The Clash of Barbarisms*, New York: Monthly Review Press.

Morris Adelman (2004) 'The Real Oil Problem', in *Regulation* 27: 1.

Aijaz Ahmad (1992) *In Theory*, London: Verso.

Greg Albo (2003) 'The Old and New Economics of Imperialism', in Leo Panitch and Colin Leys, eds, *Socialist Register 2004*, London: Merlin Press.

Jeffrey Alexander (1995) *Fin de Siècle Social Theory*, London: Verso.

Graham Allison (2005) *Nuclear Terrorism*, London: Constable.

Perry Anderson (2002a) 'Internationalism: A Breviary', in *New Left Review* II: 14.

Perry Anderson (2002b) 'Force And Consent', in *New Left Review* II: 17.

Giovanni Arrighi (2005) 'Hegemony Unravelling', in *New Left Review* II: 32.

Robert Axelrod (1984) *The Evolution of Co-operation*, Harmondsworth: Penguin.

Andrew Bacevich (2002) *American Empire*, Cambridge, Mass.: Harvard University Press.

David Baldwin (1989) *Paradoxes of Power*, Oxford: Basil Blackwell.

Yoram Barzel (2002) *A Theory of the State*, Cambridge: Cambridge University Press.

William J. Baumol (2002) *The Free-Market Innovation Machine.* Princeton: Princeton University Press.

Owen Bennett Jones (2003) *Pakistan*, New Haven: Yale University Press.

C. Fred Bergsten (2002) 'The Euro Versus the Dollar', presented at the annual meeting of the American Economic Association, Atlanta, USA, 4 January.

C. Fred Bergsten (2004) 'The Risks Ahead for the World Economy', in *The Economist*, 11 September.

John Blair (1976) *The Control of Oil*, New York: Pantheon Books.

Barry Bosworth and Susan M. Collins (2007) 'Accounting for Growth: Comparing China and India', available at *http://www.tcf.or.jp/data/2006120607_B_Bosworth-S_Collins.pdf*.

Charles Bright and Michael Meyer (2002) 'Where in the World Is America? The History of the United States in the Global Age', in Thomas Bender, ed., *Rethinking American History in a Global Age*, Berkeley: University of California Press.

Simon Bromley (1991) *American Hegemony and World Oil*, Cambridge: Polity Press.

Simon Bromley (1998) 'Oil and the Middle East: The End of US Hegemony?', in *Middle East Report* No. 208.

Rogers Brubaker (1984) *The Limits of Rationality*, London: George Allen & Unwin.

Zbigniew Brzezinski (1997) *The Grand Chessboard*, New York: Basic Books.

Zbigniew Brzezinski (2004) *The Choice*, New York: Basic Books.

Hedley Bull (1995) [1977] *The Anarchical Society* (2nd edn), London: Macmillan.

Barry Buzan (2004) *The United States and the Great Powers*, Cambridge: Polity Press.

Alex Callinicos (2003) *The New Mandarins of American Power*, Cambridge: Polity Press.

Paul Cammack (1997) *Capitalism and Democracy in the Third World*, London: Leicester University Press.

Menzie Chinn and Jeffrey Frankel (2005) 'Will the Euro Eventually Surpass the Dollar as Leading International Reserve Currency?', Harvard University RWP05-064, available at *http://ssrn.com/abstract=806288*.

Noam Chomsky (2003) *Hegemony or Survival*, London: Hamish Hamilton.

Wesley Clark (2003) *Winning Modern Wars*, New York: Public Affairs.

William Cline (2005) *The United States as a Debtor Nation*, New York: Institute for International Economics.

Benjamin Cohen (1971) *The Future of Sterling as an International Currency*, London: Macmillan.

Benjamin Cohen (1998) *The Geography of Money*, New York: Cornell University Press.

Daniel Cohen (1998) *The Wealth of the World and the Poverty of Nations*, Cambridge, Mass.: MIT Press.

Steve Coll (2004) *Ghost Wars*, London: Penguin.

Richard Cooper (2005) 'Living with Global Imbalances', Institute for International Economics, Policy Brief, October.

Robert Cooper (2004) *The Breaking of Nations* (revised edn), London: Atlantic Books.

Robert Cooter (1987) 'The Coase Theorem', in John Eatwell, Murray Milgate and Peter Newman, eds, *The New Palgrave Dictionary of Economics: Allocation, Information and Markets*, London: Macmillan.

W. Max Corden (1994) *Economic Policy, Exchange Rates, and the International System*, Oxford: Oxford University Press.

Nicholas Crafts (2000) 'Globalization and Growth in the Twentieth Century', IMF Working Paper WP/00/44.

Richard Crockatt (1993) 'Theories of Stability and the End of the Cold War', in Mike Bowker and Robin Brown, eds, *From Cold War to Collapse*, Cambridge: Cambridge University Press.

Ivo Daalder and James Lindsay (2003) *America Unbound*, Washington, DC: Brookings Institution.

Paul De Grauwe (1989) *International Money*, Oxford: Clarendon Press.

Anton DePorte (1979) *Europe between the Superpowers*, New Haven: Yale University Press.

Charles Dumas and Diana Choyleva (2006) *The Bill from the China Shop*, London: Profile Books.

The Economist (2004) 'The Dragon and the Eagle', 2 October 2004.

The Economist (2005) 'Oil in Troubled Waters', 30 April.

The Economist (2006) 'Steady as She Goes', 22 April.

Barry Eichengreen (1994) *International Monetary Arrangements for the 21st Century*, Washington, DC: Brookings Institution.

Barry Eichengreen, Ricardo Hausmann and Ugo Panizza (2003) 'Currency Mismatches, Debt Intolerance and Original Sin: Why They Are Not the Same and Why It Matters', NBER Working Paper No. 10036, available at *http://papers.ssrn.com/sol3/papers.cfm?abstract_id=459407*.

Shmuel Eisenstadt (1987) *European Civilization in Comparative Perspective*, Oslo: Oslo University Press.

Jon Elster (1985) *Making Sense of Marx*, Cambridge: Cambridge University Press.

Bill Emmott (2002) 'Present at the Creation', in *The Economist*, 29 June.

Bill Emmott (2003) *20:21 Vision*, London: Penguin.

Hans Fehr, Sabine Jokisch and Laurence J. Kotlikoff (2005) 'Will China Eat Our Lunch or Take Us Out for Dinner? Simulating the Demographic, Fiscal, and Economic Transition Paths of the U.S., EU, Japan, and China', NBER Working Paper No. 11668, available at *http://ssrn.com/abstract=819829*.

Niall Ferguson (2004) *Colossus*, London: Allen Lane.

William Fox (1944) *The Superpowers*, New York: Harcourt Brace.

Jeffrey Frankel (2006) 'Global Imbalances and Low Interest Rates: An Equilibrium Model vs a Disequilibrium Reality', Harvard University RWP06-035, available at *http://ssrn.com/abstract=902385*.

Lawrence Freedman (2004) *Deterrence*, Cambridge: Polity Press.
Thomas Friedman (1999) *The Lexus and the Olive Tree*, London: HarperCollins.
Thomas Friedman (2003) *Longitudes and Attitudes*, London: Penguin.
Francis Fukuyama (1989) 'The End of History', in *The National Interest*, Summer.
Francis Fukuyama (1992) *The End of History and the Last Man*, London: Penguin.
Francis Fukuyama (2006) *After the Neocons*, London: Profile Books.
John Lewis Gaddis (1982) *Strategies of Containment 1982*, Oxford: Oxford University Press.
Anthony Giddens (1982) *Sociology*, London: Macmillan.
Stephen Gill (2004) 'The Contradictions of American Supremacy', in Leo Panitch and Colin Leys, eds, *Socialist Register 2005*, London: Merlin Press.
Andrew Glyn (2005) 'Global Imbalances', in *New Left Review* II: 34.
Andrew Glyn (2006) *Capitalism Unleashed*, Oxford: Oxford University Press.
Wynne Godley (2003) 'The US Economy', Jerome Levy Economics Institute.
Wynne Godley and Marc Lavoie (2004) 'Simple Open Economy Macro with Comprehensive Accounting', Cambridge Endowment for Research in Finance, University of Cambridge, April.
Ran Goel (2004) 'A Bargain Born of a Paradox', in *New Political Economy* 9: 4.
Avery Goldstein (2001) 'The Diplomatic Face of China's Grand Strategy', in *The China Quarterly* 168.
Morris Goldstein (2004) 'Adjusting China's Exchange Rate Policies', paper at IMF seminar on China's Foreign Exchange System, Dalian, China, 26–7 May.
Peter Gowan (2002) 'The American Campaign for Global Sovereignty', in *Socialist Register 2003*, London: Merlin Press.
Peter Gowan (2004) 'Contemporary Intra-Core Relations and World Systems Theory', in *Journal of World Systems Research* X: 2.
John Grahl (2001) 'Globalized Finance', in *New Left Review* II: 8.
John Grahl (2004) 'The European Union and American Power', in Leo Panitch and Colin Leys, eds, *Socialist Register 2005*, London: Merlin Press.
Antonio Gramsci (1971) *Selections from the Prison Notebooks of Antonio Gramsci* (edited and translated by Qunitin Hoare and Geoffrey Nowell Smith), London: Lawrence and Wishart.
Colin Gray (2005) *Another Bloody Century*, London: Weidenfeld and Nicolson.
Joseph Grieco (1993) 'Anarchy and the Limits of Cooperation', in David Baldwin, ed., *Neorealism and Neoliberalism*, New York: Columbia University Press.

Lloyd Gruber (2000) *Ruling the World*, Princeton: Princeton University Press.
Ian Hacking (1999) *The Social Construction of What?* Cambridge, Mass.: Harvard University Press.
Fred Halliday (2001) *The World at 2000*, Basingstoke: Palgrave.
Fred Halliday (2002) *Two Hours That Shook the World*, London: Saqi Books.
Fred Halliday (2005) *100 Myths about the Middle East*, London: Saqi Books.
Stefan Halper and Jonathan Clarke (2004) *America Alone*, Cambridge: Cambridge University Press.
Russell Hardin (1999) *Liberalism, Constitutionalism, and Democracy*, Oxford: Oxford University Press.
Michael Hardt and Antonio Negri (2000) *Empire*, Cambridge, Mass.: Harvard University Press.
John Hartshorn (1993) *Oil Trade*, Cambridge: Cambridge University Press.
David Harvey (2003) *The New Imperialism*, Oxford: Oxford University Press.
Robert Harvey (2003) *Global Disorder*, London: Constable & Robinson.
Ricardo Hausmann, Elim Lim and A. Michael Spence (2006) 'China and the Global Economy: Medium-Term Issues and Options – a Synthesis Report', Harvard University, KSG Working Paper No. RWP06-029, available at *http://ssrn.com/abstract=902379*.
Ricardo Hausmann and Frederic Sturzenegger (2006) 'Global Imbalances or Bad Accounting? The Missing Dark Matter in the Wealth of Nations', Centre for International Development Working Paper No. 124, Harvard University, January, available at *http://www.cid.harvard.edu/cidwp/pdf/124.pdf*.
Gary Hufbauer, ed. (1990) *1992: An American Perspective*, Washington, DC: Brookings Institution.
Samuel Huntington (1968) *Political Order in Changing Societies*, New Haven: Yale University Press.
Samuel Huntington (1993) 'The Clash of Civilizations?', in *Foreign Affairs* 72: 3.
Samuel Huntington (1996) *The Clash of Civilizations and the Remaking of World Order*, New York: Simon & Schuster.
Michael Ignatieff (2003) *Empire Lite*, London: Vintage.
G. John Ikenberry (2004a) 'A Liberal Leviathan', in *Prospect*, October.
G. John Ikenberry (2004b) 'Liberal Hegemony or Empire?', in David Held and Mathias Koenig-Archibugi, eds, *American Power in the Twenty-First Century*, Cambridge: Polity Press.
G. John Ikenberry (2006) *Liberal Order and Imperial Ambitions*, Cambridge: Polity Press.
IMF (2006) *World Economic Outlook*, September, Washington, DC.
International Energy Agency (2004) *World Energy Outlook 2004*, Paris.

Alex Izurieta (2005) 'Can the Growth Patterns of the U.S. Economy be Sustained by the Rest of the World?', Cambridge Endowment for Research in Finance, University of Cambridge, May.

Mark Jaccard (2005) *Sustainable Fossil Fuels*, Cambridge: Cambridge University Press.

Robert Jackson (1990) *Quasi-Sovereignty*, Cambridge: Cambridge University Press.

Chalmers Johnson (2002) *Blowback*, London: Time Warner.

Robert Kagan (2002) 'The Power Divide', in *Prospect*, August.

Robert Kagan (2003) *Paradise and Power*, London: Atlantic Books.

Robert Kaplan (1994) 'The Coming Anarchy', in *Atlantic Monthly*, February.

George Kennan (1952) [1947] *American Diplomacy 1900–1950*, London: Secker & Warburg.

Paul Kennedy (1988) *The Rise and Fall of the Great Powers*, London: Unwin Hyman.

Henry Kissinger (2002) *Does America Need a Foreign Policy?* (revised edn), London: Free Press.

John Kitchen (2006) 'Sharecroppers or Shrewd Capitalists? Projections of the U.S. Current Account, Intended Income Flows, and Net International Debt', available at *http://users.starpower.net/jkitch/ShareShrewd.pdf*.

Michael Klare (2003) *Blood and Oil*, London: Hamish Hamilton.

Gabriel Kolko (1986) *Vietnam*, London: Allen & Unwin.

Gabriel Kolko (2002) *Another Century of War?* New York: The New Press.

Stephen Krasner (1999) *Sovereignty: Organized Hypocrisy*, Princeton: Princeton University Press.

Anne Krueger (1993) *Economic Policies at Cross-Purposes*, Washington, DC: Brookings Institution.

Paul Krugman (1992) *Currencies and Crises*, Cambridge, Mass.: MIT Press.

Paul Krugman (2007) 'Will There Be a Dollar Crisis', in *Economic Policy* 22: 51.

Paul Krugman and Maurice Obstfeld (1997) *International Economics* (4th edn), Reading, Mass.: Addison-Wesley.

Bruce Kuklick (2006) *Blind Oracles*, Princeton: Princeton University Press.

Krishan Kumar (1978) *Industrial Society*, Harmondsworth: Penguin.

Charles Kupchan (1987) *The Persian Gulf and the West*, London: Allen and Unwin.

Charles Kupchan (2003) *The End of the American Era*, New York: Random House.

Christina Lamb (2002) *The Sewing Circles of Herat*, London: HarperCollins.

Robert Lawrence (1996) *Regionalism, Multilateralism and Deeper Integration*, Washington, DC: Brookings Institution.

Melvin Leffler (1994) 'National Security and US Foreign Policy', in David Painter, ed., *Origins of the Cold War*, London: Routledge.

Bernard Lewis (1994) *The Shaping of the Modern Middle East*, Oxford: Oxford University Press.

Keir Lieber and Daryl Press (2006) 'The Rise of U.S. Nuclear Primacy', in *Foreign Affairs* 85: 2.

Anatol Lieven (2004) *America Right or Wrong*, London: HarperCollins.

Dominic Lieven (2000) *Empire*, London: Pimlico.

Geir Lundestad (1998) *'Empire' by Integration*, Oxford: Oxford University Press.

Ronald McKinnon (2001) 'The International Dollar Standard and Sustainability of the U.S. Current Account Deficit', available at *http://www.stanford.edu/~mckinnon/*.

Ronald McKinnon (2003) 'The World Dollar Standard and Globalization', available at *http://www.stanford.edu/~mckinnon/*.

Ronald McKinnon (2005a) 'Trapped by the International Dollar Standard', available at *http://www.stanford.edu/~mckinnon/*.

Ronald McKinnon (2005b) 'China's New Exchange Rate Policy', available at *http://www.stanford.edu/~mckinnon/*.

Ronald McKinnon and Gunther Schnabl (2004) 'The East Asian Dollar Standard, Fear of Floating, and Original Sin', in *Review of Development Economics* 8: 3.

Thomas McNaugher (1985) *Arms and Oil*, Washington, DC: Brookings Institution.

Angus Maddison (2006) *The World Economy, Volume 1: A Millennial Perspective*, Paris: OECD.

Charles Maier (2006) *Among Empires*, Cambridge, Mass.: Harvard University Press.

Michael Mann (2003) *Incoherent Empire*, London: Verso.

Karl Marx (1973) [1858] *Grundrisse* (translated by Martin Nicolaus), Harmondsworth: Penguin.

Leonardo Maugeri (2006) 'Two Cheers for Expensive Oil', in *Foreign Affairs* 85: 2.

Walter Russell Mead (2002) *Special Providence*, London: Routledge.

Walter Russell Mead (2005) *Power, Terror, Peace, and War*, New York: Vintage Books.

John Mearsheimer (2001) *The Tragedy of Great Power Politics*, New York: W.W. Norton & Co.

Gerald Meier (1998) *The International Environment of Business*, Oxford: Oxford University Press.

Ellen Meiksins Wood (2002) 'Infinite War', in *Historical Materialism* 10: 1.

Ellen Meiksins Wood (2003) *Empire of Capital*, London: Verso.

Gian Maria Milesi-Ferretti (2007) 'IMF Offers Compromise Path on Imbalances', in *IMF Survey*, 7 August.

John Stuart Mill (2002) [1859] 'A Few Words on Non-Intervention', in Chris Brown, Terry Nardin and Nicholas Rengger, eds, *International Relations in Political Thought*, Cambridge: Cambridge University Press.

Alan Milward (1992) *The European Rescue of the Nation-State*, London: Routledge.

Sylvia Nasar (1998) *A Beautiful Mind*, London: Faber and Faber.

National Energy Policy Development Group (2001) *National Energy Policy*, The White House, May.

Bary Naughton (1995) *Growing Out of the Plan*, Cambridge: Cambridge University Press.

Joseph Nye (1990) *Bound to Lead*, New York: Basic Books.

Patrick O'Brien (2003) 'The Myth of Anglophone Succession', in *New Left Review* II: 24.

Maurice Obstfeld and Kenneth Rogoff (2005) 'The Unsustainable US Current Account Position Revisited', NBER Working Paper No. 10864, available at *http://elsa.berkeley.edu/~obstfeld/NBER_final.pdf*.

James O'Connor (1970) 'The Meaning of Economic Imperialism', in Robert Rhodes, ed., *Imperialism and Underdevelopment*, New York: Monthly Review Press.

William Odom and Robert Dujarric (2004) *Inadvertent Empire*, New Haven: Yale University Press.

Mancur Olson (2000) *Power and Prosperity*, New York: Basic Books.

Tommaso Padoa-Schioppa and Frabrizio Saccomanni (1994) 'Managing a Market-Led Global Financial System', in Peter B. Kenen, ed., *Managing the World Economy*, Washington, DC: Petersen Institute.

Anthony Pagden (2001) *Peoples and Empires*, London: Weidenfeld and Nicolson.

Kenneth Pollack (2002) *The Threatening Storm*, New York: Random House.

Robert Pollard (1985) *Economic Security and the Origins of the Cold War*, New York: Columbia University Press.

Edward Porter (2001) 'U.S. Energy Policy, Economic Sanctions and World Oil Supply', Policy Analysis and Statistics Department of the American Petroleum Institute.

Robert Powell (1994) 'Anarchy in International Relations Theory', in *International Organization* 48: 2.

Clyde Prestowitz (2003) *Rogue Nation*, New York: Basic Books.

Thomas Quint and Martin Shubik (2004) 'Gold, Fiat and Credit: An Elementary Discussion of Commodity Money, Fiat Money and Credit', Cowles Foundation Discussion Paper No. 1460, available at *http://ssrn.com/abstract=546682*.

Ahmed Rashid (1998) 'Pakistan and the Taliban', in William Maley, ed., *Fundamentalism Reborn?* London: Hurst & Company.

Robert Reich (1990) 'Do We Want U.S. to Be Rich or Japan Poor?', *Wall Street Journal*, 18 June, A10.

Michael Renner (2003) 'The New Oil Order', in *Foreign Policy in Focus*, 14 February, available at *http://www.agitprop.org.au/nowar/20030214_renner_the_new_oil_order.php*.

Christian Reus-Smit (2004) *American Power and World Order*, Cambridge: Polity Press.

Dani Rodrik (2006) 'What's So Special about China's Exports?', Harvard University Faculty Research Working Papers, available at *http://ksgnotes1.harvard.edu/Research/wpaper.nsf/rwp/RWP06-001*.

Paul Rogers (2000) *Losing Control*, London: Pluto Press.

Kenneth Rogoff (2002) 'Why Are G-3 Exchange Rates So Fickle?', in *Finance and Development* 39: 2.

Alessandro Roncaglia (1985) *The International Oil Market*, London: Macmillan.

Justin Rosenberg (2001) *The Follies of Globalization*, London: Verso.

Walt Rostow (1954) *The Dynamics of Soviet Society*, New York: W.W. Norton & Co.

Walt Rostow (1960) *The Stages of Economic Growth*, Cambridge: Cambridge University Press.

Walt Rostow (1971) *Politics and the Stages of Growth*, Cambridge: Cambridge University Press.

Walt Rostow (1990) 'Preface to the 3rd edition' of *The Stages of Economic Growth*, Cambridge: Cambridge University Press.

Olivier Roy (2004) *Globalized Islam*, New York: Columbia University Press.

Ian Rutledge (2005) *Addicted to Oil*, London: I.B. Tauris.

Thomas Schelling (1960) *The Strategy of Conflict*, Cambridge, Mass.: Harvard University Press.

John Searle (1995) *The Construction of Social Reality*, London: Allen Lane.

Edward Shaffer (1983) *The United States and the Control of World Oil*, London: Croom Helm.

Avi Shlaim (1995) *War and Peace in the Middle East* (revised edn), Harmondsworth: Penguin.

Matthew Simmons (2005) *Twilight in the Desert*, London: John Wiley.

Ian Skeet (1988) *OPEC*, Cambridge: Cambridge University Press.

Steve Smith (1985) 'International Relations', in Lynton Robbins, ed., *Introducing Political Science*, London: Longman.

Tony Smith (1981) *The Pattern of Imperialism*, Cambridge: Cambridge University Press.

Duncan Snidal (1993) 'Relative Gains and the Pattern of International Cooperation', in David Baldwin, ed., *Neorealism and Neoliberalism*, New York: Columbia University Press.

George Soros (2004) *The Bubble of American Supremacy*, London: Phoenix.

Gareth Stedman Jones (1972) 'The History of US Imperialism', in Robin Blackburn, ed., *Ideology in Social Science*, Glasgow: Fontana Collins.

Lawrence H. Summers (2004) 'The United States and the Global Adjustment Process', speech at the Institute for International Ecomics, Washington, DC, 23 March, available at *http://www.iie.com/publications/papers/paper.cfm?ResearchID=200.*

Lawrence H. Summers (2006) 'Reflections on Global Account Imbalances and Emerging Markets Reserve Accumulation', available at *http://president.harvard.edu/speeches/2006/0324_rbi.html.*

Bruno Tertrais (2005) *War without End*, New York: The New Press.

Pierre Terzian (1985) *OPEC*, London: Zed Press.

Charles Tilly (1990) *Coercion, Capital and European States, A.D. 990–1990*, Oxford: Basil Blackwell.

Emmanuel Todd (2003) *After Empire*, New York: Columbia University Press.

Richard Tuck (1999) *The Rights of Peace and War*, Oxford: Clarendon Press.

Grahame Usher (2006) 'Musharaff's Opening to Israel', in *Middle East Report Online*, 2 March, available at *http://www.merip.org/mero/mero030206.html.*

Raymond Vernon (1983) *Two Hungry Giants*, Cambridge, Mass.: Harvard University Press.

Robert Vitalis (1997) 'The Closing of the Arabian Oil Frontier and the Future of Saudi–American Relations', in *Middle East Report* 204.

Theodore von Laue (1964) *Why Lenin? Why Stalin?* London: Weidenfeld and Nicolson.

Robert Wade (2007) 'A New Global Financial Architecture?', in *New Left Review* II: 46.

Stephen M. Walt (2000) 'Keeping the World Off Balance: Self Restraint and U.S. Foreign Policy', KSG Working Paper No. 00-013, available at *http://www.ssrn.com/abstract=253799.*

Stephen M. Walt (2005) *Taming American Power*, New York: W.W. Norton.

Kenneth Waltz (1959) *Man, the State and War*, New York: Columbia University Press.

Kenneth Waltz (1979) *Theory of International Politics*, Reading, Mass.: Addison-Wesley.

Martin Wight (1986) *Power Politics* (2nd edn), Harmondsworth: Penguin.

L. Alan Winters and Shahid Yusuf (2006) 'Introduction: Dancing with Giants', in L. Alan Winters and Shahid Yusuf, eds, *Dancing with Giants*, New York: World Bank.

Elizabeth Wishnick (2002) 'Growing U.S. Security Interests in Central Asia', Strategic Studies Institute, US Army War College, available at *http://www.strategicstudiesinstitute.army.mil/pubs/display.cfm?PubID=110.*

Elizabeth Wishnick (2004) 'Strategic Consequences of the Iraq War', Strategic Studies Institute, US Army War College, available at *http://www.strategicstudiesinstitute.army.mil/pubs/display.cfm?PubID=383.*

William Wohlforth (1999) 'The Stability of a Unipolar World', in *International Security* 24: 1.

Martin Wolf (2004) *Why Globalization Works*, New Haven: Yale University Press.

Robert Wood (1986) *From Marshall Plan to Debt Crisis*, Berkeley: University of California Press.

Bob Woodward (2003) *Bush at War* (with a new Afterword), London: Simon & Schuster.

Daniel Yergin (2006) 'Ensuring Energy Security', in *Foreign Affairs* 85: 2.

Alwyn Young (1995) 'The Tyranny of Numbers: Confronting the Statistical Realities of the East Asian Growth Experience', in *The Quarterly Review of Economics* 110: 3.

Shahid Yusuf, Kaoru Nabeshima and Dwight Perkins (2006) 'China and India Reshape Global Industrial Geography', in L. Alan Winters and Shahid Yusuf, eds, *Dancing with Giants*, New York: World Bank.

Name Index

Subject Index

DATE DUE

BRODART, CO.   Cat. No. 23-221